DEFINING
MOMENTS

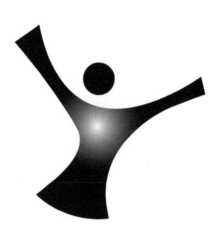

DEFINING MOMENTS

A trilogy of hope

by DEBRA KRUEGER

Set Free International
Stillwater, MN

Set Free International, Stillwater, MN 55082

Printed in the United States of America

ISBN 0-9754815-0-9

Printed by Ideal Printers, Inc.
Bound by Midwest Editions, Inc.

1. Autobiography. 2. Christian inspiration. 3. Memoir
4. Poetry 5. Psychology 6. Self improvement
7. Sexual harassment 8. Spirituality
9. Woman-United States-Social conditions
10. Women's rights-United States

To Bill,
Ben and Norma,
Andrew and Kearstin,
and Corissa.

CONTENTS

Third Awakening - My Purpose

ACKNOWLEDGMENTS

No person can be an island and survive—I have finally learned that truth. Thriving depends on the quality of relationships we hold dear. I, especially, have a debt of gratitude to pay to the many who have helped me move beyond survival. The shear number of people I owe and the wonder and awe I feel for their grace and generosity precludes adequate acknowledgement here. I ask you to please visit our website at www.setfree.biz—there you will find a burgeoning list of saints, all part of the divine community called hope.

Here, allow me to state my appreciation to the wonderful people who have helped bring this book to life. It has indeed been a shared work of passion.

Many people volunteered to read early versions of the book and give feedback: Deborah Andrews, Deb Battah, Traci Berrey, Mary and Craig Beyl, Jim Brogan, Vikki Bullock, Manuela Burge, Alison Drichta, Irene Elkins, Deb Friar, Elizabeth Gherity, Barb Hill, Lynn Hoffman, Alletta Hudgens, Scott and Carolyn Jacobson, Natalie Kilibarda, Len Kistner, Pam Klinkenberg, Corrine Kodelka, W.J. Krueger, Mark Lageson, Carol Manning, Karen McCarthy, Linda McCollough, Cindy Milford, Lisa Miller, Mike Murphy, Jim Pisula, Frank Rempel, Denise Rooney, Becky and Bill Sander, Dorene Sarnoski, Becky Serafini, Mary Timmers, Joy Tracy, Theressa Vogt, Dawn Walker, Tom Whalen, Rebecca White, Joy Whiting, Chris and Britta Wiederkehr, Pam Wigley, Mervin Winston, Pamela Wood, and Lois and Alan Yeschenko.

Editors, and there have been many, each played a role and played it well. Most have read, scrutinized, spoken aloud, and read again until I imagine they became numb. It is hard to believe people would be called to such rigor of purpose. Alphabetically, they are: Maryanne Coronna, Kim Cupelli, George Hoeppner, Corissa Krueger, Margaret Meyer, Kearstin Sullivan, and Janelle Wong.

I would like to thank Carolyn Jacobson for suggesting the subtitle and division of the book into three sections. Brilliant!

Endnotes were researched and written by Corissa Krueger.

Page layout and typesetting by Heather McInerney of Quantum Digital Design.
Page design by Margaret Meyer of MARGgraphics.

Set Free logo design by Laurie Borggreve of Swivel Design.

Greg Boyd, whose love and fearlessness in Christ helped bring me back from the edge. Thank you for endorsing the book as a testimony of God's faithfulness.

A huge amount of love and appreciation is extended to my husband, daughter, two sons and their wives for the courage and confidence they expressed in supporting this effort. They have willingly stepped into the circle of risk created by the honest nature of this book, thereby assuring I would not stand alone.

To the Trinity of Eternal Love that calls, bears, carries and saves me.

Love forever.

DK

My sincere apologies to anyone I may have missed—it was certainly not my intention.

SUGGESTIONS FOR ENJOYING THIS BOOK

Although this book is a series of vignettes, each a defining moment,
it is meant to be read straight through as you would a story.
In the beginning, the time between each vignette is long and the
memories scattered. After the first chapter, they become closer and
merge into a tighter flow.

The book is divided into three sections, each termed an "Awakening."
The style changes as the reader moves from one awakening to the next—
this is intentional.

With the exception of the proper use of italics for titles, all italicized areas
indicate text taken from actual documents that are safely stored.

This is the true story of my life, no part has been fictionalized. My intent
in publishing this book is to create understanding and generate discussion,
it is not to cause harm. Therefore, in most cases, company names have been
withheld and the names of people have been changed.

Do not lose heart—this is a book of hope.

D.K.

Preface

Life is about struggle,
if not our own,
then another's.

Is the absence of strife
our claim of victory?

Or, are trials the path to hope?

If only curiosity calls you forward,
then let me make friends with your inquisitiveness.
But, I warn you…
you will feel the wounds of battle.

I am a freedom fighter.
I cannot be otherwise.

I wrote to reveal what I could not see.

I share
because
life, love and hope
are worth the words
we dedicate to understanding.

First Awakening

MY VOICE

If I find meaning in the trials of life,
it is because they produce endurance,
and I know endurance develops character.

Character is the breath that lifts your voice,
and births a hope deep within that cannot be crushed.

Chapter 1

CHILDHOOD THROUGH ADOLESCENCE:
SCATTERED MEMORIES

REACHING A COMMON UNDERSTANDING

Dad drank heavily the first year of my life.

Caught in an act of drunken indiscretion,
Mom pointed a gun at his head and warned,
"Quit, or I'll blow your head off!"

So, he quit.

EMBEDDED RESPONSE

The first year of my life was traumatic.
Somewhere in it,
I developed an ailment that stayed with me for over 40 years.

Doctors had no explanation,
other than to say it was an effect of deep-seated emotions.

Do Not Disturb!

The broken-down beige couch, propped up on empty beer cases,
sat against the longest wall in the living room.

Dad, unable to cope with his sobriety, would often lie there.

His long arm, when provoked, could cut a wide swath into the room.

As a toddler, I feared his arm.
I would scamper in a wide arc far away from his reach.

Sometimes, however, he would be loving and peaceful,
and I would crawl up into his lap
and listen to the rumbling in his chest
as he hummed a Japanese lullaby.

We never knew what to expect.
Mom taught us to always approach him cautiously;
to judge his mood before asking or doing anything.

MALADJUSTMENT

My grandmother took the beatings from my drunken grandfather
because that is what women were expected to do;
be silent and subservient.
My mother watched, helpless to stop him.

During Grandmother's last beating,
as Grandfather was choking her to death on the bed,
Grandmother drew her knees up and, using them as a countervailing force,
she catapulted Grandfather into a chest of drawers.
He broke two ribs when he hit the furniture
and never beat her again.

When my grandmother was arrested for shoplifting,
my mother watched helplessly as the police took her to jail.
While incarcerated,
Grandmother enjoyed herself.
She talked on the phone to friends and relatives,
wrote letters, played cards and did her nails.

Meanwhile, my mother searched helplessly
for words to explain her absence from seventh grade classes.
Her absence was nonnegotiable;
Grandfather demanded she stay home and take over the role of
housewife and mother to her younger siblings.

When Grandfather, in a drunken rage,
threw my mother out of the house at 16 years of age,
she recalled feeling helpless to find her way in the world.
She learned to get tough and hard
so she wouldn't feel the pain.

Too young to understand,
I experienced her hardness
and accepted the absence of motherly tenderness as
normal because I knew nothing else.

THE PYTHON

The length of my hair
was always an issue between my mother and I:
she liked short hair,
I liked long.

She always won—
she had the fierceness to enforce her will.
She exercised her power with a great deal of determination;
my resistance was inevitably squashed.

In the summer,
she would cut my hair in the backyard.
Wrapping her legs around my upper body and holding me motionless
—like a python strangling its victim—
she would begin the shearing process.

My only defense was to scream,
a blood-curdling shriek.
The only one who noticed my agony
was the neighbor lady.
She would run out her back door,
leaving it to slam shut,
and trundle across both yards.
"Is she alright?" she'd ask, mortified by my distress.
"Of course she's alright.
She just doesn't want her hair cut."

My mother defended her position on the grounds
that I was too young to care for my hair.
Short hair was easier,
and permed, short hair was the easiest.

Mom gave home perms because they cost less.
The consistency of result was never assured,
but I was just a kid,
and no one cares what a kid looks like.

After each torturous hair contest was over,
my mother offered her form of comfort,
"Your hair will grow back..."
Or, "The perm will relax in a month.
Everything gets better with time."

One summer,
my budding female identity was demolished by a bad perm.
It was the summer girls started to notice boys,
and the cutest boy my friends and I had ever seen
just moved on the block.
Nancy, who was thin, with long straight blonde hair, captured his attention.
I did too...
but, I think it was the spring force on my curls.
Pull the curl out, let go, SNAP.
Pull, SNAP.
Pull, SNAP.
I didn't think it was funny...he did.

I wore a scarf on my head for weeks until the perm relaxed.

RIVERS

The drive to the mental health hospital was serene:
the trees along the parkway formed living tunnels,
a green canopy,
broken by shards of sunlight,
allowing random,
ever-changing openings of light to frolic along the roadway.

We drove to the hospital every night to see Dad.
It was a quiet place,
where life had an established order,
and tranquility spoke in the muffled sounds
emitted from the indoor pool just beyond the glass wall.

We never saw Dad's room—
he met us in the lobby just past the pool.

Each time we saw him,
he wore a blank, withdrawn expression on his face.
I imagined him a door:
we knocked,
but he would not answer.

He sat in the lobby chair,
feet together, flat on the floor,
knees pressed tight against each other.
His arms rested, limp on the chair's wooden arms;
hands dangling,
loose and lifeless as if hung by a noose.

It appeared Dad's mind had vacated his body.
The shock treatments had that effect.
We were promised he would eventually return to us
a happier man,
without the sullen signs of depression;
perhaps without the anger and rage that preceded each episode.

Admittedly, at 10 years old,
I didn't know much about mental hospitals.
But I did know one thing:
the rules at home changed when Dad was hospitalized.

Since he established all the laws of our household:
      the time we ate,
      what we ate,
      how we spent money,
      where we spent money,
      if we spent money,
when he was in the hospital
there was a marked relaxation of the rules.

I suspected mom relaxed the rules for multiple reasons,
not the least of which was to manage the stress she felt.
Dad's stay in the hospital oppressed Mom.
She became nervous, irritable, was easily moved to tears
and spoke aloud of her feelings:
      nervous because our poor financial condition was growing worse by
      the day;
      irritable because Dad's emotional weakness left her carrying the bag;
      was easily moved to tears because she felt abandoned.

I could sense her tension,
like a volcano waiting to erupt.
If she ever exploded,
I believed molten lava would flow from her in scalding rivers,
scorching all life in her path.
She was full of anger, fear and frustration.

As Dad's hospital stay extended,
the summer grew hotter.
It was a record August—
nothing assuaged the unbearable heat.

At night,
we slept on the living room floor
lined up in a row in front of one large fan.
Its monotonous hum and rattle throughout the night
seemed a stabilizing factor because it was known and continuous.
Mom was not able to sleep on the hard floor
and each exhausting day of heat
seemed to sap more of her strength.

One blistering day,
    temperature 100 degrees,
    humidity 98%,
Mom decided to make lunch in the basement where it was cooler.

Standing in front of the laundry tubs,
she dropped a full jar of pickles.
It shattered.
There was pickle juice and glass everywhere.

My brother and I caught our breath—
it was usually the small things that sent mom around the bend,
and a broken pickle jar qualified.
We understood a diversion was necessary.
The juice was running along the cement floor toward the floor drain.
"Look, Pickle River,"
we joked, laughing nervously.

We waited and watched her face.
Finally,
Mom slouched into a folding chair dad had "borrowed" from the school board.
She was too tired to erupt.
Crying was not an option—
it only gave her a headache.
She looked pathetic, used up, wasted.

I helped Mom clean up the mess.
I knew somehow I shared her place.
And, I would share her place for years to come.

CLASH OF WILLS

Allowed no outside interests other than her bowling league,
Mom fought with Dad each year for her freedom
to attend the annual bowling banquet.

She would start planning for the banquet weeks in advance.
Wanting to look especially attractive,
she would sew a new dress,
buy new shoes,
and, perhaps, a matching purse.

Dad feared her flirtatiousness;
        teasing men was one of my mother's favorite pastimes.

Mom resisted his reins.

The argument would always reach a fevered pitch just as she, in tears,
walked out the door for the evening.

In our early adolescence,
my brother and I were too big to find small places to hide in
when Dad was that angry.

Everyone had a miserable evening,
except Mom, who, upon reaching the banquet hall,
put on her party face and played the night away.

STICKS AND STONES

What does it mean
when your father routinely
calls your mother:

"Fucking whore,"
"Fat cocksucker,"
"Bitch?"

What does it mean
when your mother accepts the expletives?

DAD'S HARDSHIP

When he was only 15, Dad lied about his age to get into the Merchant Marines.
Without a high school diploma, later job choices were limited.

His job as a "cruddy janitor" for the Minneapolis School Board depressed him.

It was our fault:
he had to stay in a job he hated to support our "fat lazy asses."

I tried to make it better.
On weekends, I would help Dad with his second job cleaning offices.
    I took pride in cleaning things he would overlook,
    like cleaning sludge off the sides of metal desks.
    People noticed too—they told him how nice their desks looked.

Once a week,
I would put cards in Dad's lunch box,
thanking him for working so hard.
He liked the cards.

Sometimes he said these things made him happier;
most of the time, they made no difference.

TREND SETTER

Mother warned me,
"Didn't I tell you to keep your hair out of your eyes at the dinner table?"
Determined, she now asserted her obligation to right my wrong.
My straggly hair was an abomination.
It must be controlled to appease my father and thus maintain peace
in the household.

I begged and pleaded:
"No girls in junior high wear short hair.
I'll look like a dork.
Everyone will laugh at me.
I don't want my hair cut."
"Then you should have kept it out of your face like I told you three times.
Three strikes and you're out!"
My mother asserted this with her 'don't mess with me look' on her face.

My hair was going to be cut—she had made up her mind.

When Mom set her jaw,
she became rigid and brutal looking.
She talked less thereby keeping her jaw rigidly locked.

In junior high I was too big for my mother to give me a python lock.
So, when she wanted my hair cut,
she took me to a salon,
trusting I would not make a scene in public.

I didn't.

But I cried all the way to the salon.

As I sat in the chair
watching my strands of hair
fall to the floor,
I hated the fact that I had no control,
no free will,
no choice,
no power to decide for myself.

I cried all the way home from the salon.

Mom said I should learn to be a trend setter,
not a trend follower.
But who cares about that in junior high?

I questioned her,
"How can you expect me to develop independent thinking,
if I don't even have the right to choose the length of my hair?"
She answered,
"Kings and queens rule.
You're nothing in this kingdom—you don't even get to vote."

Mother was convinced other girls got their hair cut short,
just like mine,
because I started a new trend.

She was very proud of herself.

CONSPICUOUS

As far as I am concerned,
they can take the junior high years
and erase them from existence.

It is a transition time—
a time when you start becoming a woman,
whatever that means.

I felt a violating sense of discomfort
as I caught the glance of male teachers.

Maybe it was my appearance:
I wore three-inch spiked heels
because they were the only ones left in the Baker's sale bin.
My mom thought they were sexy,
I thought they were stupid.
They were cheap,
and cheap won.
The neighbor lady gave me her hand-me-down dresses
which, were cheap…actually free,
and so they definitely won.

There I was,
short haired, high heeled, in the neighbor's dress,
with a developing body,
receiving the unwanted looks of grown men.

There was no way to walk smaller…
to be inconspicuous.

Whenever I complained, my mother would bark,
"What are you complaining about?
At least you're not running around naked."

I didn't know how to tell her,
"I feel naked."

Moral Substitution

The gang of girl thugs were tough
and they traveled together—
not one could be found alone.
With their combined bodies,
their bullying behavior seemed formidable.
Like a pack of wild animals,
they looked for hapless victims to beat and harass.

They found Mary in eighth grade gym class.
(Mary was a pudgy short girl whose bangs hung in a perpetual droop over her eyes.
She usually begged out of strenuous sports by bringing a note from her mother.)

With pack instinct,
they descended upon Mary.
She was quickly imprisoned,
cut off from the rest.
While slapping and pushing her,
they mocked her fear.

She stood in the center of their ring of terror.
Her face stricken with fright.
She did not know her offense.
There was none required:
        power preys,
        mercy is for the weak.

The circle of glaring eyes started to move in closer.
One by one,
they pressed toward Mary—
in and out—
like pistons firing.
Their engine of fear was gaining power:
the power to intimidate.
Intimidate not just Mary,
but all those standing, helplessly, watching.

Abandonment has an ugly feel.
Who would take the risk?
Who would stand in the gap?

Time seemed to slow to a stop in my mind.
I judged the consequences of my options.
Should I stand,
and be beaten?
Should I do nothing,
and live with the torment in my gut:
  aching because Mary stood alone,
  burning because this wasn't right?
The aching drove my decision.

I chose to stand.

I took the hit,
not just that day,
but for months to come.

While Mary escaped their torment,
they cornered me in lonely places,
punched me in the stomach,
and threatened future harm
should I speak of the abuse.

They watched for opportunities and took every one.

My mother advised I fight the battle, "Hit them back," she'd huff.
I would plead with Mom,
"I don't want to hit back.
I shouldn't have to hit back.
School shouldn't feel like a war zone.
Besides, it would be me against all of them—
those are very bad odds."

My mother wanted me to be strong.
She lived by the motto, "Life is shit, and then you die."
"Bullies back down if you hit them hard enough," she advised.
I just wanted justice.

I did not want to be beaten to a pulp.

I dreaded going to school.
I lived in fear.

Eventually, a meeting was called with the school principal.
The girls who were involved and their parents attended.
The truth was finally out.
The ringleader was expelled.
Several years later, I asked a neighbor about her.
They said she never finished school;
she spent her time visiting judges in juvenile court.

KEEP IT TO YOURSELF

I sat sandwiched between my friends
in a church pew six rows back from the altar.
I think they invited me because they intended to save me.
It was a scary thing—sitting next to them—
being surrounded by the faithful.

The minister speaking at my friends' Lutheran church that evening
was known for his ability to reach inside the heart.

    Such evangelistic preachers were repugnant to my family.
    Excluding those who practiced the religion that brought
    alcoholics to sobriety,
    'Bible thumpers' were to be avoided at all cost.
    My folks understood just how crappy life was,
    but the faithful—they lived in delusion.
    My mother's description of the faithful,
        "They're so heavenly bound, they're no earthly good.
        They wouldn't say shit, if they had a mouth full of it."
        And finally, the worst, "They're judgmental—holier than thou!"

    Although my mother had no time for religion,
    she did feel it was her obligation
    to have my brother and I baptized Catholic and confirmed Lutheran,
    which she did without any cooperation from my father.

    I was in ninth grade and left on my own to figure out issues of faith.

I don't remember the preacher's sermon that night
but I remember asking my friends to go up with me during the altar call.
They whispered, "No, we can't go up with you.
We've already accepted Jesus.
You have to do this by yourself.
It's your decision."

The distance to the altar seemed overwhelming.
But they insisted—I must go alone.

I felt a loneliness crying out from deep within;
something in me was broken and I wanted it made whole.
I longed for a love relationship that would promise to never let me go.
I wanted something my parents didn't have.

That night, I made the decision for Christ.

As I stood to go forward,
a spiral of fog-like haze seemed to enshroud me.
I became unaware of my surroundings,
and sensed only the gravity of the decision I was about to make.
I was told my life would be hidden in Christ,
and once sealed by the Holy Spirit,
I could never be lost from Christ.

I shook uncontrollably for hours afterward.
I cried for reasons I could not explain.

Sensing a need for decompression,
my friend's parents, Mr. and Mrs. Peterson,
invited a small group back to their house.
We prayed and talked.
I suspected this couple's life story was far different from my parents.
I wish I could have held onto the beauty I saw in their faces that night—
the radiance and peace.

It faded.

Two days later,
I asked my family to join me in a common table prayer.
I was told vehemently,
"NO!
Keep your religion to yourself."

So I did.

PUBERTY AMPLIFIED

The summer before entering high school,
I had a physical exam with Dr. Streu,
whom my mother affectionately called "Dr. Screw"
after seeing him eyeball the centerfold of a Playboy magazine
while leaning against a magazine rack at the neighborhood drug store.

After completing my exam,
Dr. Streu patted my knee and gave me a piece of advice,
"Lose some weight.
You don't want to go into high school this heavy—
none of the boys will look at you."

It wasn't the boys looking at me part,
that got my attention,
it was the idea that a doctor thought I was fat.
I was embarrassed and felt humiliated,
even if it was "Dr. Screw."

I started the first of many diets that same day.

Shedding 30 pounds of fat at age 15 was revealing.
It revealed a full grown woman's body
with curves I hadn't known.

To my dad, I became a different person;
a person worth noticing.
We became best buddies: I was his friend and he was mine.
(I had no idea he was the wrong male to notice me.)

To Mother, it was destabilizing and suspicious.
Although at the time she never said anything,
I sensed the tension and jealousy.
Years later she asked me directly,
"Did you and your father ever have sex?"
I wanted to crawl out of my skin when she asked the question.
And as much as I knew a parent should ask the question if there is concern,
(it should never be buried in secrecy)
it did create a distance between us.
Becoming a young woman was confusing.

Driving Force

My older brother wrecked Mom and Dad's car.

When it was my time to drive, they said, "Get your own car."

So, I did.

Because I was only 17,
Dad had to co-sign at the credit union for the loan.
My first loan...the beginning of adulthood and established credibility.

I worked hard and saved for the car payments, insurance, upkeep and gas.

Now, I had my own transportation,
        my independence,
                an opportunity for adventure.

I loved my car.
'65 Ford, Galaxie 500,
four barrel carb,
dual exhaust,
glass packs,
oversized tires on the back.

It RUMBLED and it ROARED.

Later, I sold it and gave the money to my brother.
He was in college and broke.

WISHING ON A STAR

Community college seemed to be the only reasonable option after high school:
affordable,
achievable, considering my demonstrated capabilities,
and…
acceptable, given I saw no other options before me.

Working 30-40 hours a week in retail,
I could just about cover my costs:
car loan payments,
gas and upkeep,
tuition and books.
(Clothes were a luxury I couldn't afford.)

Mom and Dad allowed me to live at home while attending college.
This was gracious since they charged no board and room.

I didn't see myself as a student.
My purpose was not academic achievement,
but rather to make it all work while I traveled to some distant time
where everything my heart desired would come true,
magically,
like wishing on a star.

By the end of the second year,
the magic was gone.
My grades were compromised by my work schedule
and my belief shriveled and hid like a coward.

It was 1972,
and all of my female friends were getting degrees in
elementary education or nursing.
When I told them of my insecurities,
they offered,
"Well who cares if you don't become a biologist?
As the saying goes,
it's better to marry a biologist,
than to be one."

Chapter 2

Engagement and Marriage

WITH THIS RING

My fiancé was stationed in Germany.
I knew him in high school,
but did my best to ignore him.
His withdrawn, antisocial behavior troubled me.

So the first time he wrote me from Germany,
my instinct told me to throw the letter in the trash.
My mother worried that I would be an old maid,
prodded me, "Just write him back!
You don't have to marry the guy just because you write him a letter."

I wrote back.

We dated on his first leave home.
He told me of his grand dreams of far off places,
and explained his quiet behavior was a reflection of his superior intellect.
Although he bragged about a full ride to a private college,
which was awarded him because of his intelligence,
he chose to join the Army.

He had everything planned out.

On his second leave home,
we took the city bus downtown to shop for an engagement ring.
After depositing our fares,
he started for the rear of the bus.
I followed him.

His plan was coming together.
My life was disintegrating and I felt hopeless to stop it.

My intuition told me I should not marry him,
but I could not tell him for fear of hurting him.
And, I had committed the ultimate sin of having sex with him
prior to marriage.
I felt I now had no other choice but to marry him—
we were bound in the eyes of God,
and that was irrevocable.

As if I had just pled guilty to a heinous crime
for which I would be sentenced to life imprisonment,
I sat motionless, trying to squelch the feelings that were begging to be heard.
Yet, I had no idea I had the right to express them.
I could not even label them.
My stomach knew what my head would not allow;
it ached,
a horrific pain,
a desperate moaning within.

If a small child had cried the same despairing cry,
I would have swept her up in my arms
and carried her to safety.

But I was not a child.
In my mind,
I became an adult the moment I had sex and disappointed my father.

Similarly, I felt my Father in heaven was disappointed and distant;
God had rules and I had broken them.

I stuffed everything I was feeling
while my fiancé purchased my quarter-carat diamond ring
from a jeweler who feigned respect for my modest taste.

THE WRONG MEDICINE

There was no celebrating at my parent's house the night of my engagement.
I did not understand why Dad was so upset.
My husband-to-be was just like him:
socially reclusive,
intelligent,
moody,
emotionally disabled.

Shouldn't Dad be happy I chose to marry a man just like him?

Yet, from the moment I started dating him,
Dad withdrew, angry and hostile, into his own temperamental corner.
From behind the bars and locks of his own making,
he made himself inaccessible.
Within his emotionally constructed cage,
he growled and roared,
ferocious and mean.

As if standing, helpless, in front of a lion,
I felt his words could maim or kill me.
And they did...nearly:
>"You're a whore!
>A loser!
>A quitter!
>You're not my daughter."

His words were vile and forceful, possessing animal,
not human attributes.
He went on for hours, for days.
His scornful looks seemed to tear the flesh from my bones.

I could not sleep.
I could not eat.
I could not understand.

My mother suggested I see a psychiatrist.
The doctor described it as response to significant loss,
and put me on tranquilizers.

My mother commiserated with me,
her new companion in misery,
since now we both used medication
to endure his raging moods.

BEREAVEMENT

From the time of my engagement,
I was disowned by my father.
Throughout my life he would periodically become involved,
yet, he rarely spoke to me.

The intensity grew with passing years.

Eventually, my name could not be spoken in his house.

As Mom explained later,
Dad was jealous.
Whenever another man was in my life,
I could not be his.
I was to belong to him only,
until death I suppose.

Well...
something did die.

DEFUNCT FAIRYTALE

Dad wanted nothing to do with the wedding.
His hostility waged war on the myth of "princess for the day."

Still, Mom and I tried hard to wrap the day up with a pretty bow.
    I wrote each invitation by hand and ornamented them
    with dried wildflowers.
    Mom made the dress of velvet and lace by hand.
    Together, we created the flower arrangements the day
    before in our kitchen.
    We labored weeks for this special day—sweat equity on a small budget.

When the momentous day arrived, the illusions were shattered.

As Dad and I stood waiting for the processional,
there was no
        love shared,
        congratulations expressed,
        tears spilled,
        hugs exchanged.

There was only
        frozen silence,
        two actors,
        both wanting a different script.

Nuptial Evening

He got drunk and passed out.

We slept in separate beds.

THE HONEYMOON IS OVER

After the wedding, we flew to Germany.

At 20 years of age,
I was feeling fortunate to see the world.
The potential for excitement was enormous.

Two days after arriving,
and one week before Christmas,
I was visited by an Army alcohol and drug counselor.
He told me my new husband was an alcoholic.
Reported for alcohol abuse by his commander,
and owing excessive debt to a German proprietor,
his behavior had to change.

I wondered;
was I to be held responsible for changing his behavior?

The counselor left me alone with my thoughts,
and the plate of ornate Christmas cookies
I had just received from our German landlady.

I ate the cookies and pretended everything would be all right.

OWNERSHIP OF THE PROBLEM

It was three in the morning
and he still wasn't home.
I had no idea where he was.

Worried,
I called his Army commander.

The next day,
we learned my husband had gotten drunk
and passed out in another town.
I could imagine him,
tall, rail thin, with his reddish blonde hair and freckled face
lying nose down in his own vomit.

Six months passed with more warnings of his alcohol abuse,
and yet he still claimed his drinking was not the problem.
The problem, according to him, was me.

MISCARRIAGE OF LOVE

I tried to put my first of many miscarriages into perspective.
It was a struggle to accept my thoughts and emotions as rational
when viewed from within the callousness that surrounded me.

Many of the women on my mother's side told of abortions on toilets,
of coat hangers,
and talked of conception as the plague.
They found no joy in children.
One completely disavowed knowledge of her own offspring.

Indeed, I come from a long line of women who lack sensitivity to wonder.
The wonder of life being created in the womb.
The mystery of birth—
        the end of one very miraculous process,
        the beginning of yet another.

They did not understand my grief
when my first child died.

Conceived in Germany,
the baby was taken from my womb in Spain.

Seventeen weeks of pregnancy
seemed a lifetime to me,
and was a lifetime for my child.

I followed the development of this baby.
Each week a new phenomenon:
        head, eyes and arms forming by week seven;
        heart beating in week eight;
        all organs in place by week ten;
        feet and toes in week 11;
        and five tiny fingers on each hand by week 13.

Anything that could jeopardize this child was up for scrutiny.
"Doctor, should I quit my job at the commissary?
I am concerned about the heavy lifting."

"No, if you were doing lifting before pregnancy,
there is no reason to quit now," replied the doctor.

"Doctor, I am spotting.
Is it from the lifting?"

"There's probably no correlation," he answered.

Nonetheless, I quit the job at the commissary.

"Should I be having sex with my husband?"

He answered, "Obviously, you were doing that before, so I'd say it is safe to continue."

"Is traveling okay?" I asked.
"My parents are visiting.
We had planned to travel to Spain together.
My aunt lives in Spain—Mom wants to see her."

The doctor gave the trip his blessing.

Everything in the world seemed suspect.
A hotel in France.
A dirty bidet—no, not for me!
Stained sheets.
My skin crawled.

The spotting increased.

In Spain there were
        chickens hanging,
        flies buzzing,
        snails crawling.
The outdoors and indoors were one.

I was told by my mother not to be such a prude.
But I couldn't help myself.

The spotting grew heavier still.

At the naval base in Spain,
the women sat at the kitchen table.
I told my aunt about my bleeding.
She advised,
"It's no big deal.

You just bleed and bleed,
until you drop the kid in the toilet."

I lay in the bedroom.
I could hear them playing poker in the other room.

My husband did not join me.
I was alone with my thoughts.
       Won't someone care?
       What is wrong with me?
       Why do I want someone to care?
I had been told I was oversensitive.
I should be tough and strong.

My mother told me this is the fate of women;
to be alone with birthing issues.

I could hear them as they laughed,
ate,
and played poker.

In the bathroom,
the toilet filled with blood.
I looked for my baby in the blood.
It was dying in me.
I could feel its death.
My body was killing this baby.

Alone, again.
I cried,
"Please care about us."
No one came.

At the hospital
the doctors informed me that the proper term for miscarriage is
"spontaneous abortion."

During one of his rare moments of involvement,
my dad stood at my bedside,
looking morbid.

I couldn't think of the pain.
I buried it deep within.

STANDING ROOM ONLY

Fourteen months after our wedding,
my husband's tour of duty was coming to an end.
I traveled back to Minneapolis ahead of him
and found an inexpensive basement apartment in Brooklyn Park
and furnished it with hand-me-downs and garage sale finds.
Alone, I waited for my husband to join me.

At five months pregnant,
everyone was predicting I would have twins.
"How can you be so huge, if it's not twins?"
The doctor also suspected the possibility.
But...no, the tests showed only one fetus.

It was the seventies and natural childbirth was promoted as the
only responsible way to deliver a child.
Wanting to be responsible, I decided to give birth without pain medication,
and took several classes to prepare myself.
The childbirth classes spelled out each phase of labor and delivery.
I practiced all of the suggested breathing and focus techniques
and was confident I could handle things.
Besides, I had just finished reading, *The Grapes of Wrath*
and had absorbed all the tenacity and grit given its characters as my own.

When my water broke,
I knew what to expect.
The contractions started and came hard.
I progressed all the way to transition as anticipated.
Everything was according to plan.
The head was nearly completely crowned.
Statistically, most babies are delivered shortly after the head crowns.
But this was not to be a textbook delivery.

"Okay, push," the nurse coaxed, patting my arm reassuringly.
 She added, "It should only be a couple of hard pushes and we'll be done."
The nurse took a deep breath, and puffing her cheeks up, she said,
"Push, push, push, push, push, push, push,
keep pushing, keep pushing, keep pushing, okay."
"Let's do it again," she exhorted, as she took another deep breath.
"And again.
And again.
And again."

"Hmmm," I heard the doctor say.
The nurse walked to the foot of the delivery table
and exchanged a furtive look with the doctor.
When she came back, she had stopped taking her own deep breaths,
and instead, starting pushing hard on my abdomen.
Another nurse took over coaching,
"Push, push, push, keep pushing, keep pushing, keep pushing…"

"Again, let's do it again.
and again,
and again,
and again,
and again."

"Hmmm," the doctor said again and then whispered something to the nurse.
She came to the head of the delivery table and asked,
"Would you mind if interns were allowed in the room?
The doctor believes your delivery will offer them an excellent opportunity to learn.
If you prefer, they will not be allowed in. It's your choice."

The room became an amphitheater:
the interns formed a semi-circle behind the doctor, two deep and
slightly to his right;
all male, all young.
Two additional female nurses joined the group and stood at my bedside.

"Let's try this again.
This time both of you push on her abdomen," the doctor ordered the two nurses.
"Okay, ready…push, push, push, push, push, push, keep pushing, keep pushing…"

Almost an hour had passed with pushing intervals every minute and a half.
Still, the head was not delivered.
The interns started whispering among themselves and moved in a little closer,
bending forward to get a better look.

The mirror was repositioned so I could not see.

The doctor was now explaining a device to the interns.
I asked the nurse, "What is he showing them?"
"A forceps," she answered.
"Oh," I replied, "I know why they are used."

All side conversations were down to a minimum
and I was told to conserve my strength.
Between contractions,
I closed my eyes and rested in a quiet place somewhere deep within my mind.

When the next contraction was about due,
the interns all moved in closer.
I felt the long metal tongs inserted along either side of my vagina.

Two nurses propped up my back,
two nurses pushed on my abdomen,
a fifth called out the pushing cadence.
The doctor pulled,
I pushed,
the interns watched.

An hour and a half had now passed;
still the head was not fully delivered.
Everyone was getting a bit tense.
This wasn't exactly what the doctor had wanted the interns to witness.

I was exhausted.
Pain was no longer an issue—I was numb—
numb to everything:
the demands to push, the gawking interns, even my baby.

The doctor ordered oxygen.
After the mask was placed over my nose and mouth,
I sensed my thoughts return and a gray void left my mind.

The next push successfully delivered the head.
There were cheers from the amphitheater,
the nurses let out a sigh of relief
and the doctor said the body should be out in two more pushes.

I was left on my own for the first push.
The second push had the nurses on my abdomen again.
On the third push two nurses propped me up and two pushed on my abdomen.
By the fourth push the spectators had crowded in closer again.
After 50 more minutes had passed,
everyone was bellowing for me to push harder.
I heard the doctor's voice over the others,
"God damn it! I told you to push harder!"

I wanted to cry and told the nurse I was pushing as hard as I could.
"I know honey," she soothingly responded.
"It is just that the shoulders are not coming out—
your baby is half in and half out
and is showing signs of stress.
You are going to have to try with everything you have left—can you do that for me?"

"Yes."

"Come on, make this next one count,"
I heard the doctor's voice, but couldn't see him any longer.
"Where is he?" I asked the nurse.
"Well," she explained while mimicking his posture,
"he is leaning way back on the stool.
His feet are planted on the bottom of the delivery table,
and he is bracing himself to pull hard."
She paused, then added,
"One way or the other, this baby has to come out."

"Are you ready to push?" she asked.
I had lost complete sense of the contractions and couldn't tell when each started.
The nurse cued me.
"NOW... PUSH NOW!
COME ON...HARDER, HARDER, PUSH, PUSH...
You can do it, I know you can."

I knew she had confidence in me,
but by now I was exhausted.
I began to release my breath somewhere short of the complete contraction.

"NO! YOU CAN'T STOP!!!" barked the doctor.
"TAKE A QUICK BREATH. NOW! RIGHT NOW!!"

"Watch me," the nurse pulled my face to hers.
She took a quick breath, her face turned crimson red, she pushed like life
depended on it.

Her urgency startled me and I started pushing, hard.
I was still pushing long after she said, "Stop."
With each successive contraction,
my determination swelled.
The doctor no longer had to chastise me for quitting
before the contraction was finished.

42

It seemed another eternity until the nurse finally announced,
"You have a son—a big son at that!
No wonder you had a time of it—he's huge!"
The soothing nurse added,
"You poor thing."

The interns moved from behind the doctor
to the bassinette,
and followed it as they rolled my son into another room for evaluation.
They came back to explain he was responding well and would be fine.
They thanked the doctor and me
and then left the room.

All that remained was clean-up and stitches.
From the foot of the bed,
the doctor cautioned,
"It is going to be hard to sit for several weeks.
I suggest you take an inflatable doughnut with you wherever you go."
(He was right.)

The nurses chatted among themselves,
"Well, my God, the chest is never as big as the head.
This baby's chest measures the same as his head.
It would be like delivering a second head the same size as the first!"

Visitors looking through the glass said,
"Look at that one.
Wow, he's a big one—he can't be a newborn.
Wonder why they brought him back to the hospital?"

My mother and her sisters made lewd comments
about my presumably cavernous hole caused by his birth.

And, of course, there were all the jokes about his trophy size,
"He's a keeper.
Don't throw that one back."

I didn't laugh.
I wanted my trophy!

GREENER GRASS

My husband got a job at the post office;
the additional points for being in the military helped his score.
He was assigned the night shift.

Things seemed to level out.
We bought a "starter home" in north Minneapolis,
and bought a couple of pieces of furniture.

At a year old, our son Ben was developing right on schedule.
Since things seemed stable,
I decided to return to the community college I had left before marriage;
take a couple of classes,
perhaps finish my Associate's degree.
I had a period of trepidation;
nevertheless, I pushed past my fear and registered.

Throughout high school, math and science were extremely difficult for me.
With the exception of biology, which I loved,
the sciences caused me heartburn.
The study of biology, however, disclosed the mysteries of life:
the miracles of divinely inspired creation.
How fascinating that cells, tissues, and organs
are all organized to function in concert for the purpose of living.
Even the single cell revealed a design of eternal magnitude.
I really loved biology!!

Nonetheless, I knew if I wanted to be a biologist,
I would have to reconcile myself to the remaining sciences.
With that in mind,
I registered for chemistry and physics.

To my greatest surprise,
I was having a blast.
Other students were asking me for help.
How could that be?
I wasn't brilliant, and it was only a community college.
Nonetheless, it felt great.
I made new friends and felt fully alive and hopeful.
The sky looked bluer, the grass greener.
I felt I had crossed a threshold and now nothing could hold me back.

SHARED RESPONSIBILITY

Like my father, my husband said his job was driving him crazy.
He wanted to quit the post office and return to college;
this time without the full ride he supposedly had before joining the military.

I was willing to do my part.
So I quit college (again)
and got a job working full-time at a dental office as the office manager.

Leaving the house at 6:30 in the morning,
I walked six miles to and from work each day
so my husband could use the car to get to class.

But he usually didn't wake up for classes.
The way he reasoned,
he didn't need to go—
he already knew it all.

He usually slept until noon.

While he watched midday reruns of Mayberry, RFD
Ben was in day-care.

I didn't understand this form of shared responsibility.
        I gave up my dream of college—
        he was living his.

        I got up early every day for work—
        he slept right through classes.

        I was trying to make financial ends meet—
        he refused to even work part time.

        I wanted to talk—
        he ignored me.

        I was home at night with our son—
        he was drinking with his buddies.

        I was performing well at work—
        he was doing poorly in class.

So we started to go to group marriage counseling at the hospital;
not that he was anxious to go—
        I more-or-less dragged him.
It was a Christian-based counseling service provided at a discount by the hospital.
Because of our low income,
our participation was free,
offering him no excuse.

The group heard my frustration and attempted to
communicate my concerns by
        coaxing,
        coddling,
        encouraging,
        but to no avail—
        he was immovable.

I wanted more from marriage than he was willing to give.

When the group ended,
we were exactly where we began,
except I felt even more hopeless.

Fetal Remains

The following year passed excruciatingly slow.

I endured one more "spontaneous abortion;"
my body was rejecting another baby.

I thought I could handle it better this time.

The doctor advised,
"Breathe deeply because this is going to feel very uncomfortable."

The suction hose he was using went past my view into a glass jar,
which sat on a stand next to the procedural table I was lying on.
Somewhat like a vacuum process,
the uterus was sucked clean.
What would have been my baby
was probably in the jar,
if it had not already been discharged by my body.

It was gruesome and cruel
to be placed in view of the glass jar.

BRUISES

I began an exercise class two nights a week after work.
I wished coming home could have meant relaxation,
but it never did.
I wished household chores would be done,
but they never were.
It was no surprise
to find my husband in his usual position,
       sitting in the overstuffed chair,
       watching TV.

It was 7:30 p.m.
Ben, a toddler now,
had not yet been fed or bathed.
This angered me,
but I said nothing—
it wouldn't change anything.

I fed Ben in silence as I watched him squish baby food between his fingers.
Blonde haired, with big hazel eyes accentuated by his adorable long eyelashes,
he had a chubby baby belly that I loved to kiss.

When he had finished,
I brought him into the bathroom,
and started running the water in the tub.
He loved bath time.
I loved the time together—it was quiet and relaxing.
As I laid him down on the fluffy, yellow rug,
I remember thinking how much I loved the color yellow.

I removed the safety pins from his cloth diaper.
While lifting both of his legs with one hand,
I slid the diaper out from underneath him.
That is when I noticed...

There were red, swollen welts
and black and blue marks
in wide, long strips
completely covering his back, buttocks and thighs.

I stood him up and turned him around.
Gasping in horror,
tears streaming,
my guts knotted.

Picking Ben up
and holding him diaper-less in my arms,
I ran into the living room.
Standing between the TV
and the overstuffed chair,
I demanded to know,
"How did this happen?
Didn't you see it when you changed his diaper earlier?"

There was no response.
No explanation.
He didn't even get up off the chair.

I headed for the kitchen,
Ben in my arms.
Calling the doctor's answering service,
I begged,
"Please have the doctor call me at home right away.
It is an emergency!"

I waited by the phone,
rocking him in my arms.
Crying
and rocking.
Crying
and rocking.
Finally, the doctor's return call came.

I described the bruises
and asked,
"Should I take him to the hospital?"
No, I was to bring him into the office first thing in the morning.

The next morning,
my husband was too tired to get out of bed.
I went to the doctor's office alone with Ben.

The doctor said the evidence indicated abuse.
He would have to file a police report.[1]
I encouraged him to do whatever was necessary.

One week later,
everyone had been interviewed by the police.
No one admitted involvement,
including my husband.

Officially, yet unofficially,
the findings implicated my husband as the prime suspect.
When challenged with the information,
his response was hostile and defensive.
In his mind
he had done nothing wrong.
His expectation of me:
I, his wife, should believe him.

My response was to quit working full-time.
Never again would I let this happen to my son.
If our family were to eat,
my husband would have to get a job;
        it was long past due.
My son would remain by my side or with someone I trusted.
My first obligation was to his safety.

AGAINST THE ODDS

When I was informed I was pregnant again,
I was shocked.
Confused and bewildered,
I queried the doctor,
"I thought you said my condition would make it extremely unlikely to
become pregnant."
"Yes, that's true. But, statistics are just that—statistics," he answered.

My mother suggested abortion.
Others echoed her sentiment.

I could not consider abortion.

I understood their rationale:
our marriage was failing;
financially we were destitute;
we had no insurance coverage for the pregnancy and delivery;
I could not promise this young one a happy home.

Was this a responsible way to bring a life into the world?
I could not answer that question.
I did not care to answer that question.
I knew the burden of providing for my children would be squarely
on my shoulders,
and I had no guarantees.

But there was a child in my womb
who floated peacefully,
never becoming perturbed or fitful.

I would carry this baby,
no matter what the outcome.

MURKY WATERS

I really had no idea how to make it work.
Pregnant again.
No insurance.
My husband refusing to work more than weekends.

One day led to the next,
without thought,
without hope.
I lived as if the mere act of breathing were enough.

In the evenings
I boarded the city bus for the ride downtown to my part time job.
The ride always seemed interminably long.
I inevitably arrived feeling nauseous and dizzy.

Doing bad debt collection for a major department store was a depressing job.
Everyone had a story to tell of hard luck or a useless spouse.
Usually, the debtor simply avoided the call,
instructing their children to lie for them.
I could hear them in the background;
"Tell them we're not home right now."

I took the job because we needed the money
and the evening work meant trusted friends would be available to watch Ben.

I hated the job and the endless summer days.
A stretch of days hovering at 100 degrees became unbearable to me.
The house seemed a living inferno.

One day,
my husband finally looked past his own miserable existence
long enough to notice life was evaporating from mine as well.

His suggestion,
"Let's go to the bar for beer and pizza."

Sitting across from each other in the booth,
we had nothing to say.
No remedies.
No shared visions.
Few shared words.

Everything led to nothing.

Our mutual aloneness rang a toll of deafening silence.

Outside the bar window,
the dark sullen waters of the Mississippi River
seemed to languish in the August doldrums.
Its murky darkness echoed my own.
I longed to escape within the flow of this kindred spirit.
Once beautiful and majestic,
the mighty Mississippi appeared a cesspool—
a dumping ground of society's reckless disregard.
Dour looking,
it endured because it had no choice—
can a river stop flowing because it wills to do so?
No.

I wanted so much to stop—to cease existing.
I imagined jumping from the Broadway Street bridge into the turbid waters below.
How sweet the respite:
no more loneliness,
no more hopelessness,
no more forcing myself to wake up each day and move.

As I imagined my dead body floating downstream,
perhaps becoming ensnared on a deadfall,
the baby within me began thrashing about.
Arms and legs everywhere, rolling, turning, thumping.
Normally so docile,
its sudden unexplainable movement
called me back to reality.
Was it the pizza I ate?
Maybe my emotions transferred?

Rubbing my abdomen as if to console it,
I realized I couldn't hurt this little one within me—
I already knew it to be sweet natured.

There had to be a way,
even if I couldn't see it.

A week later it came to me.
It was genius of a demented sort.
As if participating in a burial ceremony,
I threw pictures of friends and a trip west, my yearbook, scrapbooks
and journals into the river.

Remnants of my former life floated downstream
and sunk slowly to their burial ground.

As the only mourner at the funeral,
I stood alone and watched.
Watched with a cold and indifferent heart.
Maybe this would make the pain stop.
Maybe this would kill the longing.

Culpability

It had helped some—throwing my life in the river deadened the longing.

The summer heat was still bearing down like a relentless nightmare;
inescapable, sweating and feverish,
it siphoned energy from mind and body.
I feared the prospect of listless, unfilled time;
time where I might start thinking and feeling again.
So, I kept moving, doing anything that filled the day.

To avoid the heat, I spent as much time in the basement as possible.
I ignored the fact that the basement was dank and dreary.
I ignored my husband's increasing withdrawal into alcohol.
I ignored the amniotic fluid slowly leaking from its sack.

I acted tough.
I was tough.

Perching myself on a gallon paint can that was stored in the basement,
I allowed my feet to absorb the cool dampness of the gray cement floor.
I wondered how we would pay for a premature birth—
we had no medical insurance.

It was still seven weeks until the due date.
The unending discharge of amniotic fluid was now beginning to alarm me.
Could I be injuring my baby?
I researched the subject in a medical encyclopedia.
It said the patient is normally hospitalized
and monitored closely for the first sign of fever.
I could do that at home.
Lying in bed, I took my temperature every two hours.

If only it would stop.
The baby's movements seemed normal.
The temperature stayed constant.
But the contractions started.

Now, there was no option.
I went to the hospital.
Mom watched Ben.

My doctor was out of town and another doctor,
whom I had never met, was filling in.
Waiting for the next contraction to start,
he stood with a cigarette in one hand
and an examination glove on the other.

I started explaining the events of the past couple of days.
As I got to the part about my fluid leaking, the next contraction hit.
With his hand inside my cervix
he began his tirade, using vulgarities to exclaim
his extreme disapproval of my choices,
"What the fuck were you thinking?
You may have endangered the fetus."
And, "You mean you stayed home because you didn't have insurance?!
Don't you know it's irresponsible to not have insurance?"
It seemed like the wrong thing to say
while his hand was fully engaged in my cervix.
I thought he would never leave the room,
let alone remove his hand from my cervix.

I was petrified!
I was guilty.
I was horrible.
I was miserable.

I wanted to see my baby.
Each contraction brought me closer to seeing it, holding it.

During the next contraction something slipped…changed.
I felt a sense of urgency,
but couldn't explain it because I still wasn't in transition.
I called the nurse and asked her to check.
I informed her, "Something has happened. Something very weird."
She wanted to put me off (everyone there seemed irritated with me).
I insisted, "You really have to check!"

That was when she noticed the blood hemorrhaging from between my legs.
Her face became stone, her words few.
She exited the room with haste,
without addressing my questions,
"What is happening?

Why is there so much blood?
Is my baby okay?
Oh, God.
My baby.
Please help my baby."

Within three minutes a surgical room was made available
and I was transferred by gurney into surgery.
Still, none of my questions had been answered.

I tried to fight the anesthesia—
I wanted to see my baby alive.
But my determination was no match for its potency
and I began to slip into unconsciousness without knowing—
had I killed my baby?

The Gift of Life

Waking from the anesthesia seemed impossible.
In waves of decreasing intensity,
voices ebbed and flowed from my consciousness.
"Open your eyes," I heard them say.
"Sit up."
"Okay," I responded with a feeble attempt to lift my head from the pillow.
The room went black.

"You need more blood," the nurse explained.
A fresh bag was exchanged for the empty.
Finally, the voices seemed to stay in the room instead of dissipating into the void.
I was told I could thank my father's AA group for the blood donations.

"How's my baby?"
"Oh, he's a strapping young fellow, nine and a half pounds.
You should thank your lucky stars you didn't go full term—
he would have went 14 pounds," chortled the nurse.

"Is he alright?"
"Yeah, a little jaundiced. He'll have to stay a couple of days, but he'll be fine."

"When can I see my baby?"
"Later this afternoon—we wanna make sure you won't be
passing out while holding him."

"When can I go home?   We don't have insurance and I can't afford to stay."
"Why don't we worry about that tomorrow?"

"I have to go to the bathroom."
"We've already taken care of that—just relax—you have a catheter."

"Do you know the doctor who delivered me?" I asked.
"He's not a regular here. Why do you ask?" she looked at me quizzically.
"Because he is a jerk!"

"Oh," she murmured. "I heard he had some troubles.
I think your doctor's office is trying to help him get back on his feet."
Fearing perhaps she had overstepped her bounds,
the nurse closed the discussion.
"Why don't you rest now?
Goodness knows you aren't going to get much of that when you leave here,"
she whispered,
as if to lull me to sleep.

STRONG-MINDED

She was right.
Soon after we were both home,
the baby developed an abscess on his chest and I, a sinus infection.
The doctor ordered hot packs to his chest and my head,
rotating between us every hour.

At 3:00 in the morning, the cheap olive-drab carpet cast its
putrid reflection on us both.
My baby's skin, still jaundiced, looked gangrenous.
My limp hair hung in clumps around my face
serving only to accentuate my dark and sunken eyes.
We were fit company for each other.

Each day his abscess moved closer to the surface.
The area around the abscess head was bright red and hot to the touch.
When it was time to lance the abscess,
Dr. Streu asked if I could hold my son, Andy, firmly down on the exam table.
"Mothers usually can't tolerate something like this.
Are you sure you can handle it?
Where is your husband? Maybe he should do it?" he offered.
"Dr. Streu, my husband didn't come; he's in bed sleeping.
I can handle it. I'm sure," I said with exhausted confidence.
His skeptical look disclosed his disbelief.

Shrugging his shoulders, he began to prep the area.
Using the razor sharp point of the scalpel,
he started to cut through the breast tissue.
He continued cutting in a line across the fullest part of the abscess.
As he proceeded, sticky yellow pus oozed from the incision.
It was wiped clean several times and still more drained.
Using cotton gauze, the doctor pushed gently around the incision
forcing excretions until blood began to flow.
All the while, I held Andy still
as he wailed a breathless, gasping, suffocating scream.

Dr. Streu affirmed, "You are quite a strong-minded woman."

I didn't think I had any other choice.

GOVERNMENT SURPLUS CHEESE AND TURKEY CARCASSES

By now,
all the relatives knew of our condition;
hospital bills that could not be paid,
doctors' bills that could not be paid,
and an income at the bottom of the poverty level.

The relatives tried to help out.

Grandma always took the cheese from the government surplus program.
She didn't want it. She didn't even like it.
The stuff was dry and broke apart in irregular shapes when she tried to cut it.
But she figured it was good enough for us.
"Beggars can't be choosers," she'd snap.
And, she was right.

During the holidays
everyone would save their turkey carcasses for me.
There was always meat left on the bones—enough for two meals.
The bones and skin, when simmered slowly, made great soup.
I would collect three or four carcasses each holiday
and double wrap them for storage in the freezer.

A cousin who worked at a pharmaceutical company
brought me expired infant formula.
"It's still good long past the expiration," she said.
"They do that as a safety precaution.
It's still good though,"
she added to clarify.

I set my sewing machine up in the basement and sewed the boys' pajamas
and made their comforters from old sheets.

Cloth diapers were donated.

I don't know how he did it,
but my husband always had money to stay out drinking at night.

The relatives had some advice:
make the bum get a job!

Chapter 3

THE LONG DARK TUNNEL

GONE FISHING

He didn't want to talk about our marriage;
he never did.
I, on the other hand,
couldn't avoid the pain.

I told him we needed to talk.
He had no time—
he was going fishing with a drinking buddy.

I urged,
"It is important.
If we can't talk now, when can we talk?"

His response, "All right, make it fast. I want to get out of here."

So, after taking several deep breaths, I burst out,

"I want a divorce."

He did not bargain, nor plead, nor cry.
He went fishing.

The basement was dark
and smelled of the dirty diaper pail I had just emptied into the washer.
As the washer started to fill with hot water
I stood alone and cried.

CRUSHED BY DECREE

Prior to the hearing
I explained to my lawyer the history of my husband's alcoholism,
the police report on abuse,
and the lack of work history.

We went before a referee;
a pre-court hearing.
The referee was known for his negative judgments against women.

I was ill prepared;
not because I was negligent,
my lawyer was.
He was no longer professionally disciplined.
His career over,
at 70 plus, he volunteered through Legal Aid.

I had no money to pay for a top-notch lawyer.
Stuck in a hard spot,
I decided to trust justice.
I was sure my case would be presented
even if my lawyer was a compromise.

Aghast, I sat in the courtroom and listened
as my lawyer failed to present my concerns.
I requested that the referee hear my story,
but he would not allow any personal testimony in the hearing.

The referee's judgment hit like a swift blow to my head.
I reeled under the concussion.

The referee's face was free of emotion as he said,
"Your husband has the degree.
He can earn a living.
You, on the other hand,
sell women's home decorations at house parties.
I don't support creating a welfare state.
For that reason, he will have the kids,
and, it follows, also the home.
He will also need the good car to get to work."

The referee added, with a final crushing strike,
"If you want custody of your kids, I suggest you get a real job."

I left the courtroom with my lawyer.
"It's not hopeless, there is still a final hearing," he mumbled.
Then in the mood to discuss something of more interest to him,
he described his exhilaration when past female clients
performed oral sex on him.

In my shock, it took me a while to catch on.
Could it be?!
Had I lost everything?
Was I really standing next to a pervert
after I had just lost everything?
No.

No! I didn't want to believe it.

I ran out and clung to the balcony rail.
The blood seemed to drain from my body.
I could not see.
I could not think.
I could not hear.

"Please, Dear God, help me!
Help me. Help me.
PLEASE, DEAR GOD.
PLEASE, DEAR GOD.
PLEASE, DEAR GOD."

Once a man jumped to his death from the same county balcony.
They had to put up high glass walls to eliminate the problem.
It's understandable....why it happens.
It's a dismal place.
A place of inhumanity,
                gasping,
                        sweating,
                                crying,
                                        on the edge.

VIEW FROM BENEFICENCE

The shocking nature of my legal counsel's presentation,
and later his lewd suggestions,
amplified my despair to a level where life became surreal.
Everything I heard and smelled seemed of another world.
I stopped seeing things as real and concrete.
Buildings appeared like paper facades.
People walking in the street resembled mannequins formed from dust;
I imagined my touch could cause them to disintegrate before my eyes.

My mother had been waiting outside the court for the referee's decision.
She confessed a desire to live her own escape vicariously through me.
But this wasn't the way she envisioned escape,
nor was this the outcome she expected.

Without doubt, I needed a new attorney.
Yet, I had no money,
and I personally knew of no attorney willing to take my case.

A thought occurred to Mom;
Sandy, one of her sewing customers, worked for an attorney.
Maybe Sandy could convince him to help us.

Sandy talked to her boss.
The attorney agreed to meet with us.

His office, housed in a historic building near the Walker Art Center,
was large with built-in, floor to ceiling, mahogany bookshelves.
I sensed I had entered yet another entirely different world,
as surreal as mine had become.
A world of intellectuals and professionals where the cruelties of life
are somehow assuaged by education and self worth.

He was a man of large stature and quiet disposition.
The secretary ushered us into his office and closed the door when she exited.
As he listened earnestly and intently,
some of my distortions of reality dissipated.
Focus and hope returned.
It seemed like magic—
magic only the human heart can give and receive.

He agreed to take my case,
and would wait payment of his fees and expenses
until the final divorce settlement was reached.
At that time, I hopefully could pay him from the meager
equity we had in the house.

Never before had I experienced this kind of affirmation of my worth.
In the gift he gave,
I suddenly saw value in my existence.

I wanted to enter the world where he lived;
a world of quiet confidence,
assurance,
maturity,
stability,
purpose.
A world where I could gift others as I had just been gifted.

ABSOLUTELY NOTHING

My new attorney advised me that the referee's decision still stood;
I had to leave the house.

Allowed the indulgence of taking only personal items,
I put the few clothes I owned in a paper bag,
grabbed my toothbrush and shut the front door behind me.

My parents allowed me to stay with them until I could find an apartment.

I had no furnishings, no dishes, no towels, no cooking utensils;
I had absolutely nothing.

Grandmother, Mom and I,
as the kindred sisterhood of the downtrodden,
went garage sale shopping to acquire the necessities.
We found a clean sofa sleeper for $25,
piecemeal dishes, pots and pans, and glasses for an additional $5.

The county gave me a list of low rent apartments,
the kind that accept welfare recipients.
It seemed welfare-friendly apartments were a dime a dozen,
so I had little difficulty finding one.

The county also informed me I was qualified for additional help.
It appeared I was a unique class:
thrown out of my house by the court,
no money,
no belongings—
I was classified under some seldom used disaster relief category.
I was advised to register at the welfare office downtown—
they would help me out until things got in place.

Safety Net

I stood in line an hour with people waiting for welfare.
Upon entering the clerk's office
I explained I needed only a negligible amount,
just enough to get me through this state of emergency.
I could make it.
You see, I would work.

"No, no," they counseled.
"If you get custody,
 you'll have no need to work while the children are young.
The county will provide assistance for rent, food, etc.
It is important for parents to be home when the kids are young."
I didn't disagree with the importance of parenting,
I just disagreed with the concept of no responsibility to work.
After all, I was brought up with a work ethic.
It would not be right.
I must work.

Being considerate,
they reminded me I had no degree;
finding work to cover day-care costs would be difficult.
I appreciated their thoughtfulness.

"Thank you, but no thank you," I argued.
"I don't think the government owes me a living.
I just need help getting on my feet."

They gave me an initial sum under the classification of emergency aid
and explained the way the system worked.
Later, when I had custody,
I would receive a monthly check that covered child support.
Then the county would collect the amount due from my husband.
That way, if he didn't pay, we wouldn't be compromised.

ON THE JOB LEARNING

The small amount of emergency relief the county gave me
did not cover the essentials.
I still had an urgent need to make quick cash.

My mom's sisters each offered a suggestion,
    "Sell your blood—that's easy."
    "No, sell your body—that's more profitable."
    "How about selling drugs? That's where the big bucks are."

My lack of flare surely disappointed my aunts.
Instead of taking their advice,
I cleaned homes, cars, pools, yards;
whatever I could find that was legal.

When strangers heard of my circumstance,
they went out of their way to think of odd jobs for me.
    "Oh, the leather seats in my car are filthy, disgusting!
    Would you mind cleaning them?"

    "I'm not in the habit of worrying about how the yard looks,
    but I imagine the neighbors would appreciate your efforts
    to spruce up our yard."

    "A pool service cleaned the pool last year,
    but I wasn't satisfied.
    Would you have time to do that as well?"

This kind of understanding from complete strangers
diminished my sense of isolation.

Mae, a Jewish woman who lived in St. Louis Park,
supervised me oppressively close the first day I cleaned her house.
    She stood outside the shower stall
    watching,
    while I stood inside
    cleaning.

    She immediately inspected each room I finished.
    All floors were scrubbed on my hands and knees.
    I used a toothbrush to clean the edges and corners of her kitchen floor.

After finishing the first day,
I lay on the front seat of my car
too exhausted to drive myself home.
I considered sleeping in the car overnight,
but decided against it,
suspecting the neighbors would call the police
and complain about a rusted-out vehicle
abandoned on their street by a transient worker.

After the second full day of cleaning,
Mae and I developed a rapport and respect for each other.
I discovered her toughness was only exceeded by her generosity.
Each week there was something else she no longer needed
that I "should" take home.
When her new china arrived,
she packed up her old service for 12,
and left it by the door, insisting,

> "Are you kidding? There's no one in the family
> who wants this old stuff.
> Take it! Take it!
> Please, it's yours!
> Take it!"

Mae usually made tuna and sweet pickle sandwiches for lunch.
We'd sit together,
Mae, her husband, Julius,
and I,
and talk about life.
How sweet pickles are so great with tuna.
What it is like to have nothing.
They understood and passed no judgment;
life had taught them that things can be taken away.
"You just have to start over," they said, as they patted each other's hand.
"That's all. Just start over."
I'd ask Julius how his cancer treatments were going.
Usually, I already knew the answer.
I could tell by the clumps of hair on the bathroom floor,
and the blood and vomit splatters in the toilet bowl.
He never complained.

Cleaning their home was a profoundly intimate experience.
I came to know the rhythm of their struggles
in ways that others lacking my proximity could not.
Through this unexpected bond of closeness,
I learned that hardship makes grace shine brighter.

The psychologist wanted her backyard pool cleaned
for her daughter's wedding.
Because she was a compassionate woman,
she made a laundry list of things for me to do to earn money.
She didn't mind paying me to do the chores—
they had the money.

I was hired to clean the pool,
rake the yard,
clean the house,
and serve drinks the evening of the wedding.

The evening of the wedding
groups of people stood poolside,
admiring the setting that had been painstakingly created.
The drinks flowed freely,
while yard lights shone across the pool
creating glimmering trails of light
that bobbed playfully across the water's surface.
A group of tuxedoed gentlemen,
champagne bottles in hand,
jumped into the pool
sending the trails of light into frenzied undulations.
Soon the women followed.
They celebrated long into the night,
until exhaustion forced an ending.

The next morning, I came back to clean up.
Understanding the enormity of the job in front of me,
the bleary-eyed mother of the bride expressed her sincere
gratitude for my return.

The newlywed bikini-clad daughter,
who was near my age,
came in the house after her morning swim
and sat sprawled on the sofa watching me vacuum.
Her look of disdain and detachment withered my struggling self worth.

When I attempted to vacuum a small pile of grass and
leaves discarded at her feet,
she refused to move,
and snapped,
"You're annoying me!
Go somewhere else and vacuum."

Her mother apologized
explaining she had lost influence over her daughter many years ago.

Feeling the effects of her daughter's disregard,
I wondered if my sons would grow to display such contemptuousness.
I admitted our lives were uncertain and fragile,
but no one deserves the contempt I felt from her.

LOST AT SEA

Surprisingly,
when I asked for the divorce,
I never thought of the issue of child custody;
I simply could not live any longer,
if it meant living with him.

Now,
custody was an ocean
and I was adrift at sea in a ship without a rudder.

Instead of caring for my boys daily,
I was now visiting them twice a week.
It seemed ludicrous;
the man who couldn't even care for himself
was now fully responsible for my sons.

But I wasn't laughing—
I was lost.

I felt as if the boys had been tossed overboard during a raging storm;
I tried desperately to reach their tiny hands
as they careened helplessly in the voluminous swells.
Yet I was completely without means to save them.
Each time visitation was over,
I watched their faces grow distant as I walked away
and my heart sank
into the deepest, darkest, depths;
to the bottom of the ocean,
where I could do nothing
but let go of my tenuous grasp.

A Job with Clout

I detested feeling helpless.

I asked myself what I could do to get custody of my kids.

The referee had made it perfectly clear:
if I were to gain custody,
I would need a "real" job.
This was no time to question why the referee did not understand
my reluctance to leave my children unprotected,
and that was why I sold decorating products in home shows.
Even if I did consider the referee an insensitive reactionary,
I had to play the game by his rules.

Fortified with almost an associate degree in nothing,
I hit the streets.
I found nothing other than waitress jobs and temporary placement positions.

But just when things began to seem dark and hopeless,
my father's AA group came to rescue the daughter of one of their own again;
first it was blood, and now it was a job.

I was interviewed for the position at the AA club picnic.
Held every summer at Fort Snelling,
the picnic was an event filled with the customary games and food,
but no alcohol.

The professor was sitting on top of a picnic table
watching my brother and I play badminton.
My shorts were exceptionally short and my
body down to an "attractive" weight;
judging by the direction of his gaze,
I was sure he noticed.
After the set, he called me over.
"Your dad tells me you are looking for a job."
Pulling my shorts down in back, I sat next to him on the table.
"Yes, I am."
"What do you know about biochemistry?"
he asked, looking over the top of his glasses.
"I had biology, chemistry, anatomy and physiology."
"Do you know what a lipid is?"
"Yes, it's a fat molecule."

Two more questions and the interview was over.
I suspect it had something to do with my shorts
and Dad's brotherhood in AA.
It had nothing to do with my intellect or capability,
which were entirely unknown commodities,
to him as well as to myself.

I began work in the biochemistry department at the university
just one week after the picnic.
Each day I stood at the lab bench
filled with trembling timidity.
Although I felt totally inferior for the job,
I knew my children hung in the balance;
there could be no excuses—
I had better learn quickly and perform well.

CLUBBING CARP

I would do whatever was required
to find my way out of the mess I was in.

There was no doubt about it,
getting my new job at the university
meant overcoming a major hurdle—the "respectability" hurdle.
Even if I couldn't say I loved every aspect of the job,
I was grateful to have it.

So on that bright, early Monday morning,
when the professor handed me a pair of rubber gloves designed for gripping
and a large rubber mallet,
I decided to remind myself just how grateful I was.

"Okay, now what?" I asked, looking stupidly at him.

"Here, you probably should wear this plastic apron," he said with a grin.

I put it on, tying it in the back.

"Yeah, now what?"

"Grab one of the carp,
hold it tight on the board here,
and hit it real hard on the head with the rubber mallet to stun it."

Looking a lot like a stunned carp myself,
I asked, "Are you kidding?"

"Nope."

"What do I do with it after that?"

"Milk it by running your hand along both sides of its belly, like this,"
he smirked,
demonstrating the motion on a carp.
"Then count the sperm in each sample and record it in the book."

"Hum, so that is sperm in that creamy white fluid?" I noted aloud,
while trying not to look repulsed.

"After that, cut the carp open along its belly
and take out the testes and liver.
Grind them up separately following the procedure I gave you last week.
Remember to mark and record all samples specific to each fish."
He left the lab for the comfort of his office.

I took a deep breath as I began my carp assault.
It seemed a putrid price to pay for a respectable job.

I swung the rubber mallet downward.
The carp's head flipped sideways.
The mallet missed the carp and hit the board with a resounding thud.
I heard chortling from the professor's office.

I got mad.

I grabbed the carp with an iron grip,
this time near its head.
Its tail thrashed violently until eventually I lost my grip.
It hit the floor and took off down the lab corridor.
Skittering along the floor,
the carp had almost reached the exit by the time I corralled it.

People in the adjacent lab were laughing.
I shrugged my shoulders and turned red.
This really was too much to pay for respectability.

From his office
I heard the professor mockingly say,
"What's the matter,
that carp getting the better of you?"

Under my breath, I muttered:
"Glad you think it's so funny.
I'd rather clean toilets than do this!"
I kept muttering while maintaining a headlock on the runaway carp.

This had to be a matter of will.

I steeled myself for the day-long assault.
Eventually, my will won
and all 20 carp had sacrificed themselves to the cause of research.

Although offering up carp in the hope of an eventual good
was not high on my list of accomplishments,
my self-confidence did develop a perkiness after that day.

MEDIATED TORTURE

My attorney was pleased with news of my job—
it was a big step in the right direction.

He had something to share with me as well.
Court Services had been ordered to provide custodial mediation,
which meant my husband and I would be allowed a reasonable length of time
to resolve our differences on custody.
If we could find a solution,
it would be presented to the court.
If we could not come to an agreement,
the court would order a custody evaluation.
"If that happens, the court will be making the decision for you," he said.
"Obviously, it is in everyone's best interest for the mediation to work."

I really wanted the mediation to work;
I never wanted to cause so much trouble;
I just wanted to feel life within me again.

Each session, however,
proved to be an inhumane form of torture—
an insane, mind crushing, abhorrent exercise in futility.

My husband's wounded pride and initial court victory
fueled his demand for custody.
Engorged with anger,
he asserted, while pointing his finger, that I was the guilty one.
I was the shameless whore who brought this disrespect upon his family.
"Your leaving me is going to kill my father.
Why can't you wait until he has beaten his cancer?
You're kicking him while he's down.
You know my mother is a good Catholic—
they don't get divorces.
This is destroying her.
You're killing everyone in my family."
There was no end to his tirade.
Drenched in shame,
I was willing to give anything just to stop the torture.
However, that would not have been a mediated solution,
that would have been surrender.
So, after 60 days
the court was told a resolution could not be reached.
A custody evaluation was consequently ordered.

Home is a Concept

While the evaluation was in progress
the court ordered the boys remain in the home;
the parents would be moved in and out and monitored with the children.
Accordingly, it was now my shift in the home.

Before the referee had forced me out,
the boys' bedroom had seemed like a safe haven.
I was proud of the way their room turned out;
the bed quilts and curtains sewn by hand,
walls, crib and dresser painted with patterns in bright and lively colors,
a discarded hard hat turned into a light fixture
proved to be the finishing touch.
Standing back to view my work, I was pleased.
So little money—such big results.

When I was allowed to return home several months later,
it was different.
The house was dark, closed up, dirty, and smelled of stale cigarette smoke and beer.

I was enraged!

The place had become a pigsty—
and I had to clean it up!

I started cleaning and didn't stop until the skin cracked and bled on my fingertips.
I washed the walls and ceilings,
light fixtures,
cupboards and closets,
windows and woodwork.
I also rented a steamer and cleaned the carpets,
moved and cleaned underneath all the appliances,
washed all the curtains, bedding, and linens.

Since the custody evaluation would consider the cleanliness of the house,
I persisted until there was no spot left untouched.

I thought the sinking feelings I had during my period of visitation would vanish
when I returned home.
They didn't.
Now, even my concept of "home" felt violated.
Nothing seemed secure and we were still adrift at sea.

KEYS TO ENTRY

When the court ordered my return to the house,
my husband had been told to turn over the extra set of keys.
He refused.
He said it was still half his house
and that meant he should have a set of keys.

My attorney documented my request
in writing to my husband's attorney.

He still refused to comply.

The keys meant reentry into my life
anytime he chose.
Theoretically, I could not lock him out.

Because there was no other "man" in my life,
my dad gradually reentered.
He changed the locks on the doors.

Amazing Grace

Things were not going as smoothly as my husband expected.
No longer in the house,
he was now in the position of visiting parent.

Just like my father,
when he discovered he had lost control
his behavior became more vile and evil.

Each time he picked up the boys:
he threatened to never return them;
he would leave the state;
he would hide in obscure parts of the country where no one would find him;
he told me I would never see the boys again;
he would keep moving;
and no one would ever find them. [2]

I envisioned the boys without a home, school, friends;
dirty waifs, becoming faceless nobodies
because their father kept them moving.

I informed Court Services of his constant threats.
I told them he vowed, "I'll kill you before I'll let you take my kids."
They told me it was very important for children to have both parents in their
lives, and it was nearly impossible to restrict a parent's visitation rights.

I was advised to talk to a counselor who could help me develop coping skills.

But there wasn't a counselor on earth who could have helped me that night—
the night I waited and watched as the clock ticked by slowly
and still the boys were not returned.
Hour after hour.
Miserable.
Hopeless.

I paced.

I called my husband's mother.
She had no idea where he was.

I called his sister.
She had no idea.

He was six hours late.

I called the police.

They advised me I had to wait 24 hours before reporting a missing person.

I watched the clock again.

"Is there no one who can help me?!!" I shouted aloud.

I resumed my pacing and began praying.

I cried,
"Oh God,
please don't let this happen.
Jesus, the panic I feel could swallow me up.
Please bring my children back.
I have nothing.
Please, please, not my children.
Lord, oh God,
I could die from this grief.
Speak to me—say something, please.

I know everything on this earth passes away,
and to invest my soul in things that are temporal is foolish.
But I'm talking about my sons…
they are my sons.
They are my flesh.

Am I not supposed to be responsible?

You knew Abraham's heart when you tested him;
know mine.
You are not a God that sacrifices children.
Don't allow the boys to be sacrificed on this altar of insanity.

Understand that I feel so responsible, so accountable.
What happens if they are in danger?
What am I supposed to do?
I've tried everything I know.
God, I feel so helpless.
I could die.

Help me.
Please, help me."

Throwing myself on the bed,
I buried my face in the pillow and wept until I could weep no more.

And then, in the breathless silence,
I felt the Lord's presence—
beautiful, soft and peaceful.
A wave of knowing, of quiet assurance,
filled my body,
dissolving the fear that had strangled my heart.
Suddenly, I knew they were safe;
they would be returned soon.
The feeling was incredibly serene.
I allowed myself to float in this new state of knowing.
Resting, I let the assurance overtake me.

Moments earlier,
the walls and ceiling of the room
seemed to be collapsing on me,
leaving no air to breathe or light to see.
All at once
I felt as if a huge crane had lifted rubble from my body
and God stood ready to deliver me from my tomb of despair.

Everything shone light and bright.

I marveled at the love and deliverance
of this living God who heard my cry.
I felt rich beyond words,
and knew nothing on earth could replace the value of our intimacy.
I could never leave.
I never wanted to leave this place;
a place,
a state of being,
of being engulfed in God's love.

From within my haze of euphoric deliverance,
I vaguely heard a knock at the door.
The knocking, however, called me back into the moment,

the moment I had been waiting for.
I ran to the door,
and opened it to see the boys standing in front of their father.
Without hesitation, I snatched them across the threshold
and claimed the gift I had just been assured.
The intensity of my instinct to clutch them surprised me.
Had I gone over the edge?

My behavior seemed inconsistent to me.

Often I resented the responsibility;
the loneliness of all the demands.
I could be very strict and intolerant with them.

But at that moment,
I wanted desperately to attach them to my body permanently,
even if it meant one on each hip.

I asked their father why he returned them so late.
I asked why he hadn't called.

He had no reason;
he wanted them longer,
so he kept them longer.

I firmly stated my understanding of the rules of visitation;
visitation on the agreed upon days, for the agreed upon hours only.
He disagreed.
He would continue to do just as he pleased,
defying anyone to try to stop him.

In his mind,
he was not wrong.

FIGHTING PANIC

It was the day I was to be evaluated for custody.
I got out of work late
and ran four blocks to remote parking,
where, thankfully, my car started.

I would be late.
I didn't need this,
not now.
I imagined the Hennepin County family counselor
looking at her watch,
wondering if I were the irresponsible type.

This meeting meant my life,
my children's health and future happiness,
my vindication.
Truly, my world would continue
or cease,
depending on how I presented myself.
And…to my horror,
I was making the county counselor wait;
wait, while I fought time, traffic and a dying car.

"Hurry,
hurry,
hurry!" I begged the drivers in front of me.
But they had no idea of my panic.

"Don't turn red.
Please don't turn red,"
I pleaded with each stoplight.
But the stoplights had no idea of my panic.

Each time I slowed for a red light,
I urged the car,
"Don't stall.
 Please, don't stall."
But the car had no idea of my panic.
Each time it stalled,
I asked for mercy as I turned the ignition key,
"Please start.
Please start.
God, please make this pile of junk start."

Christ knew my panic when I said,
"There is no one else who can help me.
Please help me."

As I slowed the car to a stop in front of the day-care,
it stalled.
Rushing in,
sweat beading on my upper lip and forehead,
I called,
"Come on boys,
we have to hurry."

"But mom, I wanna finish this picture."

"Sorry, honey.
You can finish it tomorrow."

Sitting in the back seat,
Ben asked,
"Why are you in such a hurry?"

"Sweetie, you know how I have been cleaning the house really hard lately?
And I told you that someone important was going to visit us?
Well, she is visiting us today,
and I think she beat us home."

"That's okay," he said.

"Maybe, but I wanted to make a good impression
and being late is inconsiderate."

As we turned the corner of our block,
he pointed and said,
"She beat us."

She was sitting on the front steps,
legal case in her lap.

I whimpered,
"Oh, God, help!!"

Trying very hard to be in control of my emotions,
I apologized for my tardiness and introduced the boys.

Ben was unimpressed and wanted to play.
"Can I go outside?" he asked.

"Sure, but stay in the front yard where I can see you."
With Andy on my lap,
the counselor and I sat at the kitchen table
where I could see Ben in the front yard.

She asked me questions and watched me,
making notes at different times on her legal pad.
She never betrayed her opinion with affirming statements
or looks of disapproval.

She wanted to see the rest of the house.

I called Ben in from the front so I could walk her through the house.
He wasn't happy coming in.
But given the threats of kidnapping,
I could not allow him out of my sight.

The county worker flipped through a report from the child psychologist.
She asked the boys if they would like to sit with her for a moment.
They talked about books and their room.
She asked if they have friends nearby.

At two years old,
Andy wasn't talking yet,
so Ben spoke for him.

When she finished,
she shook my hand
and said she would make the report available to the court.
She left without providing any indication of her conclusions.

I felt miserably out of control—
helpless.

Although exhausted,
I slept fitfully, startled by every sound.

Chapter 4

RIGHTS ARE NOT GUARANTEED

CUSTODY REPORT

Soon after the evaluations were complete
I received a written copy of the custody report;
its findings and recommendations.

Findings
In my interview with him, Mr. S. told me that his wife had the primary relationship with the children during the marriage. He described her as an adequate mother.

He spoke of his current stressful emotional state. During the custody mediation process, Mr. S. was administered the Minnesota Multiphasic Personality Inventory. He refused permission to access those test results. He took another for the purpose of the custody study. The second test results were found to be technically invalid because of his guardedness and defensiveness.

Toward the end of my interview with him, he raised the possibility of some violent behavior on his part, or absconding with the children, but indicated that neither of these would occur until after the court hearing. The clear implication was that the outcome of his not acquiring custody might produce either of those consequences.

In my home visit with Mrs. S., I found the house to be immaculate. The children looked healthy, and her interaction with them was entirely satisfactory.

Mrs. S. told me that she was concerned about her husband, and that she was afraid of him. "He's having a hard time emotionally. He's very upset. He has had to deal with the divorce plus the recent death of his father. He keeps telling me he is going to kidnap the kids."

Recommendations
Given Mr. S.'s statements that Mrs. S. has had the primary relationship with the children, that she is an adequate mother, that the latter was reinforced by my observations during the home visit, I am unequivocally recommending that she retain custody.

I am calling to the court's attention my belief that Mr. S.'s emotional state is precarious. I consider his threats to kidnap the children, or to commit other acts of violence to have very real potential. I strongly urge that precautionary steps be taken, particularly in the area of visitation. I have two suggestions— that visitation take place under closely supervised conditions only, or, that visitation be conditional on Mr. S.'s getting immediate psychiatric help.

SEPARATION ANXIETY

In his mind
his behavior was perfectly sane.
He had no need for psychiatric help.
But, if he were forced to choose between the two evils presented him—
supervised visitation or psychiatric treatment—
he would choose treatment.

He began seeing a counselor.

I was also encouraged by the court to see a counselor;
to separate myself emotionally from him and let go of
responsibility for his welfare.
In my mind, his hurt was a direct result of my quest for freedom.
At times my feelings of shame seemed overwhelming.
Thinking I was showing pity,
I thought of the separation process as tearing off a bandage slowly.
It only made detaching harder.

DON'T ANSWER IT!

My husband became obsessed.
Every night, three, four or five times, the phone rang.
It was always him.

Each conversation followed the same course.
He was civil at first,
until I would not acquiesce.
Then he would become hostile, violent, threatening.

My counselor admonished me for answering the phone.
He advised, "Let him fall—let go.
When he threatens suicide, you don't have to respond.
Let his counselor take care of him."

When the phone rang the next evening,
I answered it, feeling guilty and ashamed.

The conversation followed the same path.
I hated myself for answering.

Again, the counselor instructed me, "Let him fall."

Finally, I stopped answering the phone.
It rang 20 times a night—all night.
It rang and rang and rang,
until I thought I would lose my mind.
It rang for days, weeks.

Very late one evening it rang.
I answered.
It was his mother asking me to please reconsider.

She had her priest call.
He pleaded on their behalf,
"Would you please consider a meeting in my office?
Christ does not like enmity.
Can't we resolve this as Christians?
The church is praying for your marriage."

Guilt and shame are great manipulators.

PRIESTLY COUNSEL

The priest's office was in the front of the church.
My husband was waiting in the room when I arrived.
Reverence for the church, or the priest's office,
did not inhibit him,
and it didn't take long for his hostile and threatening behavior to appear.

Soon I was crying,
and wondering why I had ever let myself get suckered into this meeting.

The priest asked him to leave the room.
"I want you to take a few quiet moments and think about what you are saying.
Your antagonism is not helping.
Please leave," the priest said while escorting him to the door,
"and sit in the hall until I call you back."

I stood to help myself to the tissues on the desk.
The priest returned to my side.
Holding my hands in his,
he expressed his deep sorrow for the state of my marriage.
"I believe you need comforting my dear," he said,
as he drew me into an embrace.
He pulled me so close, I could not reach my nose with the tissue.
It was awkward and uncomfortable.
I tried to pull back,
indicating I could not reach my nose with the tissue.
He seemed to not care about my desire for greater distance.
He pulled me closer,
wrapping his arms around me.

With my nose dripping,
I told him I did not need comforting.
"Oh my dear, of course you need comforting.
Divorce can be a very difficult process," he asserted.
I felt like I was in the grip of a boa constrictor.

His embrace continued to encircle me until his hands
were resting on my breasts,
and I felt his pelvis pressed against mine.

"Let go of me!" I insisted.
"I don't need your comforting, or your counseling."

I pushed to free myself from him.

He looked flushed.

"I see no reason to stay here—
this is going nowhere.
You can explain to my husband.
Good-bye."

Holding my breath,
I hurried down the hall
and pushed the heavy double doors open with one forceful movement.
After walking a significant distance from the church,
I stopped to take a deep breath.

I could not believe it!
I just could not believe it!

ASSERTING BASIC HUMAN RIGHTS

The counselor and I talked often about what I needed and wanted.
It turned out to be a difficult subject for me.
I felt I had no rights.
No right to my own feelings.
No right to have my own needs met.
No right to hurt another if my feelings were different than theirs.
No right to change my mind.
No right to make a mistake.
My list went on and on.

He asked,
"Don't you think you deserve to live outside of this dreadful fear?"

"No.
Life is what it is.
I don't believe in the word 'deserve.'
If you ask me, only spoiled people think they deserve something."

Scratching his bearded chin, he asked,
"Why do you suppose you think that?"

"I don't know.
I expect everyone thinks that way.
Don't they?"

"No, they don't," he said, as he wrote something on his tablet.
"How are your parents supporting you through this process?"

"They are trying to be very supportive."

"How so?" he asked.

"Well, they want to take the boys and me to Disneyland
to get away from this war zone.
Dad has a house trailer, so we would drive out together and stay in the trailer."

"How do you feel about that?"

"I don't really want to go, not now—there is too much going on
and being confined with them in the car and the trailer for that long
would drive me crazy."

"Why don't you tell them you don't want to go right now,
maybe later would be better?"

"Are you kidding?
I can't say that to my mom—
she would be so hurt."

"Are you saying you want to go then?" he looked at me with a quizzical,
knowing look.

"No, I don't want to go."

"Then I suggest you tell them. It was a kind offer,
but now is not the right time."

I took a deep breath
and noticed the ache start in my stomach.

"What are you feeling?" he asked.

"Fear."

The next week, he asked me if I had told my mother.

"Yes, I did."
"How did she respond?"

"Mom said, 'My father has hurt me before.
Your dad has hurt me countless times,
and now this!!
I thought you were the one person I could count on not to hurt me.' "

"How did you respond to that?" the counselor asked.

"I told her I didn't want to hurt her,
but I just don't want to go now."

"Did she understand?"

"No. She cried."

"How do you feel now?"

"Horrible.
But I didn't back down—because I really don't want to go now.
So they are taking my oldest son to Disneyland
and I am staying home with my youngest son."

"You handled the situation very well.
Even if you don't feel great now,
that was a major positive step you just took.
I would like you to take this book on assertiveness training,
read it and practice it this next week.
It is important that you state your own feelings and uphold your own needs.
It's a good book.
It won't make you become a bad Christian.
Are you okay with what I am asking you to do?"

"Yes, I am okay with it. I'll do it."
"Good," he said, as he walked me to the door.

CREDIT WORTHY

Asserting myself involved concepts foreign to me.
I usually only sought a better situation
when my existing one proved unsustainable.
So when my sorry excuse for a car
refused to run anymore,
I had to make a decision.
Should I buy a new car or a used car?
Public transportation was not an option.
I decided reliable transportation
would remove at least one of the vulnerabilities in my life,
and that was a pleasure I might possibly allow myself.

I did some car shopping
and made an appointment at the credit union
for the next day immediately following work.

I left the lab that day reeking of fish, as usual.
I had wanted to change clothes before going to the credit union,
but there wasn't sufficient time.

Arriving on time,
I waited 45 minutes for the loan officer.
While waiting
I reminisced about the first of several loans they had given me;
my first car, the Galaxie 500.
I had paid it off early and every payment had been made on time.

As I lingered in the memory, I felt proud.
And I was beginning to feel strong.

The loan officer finally called me back to her office.
"What can I help you with?" she asked with a lilt.

"I'd like to get a loan for a new car."
I told her the details: make, model, price, etc.
It was the bare bones essentials of transportation—
nothing fancy—just reliable.

"Well, let's take a look at your financial situation," she said,
as she swiveled in her chair to reach for a pen.

I recounted the loans I had paid off previously at this same credit union,
and recalled the day I joined at age 17.
I stressed my stable income from my "respectable" job.
She nodded approvingly.
Then she asked if my husband would also be signing on the loan.
I explained the situation.

She pushed her chair back from the desk
and instructed me that I would have to find someone to co-sign on my loan.

"I don't understand.
If I have already proven myself credit worthy,
and I have a steady income,
why do I need someone to co-sign?" I asked.

"You're in a category of risk
that won't allow me to approve the loan on your income alone."

"I'm not a teenage boy!
I am a 26-year-old mother of two.
I have personally paid off numerous loans here!"

"I'm sorry," she said, as if reciting from a policy manual,
"if you want a loan through the credit union,
you'll have to find someone to co-sign."

I left the credit union feeling dejected.
The cool fresh evening air
only accentuated the permeating smell of fish on my clothes.

I wondered what a woman had to do
to prove herself worthy?

I had little choice
other than to ask my dad to co-sign.
It was degrading.

SHELTER FROM THE STORM

Every decision I made
was intended to increase our stability,
yet stability eluded us.

My husband's talk of kidnapping
had taken on a whole new intensity.
Without fear of repercussion,
he didn't care who he told about his plan to murder me and
kidnap Ben and Andy.
I felt as if I stood in the path of a developing hurricane.
Everyone within the county system
was telling me the storm was reaching epic proportions,
yet no one had any civil defense advice
other than to board up the windows.

I called the police out to my home.
They told me because he had not yet harmed me,
there was nothing they could do—
threats were not against the law. [3]

When the police left,
I felt totally abandoned.

I reasoned:
if the police would not protect me from murder
and my sons from being kidnapped,
then I would have no other choice but to assume the role of protector.

My father loaned me his pistol to use for protection.
Trained in gun safety as a teenager, I was told;
          never have a gun unless you know how to use it,
          never point a gun unless you intend to shoot it.

I had to resolve myself to the possibility of shooting my husband.
Could I really do that?
Would I really do that?
Was my aim good enough to halt him?
Not kill?

I imagined every detail of the scene;
the bullet hole,
his blood,
his look of disbelief as he stumbled and fell.

I replayed it over and over in my mind
until it became a real possibility.

Then taking the pillows from my bed,
I made a nest for myself just outside the boys' bedroom door.
I sat there, in my nest, all night long,
night after night,
with the pistol in my lap.

I slept in a state of alert.
I learned to see with my eyes closed.
Every sound,
every smell,
the feel of gun metal in my hand,
the movement of air in the house,
were all processed as vital information.
The accumulation of sensory cues ran like a continuous film in my mind.

Lights from passing cars penetrated my eyelids
causing me to wake.

Squirrels running on the roof
brought me to my feet.

Wind buffeting the windows
drove me crazy with fear.

I prayed, "Please don't let the boys get hurt.
Make me strong.
Keep me strong.
Please, keep us through the night."

Although I still felt unworthy to approach God,
in desperation I picked up my Bible and asked the Holy Spirit
to reveal a promise God meant for me.
As I opened the cover,
I pleaded, "Please let me know that I am not alone;
I want to find my strength in you.
I don't want to run away from you—
I want to run toward you."

In Isaiah I read:
> [I] give strength to the weary
> and increase the power of the weak.
> Even youths grow tired and weary,
> and young men stumble and fall;
> but those who hope in the Lord
> will renew their strength.
> They will soar on wings like eagles;
> they will run and not grow weary,
> they will walk and not be faint.

I believed the promise was given to me.

Each morning as the sun cast its subtle shades of grace
across the boys' sleeping faces
I said,
"Thank you, Lord,"
and readied myself for another day of work.

GUARD DUTY

My guard duty went on like that for days.
His threats of murder were unceasing
and became more violent with each passing day.
He gave detailed descriptions of how he would murder me,
and why I deserved to die.
He spoke in terms of my death and the boys' "deliverance"
as a holy and righteous crusade.
Anyone who stood in his way—for example, my father—
would also be killed.

Because he still had not physically harmed me,
I was left to provide my own protection.

Nesting outside their bedroom night after night
began to take its toll.
I bargained with the Lord, praying;
"Help me.
I need just a little more rest each night.
I want the boys to be secure, uninterrupted, asleep in their beds.
I don't want them to experience my panic, my worry.
I need to rest in my bed even though it's further away.
Will you keep me alert enough and quick enough?"

It seemed to me I had no other choice but to trust.

Since I didn't want to accidentally blow my head off,
I decided to keep the pistol under my pillow
and the clip separate in my left hand.

It was uncomfortable;
I felt the hard lump of the gun under my pillow,
but at least I knew where it was.

I lay awake wondering how long this would go on;
when would it end?

The nights were restless
and long,
very long.

Suspecting the darkness of night harbored unseen terrors
that were meant to harm me,
I would sit and peer out of a small slit between the curtain and window.
The streetlight shone its eerie light,
creating menacing shadows
that mocked my sanity.
I grew to envy the cars parked along the curb—
still and silent—
they seemed to rest better than I did.

Sometimes I heard noises in the basement.
Although I had nailed all the windows shut
with ten-penny nails,
it would have been an easy, inconspicuous way for someone to enter.

I hated checking the basement.
Like someone out of a cop show,
I would descend the stairs,
gun in hand,
moving side to side,
and watching my back.

I surrendered my body to a deep sigh of relief
each time I found everything secure.
But always the frustrated anger followed:
        Why can't the police protect us?

Returning to my bed,
eyes burning from exhaustion,
I would remove the clip from the pistol
and place the pistol under my pillow.

Praying again:
        Keep the boys safe.
        Keep me strong.
And, now adding:
        Keep me sane.
        Give me strength to do my job.

WAKE UP CALL

The counselor tried to help.
I had been waiting for advice,
but now that I was getting it,
I didn't want to hear it.

I vividly remember our conversation.

"You have to leave the house right now, today," he said,
maintaining a relaxed posture.

My dazed look begged a question.

"Are you hearing me? Your husband's court appointed counselor called me
today. He says you are in imminent danger. He cannot breach your husband's
confidentiality unless there is a clear danger. Obviously, he feels this is a
serious situation."

Living a life of guard duty had made me callous to concern, so I answered,
"I don't believe I'll die."

Having most likely heard this before, he responded,
"Too many women think it will never happen to them and the police find their
dead bodies later. This is real." [4]

Completely exhausted, and more angry than anything, I retorted,
"I shouldn't have to run.
I shouldn't have to hide."

And, of course, the answer:
"If you don't, your children may live the remainder of their life without you.
Is that what you want?"

"Of course not.
I hate this.
I have done nothing wrong.
Why should I be in hiding?
I'm not a criminal."

The response I loath followed quickly,
"Life isn't always fair.
Do you have a friend you could stay with until we find a shelter
for you and the kids?"

I gasped and sputtered,
"As if I would want to do that to a friend. What happens if they get shot?"

"Tell them the potential for harm. They can decide."
His stoic nature was beginning to irritate me.

"That's absurd!" was all I could think to say.

As he leaned forward in his chair, his look became very intense.
With body language, he moved into my awareness and asserted,
"I do not want you to leave this office until you have someplace arranged."

I sat breathing deeply, tunneling into myself.
I wanted to hide, to move away from him.
I wanted to be anywhere but the situation I was in.
Why couldn't it just go away?
I knew he was right, but I was angry, sad and afraid.
Finally my mouth opened and my lips moved,
"I hate this!
Okay, I'll call my brother. He recently moved and no one knows where he
lives. Maybe he'll let me stay there one night with the kids."

The counselor offered me the phone and suggested I call my brother.
"I will later," I said, thinking there was one more chance to avoid the situation.

Denial is an easy thing to spot when you see it every day.
He wouldn't let me off the hook, but insisted,
"I would rather you called him now. I am only insisting for your own good."

My voice resigned, I said, "Yeah, well it's like drinking cod-liver oil - who wants to?
Okay, okay, give me the phone."

He listened to the discussion.

"Hi.
Can the kids and I stay with you tonight?
He's gone crazy.
It is not just his threats now. It has grown more serious.
I'll probably find a shelter to stay at,
but for tonight I need a place to stay with the kids.
I have to tell you one more thing.
There is a possibility you could get shot.
Or I could get killed.
But we will be out tomorrow.
I promise."

The counselor watched me roll my eyes,
as I listened to my brother chastise me for my screwed up life.

"Can we, or not? I don't need a lecture. I know my life is messed up.
Okay. Thanks.
The kids and I will be there around 6:30 tonight.
Bye.
By the way, don't tell anyone we're staying there. Okay?
Not anyone."

ORDER OF PROTECTION

The next morning, I had an appointment
at the county's Domestic Relations Department.

I told them my life was in shambles.
I had nowhere to live.
Something had to change.

The county suggested two things:
I immediately file for an Order of Protection,
and they would help me find a shelter to live in temporarily.

I filed for an Order of Protection that morning.
An Ex Parte Order became effective immediately
pending the scheduled hearing.

The court filing for the order read:
Respondent has been calling Petitioner threatening to kill her—
and that he would kill her father. He has told the counselor he plans
to buy a handgun and a silencer.

It stated my fear:
[My husband] and I have been attending counseling sessions together
and separately. During these sessions it has become increasingly apparent
that he is becoming dangerous. He has threatened to murder me and take
the children. All counselors involved have suggested I protect myself and my
children with any means available.

It expressed the urgency of the situation:
[My husband] threatened me that if visitation were altered, he would murder
me. He will be notified by his attorney today that all visitation be restricted to
a third party situation. The Domestic Relations Department suggested I get
this order until further measures can be taken to insure my safety and the safety
of my children.

IMPRISONED WITHOUT CAUSE

All of the shelters in the metropolitan area were filled.
It would take some additional time and effort to find a place for us.
"Just hang tight," the county counselor said.
"We'll call you at this number as soon as we find something."

My folks allowed me to stay at their house until a shelter was found;
       a motel would have been safer for everyone,
      but I didn't have the money.
Dad brought out his guns and kept them nearby.

No one slept while we waited.

Startled by the piercing sound of the phone ringing,
I jumped from the sofa,
and then hesitated;
what if it was him?
"Hello," I said holding the phone at a distance
as if afraid the receiver itself could harm me.

It was a person from the county.
She had found a spot.
Unfortunately, it was in Apple Valley,
a suburb 60 miles from work and day-care.
She apologized for the strain the distance would cause,
but noted the distance would make us that much safer.
Before hanging up,
she cautioned me not to let anyone know the location.

The boys and I were surprised as we drove up to the shelter that evening.
It was an absolutely nondescript house;
a three-bedroom rambler amid hundreds of three-bedroom ramblers on an
average street.
Other than looking a bit unkempt in comparison to neighboring houses,
it blended into 1970s suburbia.

We quickly learned the rules of shelter living:
Don't let anyone know where you are—NO ONE!!
Don't give out the telephone number unless that person has an urgent need
to know.

The door must always be closed and locked.
The house attendant is the only one allowed to answer the phone or open the door.
Everyone takes turns with meals and dishes.
You pick up after your own.
You don't judge others in the house.
And, remember, if anyone compromises security, everyone is compromised.

From the moment I stepped in the front door,
I hated the place.
I hated everything about it,
including being there.
Immediately I felt suffocated, gasping for air, wanting freedom.
I pushed it back in my mind
and chastised myself for what I assumed was ingratitude on my part.

Oh, I hated the sense of being imprisoned within my own life.
I wanted to escape.

To me, the others in the shelter looked like prisoners who had given up trying
to escape;
       submissive postures,
       dull faces,
       downcast eyes.

But, that was judgment, so I kept my mouth shut.
Shut, even when I wanted to scream.
They were so docile…so beaten.
Most had endured years of beatings.

One obese woman described her weight as a buffer zone;
a protection against the blows.
She thought she could endure until one day
her drunken husband, while raging at her,
threw her infant child against the wall.
She stumbled helplessly to catch her baby
before it hit the wall.
She was too late.
It was his way of getting past her padding,
her protection.

A woman sitting next to her on the threadbare sofa,
said,
"They'll do anything.
They'll find any way to hurt.
And keep hurting.
It's like a fix—they keep needing more and more to
give them the same effect."

Someone sitting on a shabby chair across the room
got up and gave the obese woman a box of tissues.

Each day I refused to return to the shelter until bedtime.

After work,
I would pick the boys up at day-care and take them to McDonald's for dinner;
which to them was the only cool thing about being in a shelter.

Afterward, we would hang out at a park or the library until it was bedtime.
Then we drove back.

I'd bathe them and tell them to hop up into the bunk bed across from mine.
They liked the idea that we all slept in bunk beds.
And they really liked the idea that we could be alone in our little room
with the door closed,
just us,
alone.

When Andy was asleep,
Ben whispered,
"Mommy, when are we going to leave here?"

"Soon, honey.
I hope real soon."

BREAKFAST OF CHAMPIONS

The next morning I entered the lab from the back
and walked down the center aisle dividing
the rows of lab benches on the left
and gas chromatographs on the right.

There he was,
the professor,
as always,
at the front of the lab,
reclining in a chair with his feet up on the large black lab bench.
Black dress shoes,
polyester pants,
socks drooping to expose hairless white ankles.
A cigarette was propped between his tobacco-stained fingers;
the ashes dropped listlessly from the end,
missing the ash tray and falling on the floor.
He certainly was not the lofty image
I had in my mind of a professor.

One side of his mouth smiled
as he looked at his watch.
"Since when did 7:40 a.m. become the start time?"
he asked wryly, noting I was expected at 7:30 a.m.

As I peered through the glass separatory funnels hanging between us,
I searched to find a feeble excuse, any excuse that would back him off;
I couldn't take his attack this early.

Should I even bother to tell him
I started my drive to work at 4:30 in the morning?
(About the same time he was probably looking at the
Penthouse magazine he had carelessly thrown in an office drawer.)
Would he care that the battered woman's shelter
was 60 minutes from my day-care provider,
which was 40 minutes from the lab on the St. Paul campus?
If he cared,
he would know an additional 10 minutes
was required for the ever-changing route
I was obliged to take to be certain I was not being followed.

Perhaps—a thoughtful person would understand—
I must spend another 10 minutes parked a block away from day-care
watching every car, house and pedestrian,
looking for an armed man,
who, I was told, intended to shoot me and kidnap my kids.
Would not a compassionate person
realize another 10 minutes was spent debriefing day-care
on the latest warnings and/or frightening events?

Should I explain my tardiness to the professor?

No,
I thought not.
What difference would it make?
He knew I was living in a shelter,
and every morning I circumvented both cities to get there.

Instead of explaining,
I reached for the aspirin bottle on the top of the lab bench
and fortified myself in my customary manner:
three aspirins with my breakfast of strong coffee.
Additional doses at 11:30 a.m. and 3:30 p.m.
seemed to keep the monster at bay.

I knew that without this job,
I would stand to lose my kids.
Without other experience—
I was beholden to the professor.

I hated feeling so trapped.

PENALIZED

The two weeks we spent in the shelter seemed interminably long.
With a restraining order now in place,
I decided to take the risk of moving back into the house.
The shelter manager insisted I could stay at the shelter as long as I needed.
I thanked her for the offer, but declined saying,
"It will save me an hour of driving in the morning
and the boys will be back home.
Besides,
what kind of a lunatic would violate a court order?"

She bit her lip and shook her head.

On our first day back home,
I picked the boys up at day-care
and asked them if they wanted to go straight home,
or go to McDonald's for supper.
They voted for McDonald's.
After supper, we headed home.
As I reached to unlock the house door,
it pushed open without resistance.
I paused to think:
Didn't I shut and lock the door this morning?
Of course I did.

I reached to turn on the lights.

The frame had been broken off the door.
The door showed damage from a crowbar.

Confused and frightened,
I called the police who promised an investigation.
When they interviewed my husband,
he admitted breaking in.
He wanted to murder me.

He felt justified.
By his standards I was a
"selfish,
heartless,
cruel,
wicked bitch."

Because he had clearly violated the restraining order,
he was brought before a referee.

The referee did not appreciate the spectacle before him—
the violent, cursing behavior was not considered appropriate.
Physically restrained, he was taken off to jail
and given a two-day sentence out of a maximum of 90. [5]

Two days!

I felt my heart being eaten alive each time I thought of the injustice.

Escape

The county told me I needed involvement in a woman's group
to sort out some issues I could not see clearly.
The group met weekly.
All women.
All victims of some sort.
We sat cross-legged, sprawled in a misshapen circle on the floor.

I was told by the county to attend;
to work on issues,
on behaviors that trapped me in a downward spiral,
wrapped in my husband's sickness.

From the start
I was uncomfortable.
"Wasn't I different from the others?"

Each member, with a slightly different twist,
talked of their pain, their struggle.
Some of them looked hard,
some vulnerable,
most looked exhausted.

One woman in particular, captured and tortured my soul.
As I listened to her story,
I was pulled and repelled with equal emotional force.
What she said—and neglected to say—etched my psyche.

She spoke in a monotone voice
of her father's poker parties;
his use of her body for sex,
and his generous offer of the same to his poker buddies. [6]

She would hide in sink cabinets,
in closets,
under beds;
never escaping his intent.

I wanted to scream,
or vomit,

or run and hide.
Anything but listen,
and watch her face.

Looking at her,
I sensed a hollowness.
It was her eyes.
Her manner of dress.
The way she positioned her body on the floor.
She had a way of not filling space.
Even fully clothed,
she seemed stripped.

She was there, in the group, supposedly trying,
but I sensed she couldn't reach out to escape.
It was as if her soul lacked arms to grasp sustenance.

I wanted desperately to hear her shout,
"I'm worth more!
More than you can ever steal from me!!"

But she couldn't find it to say.

Her lack of protective instinct
was a vacuum drawing indiscriminately,
filling the lack of her own presence with a void.

Her pain frightened me.
I wanted to forget her face,
yet I couldn't.
The aftermath of evil was so scary.

I saw her lack of resolve
as a determinant of her fate.
I wanted to shake her.
Hug her.
It drove me,
whipped me to a fury.
I left the sessions absolutely determined
to find my own escape.

Chapter 5

VALLEY OF DEATH'S SHADOW

BLESSED ARE THOSE

After the court ordered the house to be sold,
I started looking for an apartment.

It was 1979 and no one wanted to rent to a single mother of two kids—
the risk was too high.
Could they really trust I would make the monthly payments?
They had rented to this class before and had learned better.

I felt embarrassed,
as if I should hang my head and apologize for what I might do,
or for what others had done.

I had tried everywhere and was getting desperate.
Each rental office looked the same as the last.
Each response sounded the same as the first,
"Sorry, can't help you.
You don't fit our qualifications."

Working at the university granted me some credibility,
but evidently not enough.
I would have to develop coattail credibility
by finding someone who would vouch for me.

As if by divine intervention,
the man in our department
trained to run an expensive and complicated piece of analyzing equipment
heard my pleas for justice.
I received his offer of help
as a desperate person frantically grabbing a lifeline.

He knew the landlord of a place nearby;
an old six-plex, a bit run-down, but it would do.
He had rented there many years back.

Asking on my behalf,
he heard the same questions and concerns:
          Is she reliable? Will she pay?
          Will her kids trash the place?
          Will you vouch for her?

He assured them I was a hard worker, dependable and trustworthy.
He would personally feel liable if I proved to be a bad risk.

GAINING DISTANCE

The landlord had said, "Yes!"

I saw the apartment.
It was eclectic for sure.
Shabby,
no doubt.
But it was clear on the other side of town from my nightmare life.
I was going to move and start over.

It was a beautiful fall day:
mid-seventies,
slight breeze carrying the smell of dried autumn leaves,
sunny,
perfect.
Yes, indeed, life was worth living.

I stood on the corner of Como and Carter
and thanked the Lord,
tears of gratitude welling in my eyes.

I decided that afternoon
that people were great
and life was great too.

I wanted to hug someone.
Anyone.
Everyone.

MINNESOTA NICE

What did he know?

Admittedly, not enough to make an informed decision about helping me move.

His wife later confessed to me she had never told him
his life could be in jeopardy if he helped me.
She just told him a friend at work needed help moving.
She said the same to her younger brother.

As they drove to my house,
she sat between them in the front seat of their pickup truck.
She sprang the news on them about a mile from my house.
"Oh, by the way, I forgot to tell you,
her husband is armed and dangerous
and has threatened to kill her and kidnap her boys."

Both husband and brother leaned forward to see each other's faces
struck with bewilderment,
which turned quickly to shock.

She sat unperturbed between them—calm, determined.

"Oh sure, you forgot!!
This is another one of your charity cases you just couldn't refuse to help."

"Maybe, but we're almost there,
and if you don't help,
who will?"

They shook their heads in utter disbelief.
She was always helping the less fortunate,
but this took the cake!
It was, in fact, inconceivable!

They were still shaking their heads
as they got out of the truck in front of my house.

I ran out to greet and meet them;
it was the first time I had met her husband and brother.
(Actually, I didn't even know her.
She had overheard me crying in the toilet stall at work,
and asked why I was crying.
So I told her.)

As I gushed gratitude,
husband and brother smiled a polite, reserved, almost frozen smile—
a "Minnesota nice" smile—
the kind that makes you wonder what they are really thinking.

I quickly ushered them into the house
and told them other people who came to help had
already been assigned to guard
the front and back of the house,
as well as the ends of the block.
Unfortunately, that left few people remaining to move my belongings.
Luckily, I had few belongings.

I introduced them to my dad,
who stood in the kitchen,
revolver in hand.

As they shook his free hand,
their "Minnesota nice" smile returned.
This time, the smile looked severely fake,
like Silly Putty pasted on their faces.

My dad explained he would cover them as they went
between the house and truck.

Another "Minnesota nice" smile.

Then, a prophetic look shot between husband and brother-in-law—
today we might meet our Maker!
How could my wife, your sister, do this to us?
Where is the love?

"So…"
her husband said while inhaling deeply and suspending his exhale,
"May as well make quick work of this.
Come on, Jim, help me with this sofa-sleeper."

"Yeah, good idea," Jim muttered, looking at the floor.

I glanced at my new friend to discern the level of
marital trouble she had caused.
She shrugged her shoulders,

and said, "It'll be okay—
they really like the adventure."

I opened the front door for them as they lifted the sofa.
Before allowing them to exit,
I quickly surveyed the block:
each car—parked or moving,
each house—between each house,
the length of the street,
the ends of the street.

I nodded the go-ahead.
Hastily,
they beat a path to the truck and shoved the sofa from
the tailgate to the rear of the bed.

Dad stood near the truck trying to look inconspicuous with a drawn revolver.

Everyone was quick and efficient—
niceties were suspended.

When the vehicles were loaded,
movers and guards converged in the kitchen to develop route plans.
They huddled and discussed logistics as if it were a military operation.
My new location was not to be divulged to anyone.
Each vehicle was given a different route to my new apartment.
One person in each vehicle was assigned to watch
for suspicious cars following them.
If any doubt arose, they were to abort the original plan
and take a tangled route until the suspicious car was lost.

Most said it was the only real excitement they had in their life.
For me,
it was just another day.

Amid the Mess

The move was stress-filled for everyone;
up and down three flights of stairs
carrying heavy household items,
all the while watching their backs for an armed attack.
It was much more than any had bargained for.
Yet, they were all good humored about it,
and respected my need for secrecy.

My new neighbors in the six-plex
sat out in lawn chairs watching us.
Upon overhearing talk of our harrowing experience,
they wondered aloud what they had inadvertently gotten themselves into.
Jokingly they insisted they should have been allowed to screen applicants.
I tried to face my embarrassment gracefully,
but my drooping body language told them a different story.

Upstairs, my belongings were all dumped into the first accessible room.
The movers left me alone returning to their sane lives.
Before they departed, they patted me on the shoulder and thanked me
because they now realized how good they had it.

I moved some boxes until I found the sofa-sleeper.
Slumping onto the cushion,
I felt like crying,
and, at the same time,
beating someone to a pulp—anyone—it didn't matter.

The place was a mess.

My mom had the boys for the day to keep them safe.
Returning them that evening,
she shook her head in disbelief.
"Are you really going to stay in this dump?
You don't even have a ceiling in your bedroom.
The place is filthy."

"Thanks, Mom, I needed that reality check."

"Well, it's your life," she said with a shrug.

It began to rain shortly after dinner.
It wasn't long before the rainwater was tapping out
a dance on the floor in three different rooms.

The neighbor,
the resident caretaker,
came over with buckets to catch the rain and warn me about the bats—
bats that would fly into the apartment at night through the
exposed ceiling slats.

The boys didn't like that idea at all.
Assuring them their room would be safe because the ceiling was intact,
I closed their bedroom door at night to make sure no bats could get in.

After Ben and Andy were bathed and in bed,
I began cleaning, painting and unpacking.
I worked until 1:00 a.m. every night for two months.
Each morning when I awoke at 5:30 for work,
I promised myself I would not repeat my frenzied
cleaning again that evening—
I would show restraint and go to bed early.

I lied.
Each night I continued my frantic cleaning.

Maybe it was the bat perched atop my bedroom
window frame most mornings that motivated me.

IMAGINE THE HORROR

The restraining order did not preclude visitation.
The logistics were a nightmare;
how to exchange the boys without their father and I ever seeing each other.
My dad volunteered to pick the boys up,
deliver them,
and return them.

Dad usually came back beside himself;
frightened,
shaken.

My dad couldn't explain exactly what Ben and Andy's father said
that distressed him so;
mostly it was his ranting and insane raving,
senseless,
disjointed.

Once their father declared to my dad
that he would cut me up and put me down the garbage disposal;
my remains would never be found.

Now my dad and I shared the same fear.

DISPARAGEMENT-FREE ZONE

It came as a complete shock to me
that the court believed Ben and Andy's father
suddenly posed less threat to my well-being.
In their wisdom, the court did not extend the restraining order.
Because my husband still had visitation rights,
we now met in public places to exchange the boys.
It was usually the McDonald's on University and Broadway—a busy intersection.
I intentionally took different routes each time I dropped the boys off,
so they would not begin recognizing familiar landmarks.

I told the boys,
"You must not tell Daddy where we live,
even if he asks you a lot of times.
I know that will be hard,
and maybe it seems wrong not to tell him,
but it is the best thing right now."

I was sure the situation caused stress between Ben, now five, and his father.

One day when I picked the boys up at McDonald's after their visitation,
Ben commented on a song playing on the car radio.
The song was, "Ruby Don't Take Your Love to Town".

"Daddy says you're just like Ruby, a whore.
That you had boyfriends before you left him,
and that's why you left him,"
Ben said, as he watched my face in the rearview mirror.

I think I lost sight temporarily—everything went black.

"I'm sorry your daddy said that to you.
That was very hurtful.
What he said is not true."

I recalled what the counselor with the county had advised me:
"Don't say bad things about their father.
He will always be their father
and they will be the ones to suffer if that relationship
is compromised by your words."
She went on to say,
"If the court learns that a parent is making disparaging
comments about the other parent,
it negatively affects their appeal for custody.
So even if it hurts, keep your feelings to yourself. "

SYMPATHY PAINS

It was a warm spring day,
the kind that makes all things in life seem new.
I wanted desperately to believe there was hope for us,
so I embraced even the smallest things that held promise—
the light, the sounds, the smells, the newness of this spring day.

As I walked home from work,
I inhaled the smell of spring as a dehydrated person drinks water—
gulping and eager to be satisfied.

Because of the unusual warmth,
the storm door of the six-plex was wide open.
Only the screen door separated the entry from this beautiful, budding day.

I fully heard the squeak of the screen door as it opened,
as well as the banging sound of its closing,
all of which seemed full of life.

Just inside the entry were six metal mail holders mounted on the wall.
The holders had hinged lids that did not lock,
but allowed filling to the brim, or overfilling, if necessary.
Often the mail stuck out like gifts in a Christmas stocking.
On that fine day even the overstuffed mail spoke of trust,
and other life affirming notions.

I grabbed the mail from my box,
and headed up the stairs to pick up Ben from day-care—
a neighbor agreed to watch Ben during the after school hours.
As I rounded the landing of the second floor,
I stopped; stunned and alerted.
I never left my children alone—
not even for a minute.
Yet, there sat Ben all by himself,
head in hands.

He was only five years old,
and he looked just that small and fragile sitting all alone.
"Why aren't you at the babysitter's?" I asked, as I sat on the stair next to him.
"I didn't want to go there," he shrugged.

I hadn't noticed he was crying
until I put him in my lap.
He tried hard to hide it from me,
but the tear that dropped on my hand gave him away.

I lifted his head and asked,
"Why are you crying?"

"I want to die.
I don't want to live anymore,"
he said, as he choked on his confession.

"Honey, why do you feel that way?"

"Everything," he said, summing it up.

"Sweetheart, I'm sorry.
I'm so sorry.
I wish I could make all this better,
faster,
but I can't."

I hugged him and rocked him
just as I had done the evening I discovered he had been beaten,
only this time,
there wasn't a doctor to call—
no one to call that would have a remedy.

I didn't cry with him—
all I felt was a horrific ache in my stomach.

I asked him,
"If you could pick someplace fun to go tonight, what would you pick?"
He told me, "Chuck E. Cheese's."
"Okay, that's where we'll go."

That night, after they were bathed, in bed and asleep,
I paced the living room wanting to scream, hit, bite, shoot, hurt...

I could tolerate that he was hurting me,
but the agony I saw in my son caused the pain to increase exponentially.
I wanted to make the pain stop.
I was suffocating in the torment.
Prowling the confines of the apartment like a caged animal,
I said aloud,
"I can't take this anymore."

The pain I felt in my heart and mind was throbbing stronger,
sharper, deeper;
piercing, cutting, gouging.

"Please make the pain go away.
I can't stop the destruction happening in our lives.
No matter how hard I try,
it keeps getting worse."

My mind felt ravaged and frenzied.
What can I do?
What can I do?
I can't think.
I hit my head against the wall to distract me from the pain inside of me.

I stopped to notice the dull throb on the side of my head—
it diverted my attention away from the consuming pain and the ache my
heart felt.

So, I hit my head against the wall again,
and again,
and again,
and again,
and again,
and again
and again…

My head felt jarred and numb.
I questioned my sanity.
Actually, I feared for it.
But it worked;
I had stopped focusing on the pain deep within,
to nurse the knob forming on my head.

STATE OF MIND

The next morning I awoke to find a bat
on the window ledge,
just above the couch in the living room.
I watched it in the morning as we ate our breakfast,
but I did nothing.

I had become inert.
I thought I had been paying attention
to all the details required to recover our lives,
yet I had neglected to see my son's emotional collapse.
The daily bat visits became a nagging reminder
of my ineptness and growing sense of futility.
I felt cold and hard.

I told the boys to finish their cereal
as I kept an eye on the bat.

When they had finished
and were next door playing,
I remained, looking at the bat.

I wondered,
should I catch it, or call the landlord?
After all, it was his fault;
he had promised to repair the ceiling,
which was entirely missing in places.
The rain still came through,
along with the bats.

The resident caretaker came and put the bat
in a square, sandwich-sized Tupperware container,
sealed it shut,
and threw the whole thing in the trash can out back by the alley.
It fluttered inside the container for the entire day
before it died.

TAKING

All living things die.
Who cares?

I had grown tired of giving and caring.
I wanted to take.

I met a man who was warm and alive
and I felt I was dying.

He lived out-of-state
and that seemed far enough removed from my disaster.

I knew I shouldn't have a relationship with him,
but told God to turn away.

I wanted,
so I took selfishly.

He wanted more.
I changed my mind.

WAR ZONE

The doctor asked me if I was under unusual stress.
"No, not more than normal.
My life has been this screwed up for years now."

"I'm going to give you an antibiotic that should take care of this.
Broad spectrum.
If this doesn't do it, well…."

Having had just about every conceivable microbial infection
known to a general practitioner,
I was becoming a regular at the clinic.
When we had knocked out one set of microorganisms,
another type found an opportunity to move in where it wasn't welcome.

Biology has always fascinated me—
balance is the key to homeostasis.
However, experience was teaching me
that a body living in a war zone
is not a body in balance.

Balance.
It's all about balance.
Stress depletes the energy required to keep the pesky little critters in balance.
Yet, when the force of life keeps them in check,
they are all very important.
But give them an inch,
and they'll take a mile.
This was very clear to me as I watched a dead squirrel decay on the roadside.
I saw the squirrel every day as I walked to and from work.
First it got rigid.
Then it bloated.
Then it started shrinking as the microorganisms took over the body.
Soon, there was nothing left but the tail.

I saw my macro and microbiological existence flash before my eyes.
My well-being hung in the balance as various microbes
fought territorial wars over my body parts.

I gave them fair warning:
"I'm not dead yet,
SO BACK OFF!!"

FATAL LETHARGY

Evil was having its effect on my body,
my children's young minds,
our home,
our very existence.

I lost focus on the light at the end of the tunnel.
Evil seemed everywhere.
I saw it as a vision so dark it threatened to smother the light.

Evil prevails
because it demands less energy.
It is insidious.
Evil seeps under doorways.
It oozes its way between cracks and crevices in our lives,
rupturing and overtaking the weak.

I kept struggling to find escape.
Yet the path out of my valley of death
seemed insurmountable.

I couldn't find enough air to breathe.
I gasped,
overcome with bone weary exhaustion.
I lost my thoughts.
My determination was fading.
As if slipping into unconsciousness,
I couldn't recall why I should keep moving.

I asked deep down inside myself:
"Are you still there?
Are you still alive?"

I couldn't remember who I was,
or whether I ever existed.

In my mind I believed I could die.
As I allowed myself to enter into the idea of death,
deep within me there came a rousing, an urgent insistence.
God's Spirit called and would not let me go.

So I started again,
moving in the direction of the light.

LOVING ARMS

"Please, I can't take this anymore.
I have acted in faith,
believing this would end.
I have looked toward the light,
thinking our deliverance is near.

Yet, each day is another hassle—
another hurdle to overcome.
We're all bleeding from the hurt.

Hold me in your arms
and shield me
from the fears of a future
I can't predict.

I feel so alone.
There is no one to hold me.
No one to reassure me."

Wrapping my arms around myself,
I rocked back and forth.

"Jesus, I feel so alone.
I want the warmth and affection all humans need.
I am human.
I can't be more than I am.
Oh, that you could be flesh,
or I could be spirit.
What am I supposed to do?"

I rocked and waited expectantly.

He came to me like an ardent suitor with profound affection.
He could not stand the ache, the cry of my heart
was pain he wished I did not bear.
With humility born of great love,
he is capable of being divinely eternal and
personally tender at the same instant.

I experienced his tenderness as an embrace;
a closeness that was warmth,
a touch that needed no fingers for expression.
Enraptured,
I lingered in his embrace
until my heart was calmed.

I could not comprehend such perfection
coinciding with the state I was in—
it seemed too disparate.
I apologized profusely for my errors in judgment
and the things I had done wrong.

It's okay.
I was given to know there is nothing
that could separate me from this love.

Chapter 6

THE BEGINNING OF INDEPENDENCE

NEVER FORSAKEN

Finally, his visitation rights were suspended.
The relief was palpable.
I was no longer required to surrender the boys
to the insanity that was robbing us of life.

With my telephone number unlisted,
and address unknown,
the energy once consumed
to stave off death and destruction,
was now available for life, living, and believing.

The wall of distress that had barricaded us from our future was toppled.

Only a year earlier
I remembered crying as I confided to my pastor;
"I have spiritual needs not being met—
my divorce is difficult
and I am floundering.
I need help."

He squirmed and looked across the room,
pretending something had caught his eye.

I asked, "Is there such a thing as a grief
or divorce recovery group?"

"No, I'm sorry there isn't.
I don't know how to direct you.
Really, divorce is uncommon in our congregation.
I'll give it some thought and get back to you," he promised.

A year later,
my pastor apologized,
"I am sorry I never got back to you.
The church was not yet ready to admit divorce happens." [7]

"It doesn't matter," I told him.
"Some things are clearer when forged by fire.
I now know a love that I cannot deny—
I have had unmistakable and intimate experiences of Christ's presence.
He doesn't condemn me and he will never give up on me."

The pastor's face flushed slightly.
He nodded and sighed, "I am glad you found your strength in Christ."

THE SPLENDOR OF NORMAL

It was odd to suddenly have time to reflect on all I had endured.
What shocked me was the thought of resuming my place
in the normal functioning of life.
I had watched helplessly, seemingly frozen in time,
as those around me continued their lives
while mine was taken from me in struggle.
Now, like a soldier returning from an unpopular war,
I felt I was supposed to inconspicuously blend in.
Yet, I was incongruent.
I had been permanently changed.

The neighbors in the six-plex
adjusted well to having a "case study" next door.
I think they marveled to themselves at the complexities of my life.

Patrick, the resident caretaker, fixed the ceiling so the bats no longer entered.
He and Willy lived directly across the hall.
When things started to settle down,
they asked if I would like to join them for a glass of wine on Friday nights.
As we drank wine
we watched the boys,
theirs and mine,
run between the two apartments,
laughing, yelling,
slipping on rugs as they chased each other.
It seemed nothing in life could be more grand—
I felt safe and normal.
Normal.
What a beautiful thing.
How splendid to be normal.

Sometimes Jim and Martha, who lived on the first floor,
would join us and bring their two sons.
We'd have chocolate dessert—
        Willy liked anything made of chocolate.
I can still taste the sweetness of sitting at the table,
talking about normal things,
telling the boys to stop before they break something, like their heads.

They were precious times that I will always remember.

END OF CHOICE

To secure a better future,
I made a mental list of things I needed to do—
things that would forestall future bad decisions.

So, when the doctor asked,
"Are you sure you want a tubal ligation?"
I answered firmly,
"Yes, I'm sure."

"You should consider it permanent," he advised.

"I hope so!
I want it to be permanent;
so permanent, it can't ever be undone."

With one eyebrow raised,
the doctor pressed,
"Is this the right time to be taking such a fixed position?"

"Look, my children and I have been living a hellish existence
because of the man who was presumed to love and support us.
I know you are thinking I might find a prince charming in the future,
but I don't believe in 'happily ever after' anymore.
I don't want to make myself susceptible to more pain later."

The doctor cleared his throat.

Before he could speak,
I sought to close the discussion,
"Yes, I want this procedure.
Yes, I am certain.
Yes, I want you to make it permanent.
I want you to make it irreversibly permanent!"

"Okay.
I'll have the nurse come in with the paperwork,"
the doctor acquiesced with a shrug of his shoulders.

"Thank you, doctor."

REDEFINING REPUGNANT

The future still seemed doubtful.
Nevertheless, facing uncertainty head-on appeared rational,
especially considering all I had been through.

Although monstrous insecurities
could have shackled me to the past,
I ignored their weight and clanging sounds
and dragged them forward with me in search of tomorrow's hope.

I was determined to get my degree,
and since a degree in biology required three quarters of college calculus,
I figured I'd better start now.

There was one problem.
I hate math;
have always found it abhorrent.
If my life depended on solving a mathematical equation,
I would start planning the funeral.

My thoughts on the subject convinced me;
I knew exactly what I needed to do next.

I signed up for an advanced algebra and trigonometry class.

Because I worked at the university,
my college credits were paid.
So, I reasoned,
what's the worst that can happen?
I'm not losing any money.

Undaunted Determination

Facing my fears and making decisions for myself
helped my fledgling confidence grow.
It served me well on the day the professor informed me
that his grant for fish research was running out.
This meant I could not count on having a job in his lab.
He advised me to start looking elsewhere in the system.

Openings were posted on the university's job board.
The normal procedure was to fill out the application
and wait,
for the call that would come if you were qualified for an interview.
We were told professors were too busy and their work was too important
to be interrupted by calls from unscreened applicants.

However, I reasoned that their process was too slow
and I was too dependent on a "respectable" job
to sit by and wait.

After finding a posting that most closely mirrored my qualifications,
I summoned up all my courage
and dragged my shackles of insecurity
over to a hall phone and made the call.

I was told about the hiring process for the job:

Step 1. Each applicant would be given a biochemistry exam. I was told all applicants to date were graduate students. I would be the only applicant without a degree of any kind. The test would be difficult.

Step 2. The applicant who scored highest on the exam would be interviewed by team members who were representatives from the two labs collaborating on the research.

Step 3. If that person passed the team interview, he/she would be interviewed one-on-one by the hiring professor, who was a very serious researcher and had no time for incompetence.

The voice on the other end asked if I was still interested.
Ouch!

Quickly resuscitating my confidence,
I managed to say,
"Yes, I am still interested.
When will you be giving the exam?"

"I can schedule you two weeks from now," the voice responded.

"Okay, I'll be there."

I wondered what kind of a moron I was!
Desperation is not an excuse for being rash.

No turning back now, though.

For the intervening two weeks,
I studied every minute I had available.
I checked out organic chemistry and biochemistry books from the library.
I learned basic properties, constants and values,
buffers,
acid-base reactions,
neutralization,
pH,
Avogadro's Number,
molality,
normality,
and how to make solutions and dilutions.

When the day came,
I congratulated myself for at least having the courage to try.

A lab technician with a master's degree in biochemistry
handed me the exam
and kindly wished me luck.

He called me back a day later
and told me I had scored 100%.
In fact, I was the only one with a perfect score—
I did better than all of the graduate students taking the exam.
I assumed he was being kind
and not telling the truth
because it would have been impossible for me to do
better than graduate students.

"No,"
he assured me,
"I am telling the truth."

He asked me if I was ready to begin the interview process.

The first interview was with the technician I would be replacing.
During the interview he confessed an openness to Christ.
So, I told him about my faith,
and the difference it made in my life.
We bonded immediately.

When it came to the professor, I got scared.
He was indeed serious about his research.
When he learned I lived within walking distance of his lab,
he nodded approvingly,
noting inclement weather wouldn't be an excuse to miss work.
He would not tolerate slackers.

Then he asked me if I could do research on dogs.
The dogs would be anesthetized
and wouldn't feel anything,
but my job would entail removing the heart muscle
to isolate a particular organelle.
He wanted to be certain I could extract the heart while it was still beating.

I gulped,
turned red,
felt hot all over,
and responded,
"If I can club carp to death all day,
I think I can handle dog hearts."

I suspected my answer sounded a bit flippant,
so I told him I had important reasons to make it work.
I really needed to stay in the system—
I really needed the job.

"Humph," he said,
looking unconvinced and quizzical.
"I'll talk to the others and let you know."

The next day I got a call.
They all agreed I was the best candidate—
they liked my eagerness.
I would start in two weeks.

DOG DAYS

It proved easier to say
I could cut the heart out of a dog
than to actually do it.

"Dog Days"
was my unaffectionate description for the days
that we harvested sarcoplasmic reticulum
(an organelle found within an individual cell)
from the heart of a donor dog.
This happened usually once a month.

My first Dog Day
was a feeble attempt at acting assured.
I failed.
I surrendered my task to the professor
and apologized later for my failure.

I respected the professor
and knew what we were doing was important.
But whenever I had to make the cut,
I struggled with thoughts of trespassing into the forbidden.

The dogs were unclaimed from the pound.
Bitten, beaten and scarred,
their bodies read like a map of war—
every battle visible on their hides.

The dog to be sacrificed next was no different.
As I entered the sterile-looking, concrete block prep room,
I felt nauseated and oddly driven at the same time.
Like any other unpleasant task,
the quicker I got to it,
the less discomfort I endured.
That philosophy seemed to work for the dog as well...
at least most days.

This day was different.
The dog paced nervously around the prep room,
tail between his legs,
head drooped.
His hooded look communicated apprehension.

My first job on Dog Day was to calm the dog.
I approached the dog
and in a soft and reassuring tone said,
"Come here sweetie."
Scratching behind its ears, I continued,
"You're a handsome dog, aren't you?
Sure you are...yes, you're a handsome dog.
Oh my goodness, look at those scars you have."
His tail, still stuck between his hind legs,
began a quick, yet tempered wag.

I sat on the floor and invited him to sit in my lap.
Slowly, his trepidation began to subside
and he eagerly absorbed all of the attention I was willing to give.

When the dog was finally relaxed,
the professor sat beside me on the floor,
hypodermic syringe in hand.
I focused the dog's attention toward me,
while he held its front paw and attempted to inject the anesthesia.
Usually this process was quick and painless
and the dog would drift peacefully off.

This day, however, was different.
This dog had veins that were difficult to access.
With each attempt,
it whimpered and looked at me with pleading eyes.
The more it whimpered, the sadder I became.
The professor noticed mist forming in my eyes
and asked if I would be okay.
I nodded.

Eventually, it was sedated.

Still breathing,
it was lifted onto the stainless steel table
and laid on its side with its legs facing me.
The professor stood at the head of the table.
He looked at me to determine if I could continue.

At this juncture,
there was no turning back,
no time for sentiment.
I had to be quick and precise or the dog would die for nothing—
no ultimate benefit would be gained.
I counted the ribs from the neck, down along the sagittal plane,
until I reached the place where the heart would be in the thorax.
Starting on the dorsal side and working toward the ventral side,
I made one long straight incision using a surgical scalpel.
The cut ran parallel to and between the ribs
and measured eight inches long.

There was no blood.

After making the incision,
I jabbed the scalpel into the ice bucket,
and took a deep breath before proceeding.

Inserting my fingertips into the incision,
I used all my strength to pry open the chest cavity.
Much like pulling apart the laces and flaps of snow encrusted boots,
the thick hide and rib structure felt stiff and immutable.
I persisted until I had created an opening large enough
for my hand to fit within the chest cavity.

At this point I paused a brief second,
caught by a sense of intrusion…
of entering something awe inspiring that I did not deserve to see.
I was grateful for the surgical gloves
that dampened the sensation of life within this sacred cavern.

Reaching in and coming up under the heart,
I held it beating in my left hand.
The heart rate was strong, steady, and faster than a human's.
I pulled the heart toward me to expose the aorta and held on tight.
My previous mistake was to hold it gently—
in which case, it was pulled out of my hand and back into the chest cavity by
the force of the beating heart.
With my right hand,
I grabbed the scissors standing handle up in the ice bucket,
and began severing the arteries and veins holding the heart in place.

Within seconds, the heart was freed and handed to the professor for rinsing.
Once rinsed, it was placed into a beaker containing chilled buffered solution
for transport back to the lab.
I left the prep room,
beaker in hand,
while the assistants took care of the dog's body and cleaned the room.

I looked back to see the dog lying lifeless on the table.
I felt regret, however, there was no time to mourn—
the heart muscle had to be immediately ground
if we were to achieve a sizeable yield of sarcoplasmic reticulum.
It took a full day of standing in the walk-in cooler
to isolate the organelle found within each microscopic heart cell.

While maintaining a constant chilled temperature,
the muscle was cut into tiny pieces.
Lying on the counter,
each piece continued the heart's impulse to beat independent of the whole.
The rhythm held steady no matter how tiny the piece.
It ensured a methodical, persistent, remarkable, wondrous, consistency to life.
I felt an enormous sense of grandeur as I watched.

It taught me respect and dedication;
a commitment to be purposeful
thereby assuring I would never feel
the dog had died for nothing.

UNCONVENTIONAL CONFIDENCE

The professor was interested in isolating Cyclic AMP from rabbit muscle.
He handed me a methodology another researcher had developed
and expressed his confidence in me;
"Take this and see what you get."

I had never imagined, nor could I ever imagine,
being given that kind of respect.
I knew nothing about research.
I wasn't a researcher;
I was an imposter technician who came about the
position the unconventional way.

Every aspect of the project was mine,
including killing the bunny.

I had no desire to say I couldn't,
so I conducted the experiment.

When I didn't get the anticipated results,
the professor checked all my steps.
As we stood and watched the meter read the pH of my solutions,
I prayed they would be right.

He found no mistakes.
He never criticized me,
or inferred I was at fault.

The sum of my experience in his lab
was an important determinant of my immediate future;
whenever I thought I couldn't face an intellectual challenge,
I remembered I could.

A Visit to the Zoo

Five months of bliss;
five months without the annihilating effects of their father
hardly seemed long enough.
If anyone cared to ask me,
I would have told them it was a mere blink of an eye.

No one asked me.
They simply informed me their father had hired a guardian ad litem
and was seeking to restore his visitation.

Appointed by the court,
the guardian's name was Mary.
Supposedly, her job was to protect the legal interest of the children.

My feelings were
deeper than rage—
much closer to spontaneous combustion;
more intense than afraid—
definitely moving toward emotional meltdown;
not as pliable as reluctant—
try as fixed as the petrified forest!

There was nothing I could do;
it wasn't my decision to make.

Mary came to pick up the boys and take them to the zoo to meet their father.
She told me of her confusion after talking to their father.
She was at a loss to understand how the situation had gotten to this point—
his perceptions and mine were so dissimilar.
Mary explained, "It is like hearing about two different families."

I should have said something profound,
but I couldn't think of anything intelligent to say;
the experience had catapulted me back
to my previous state of insecurity and uncertainty.

After watching them drive away
I turned,
kicked the sofa and table in the living room,
threw three pillows against the wall,
slammed two of the boys' dresser drawers closed,
threw their toys into the cardboard box in the corner of their bedroom,
fell on the floor next to their teddy bears,
and cried myself to exhaustion once again.

DEVELOPING HACKLES

As soon as his visitation rights were restored,
the threats started again.

This was an insanity I couldn't endure—
I wouldn't endure.
I made a pact with myself:
where it concerned his destructive behavior,
I would not tolerate any manipulation, control,
or harassment of the children or myself,
period.

Still, no one within the county system
seemed to know what he was capable of—
they could make no promises.
We would have to wait until he physically hurt me,
or kidnapped the children.
The same old story.
There was no one to protect me.
I asked myself how long it would take before my delusions disappeared.
I answered myself.
No more, not again.
I had learned.
I had reached a point of no return.
My resolve had become steeled.

I would make decisions and act assertively based on our best interest,
not on his emotional demands or threats,
nor anyone else's for that matter.
Maybe I had finally understood the impact of enabling behavior.

This new awareness became decisively etched into my consciousness.
I would no longer abide bullying, threats or manipulation
from anyone again.
Whenever confronted with such behavior now,
my hackles stand on end
and my protective instincts show like fangs.

PAIN IS A GREAT MOTIVATOR OF CHANGE

Previously,
I had not understood,
nor could I see
the degree to which I had accepted unhealthy behaviors as normal.

After months of therapy,
three self-help books
and daily time with Christ,
I had learned to examine each idea I held.
My new state of consciousness
was an active rewriting of my mental programming.
Is that assumption true?
How do I feel about that?
Do I have to accept what that person is telling me?
What do I need from this situation?

It was exhaustingly hard work,
mostly because everyone who was a part of my life
wanted me to stay the way I was.
I felt as if I had to leave everything
just to be healthy.
I wished others could understand,
but just as I had not previously seen the dysfunction,
they were blind to it.
In their minds, my choosing health
was synonymous with rejecting them.
Sometimes, I could not tell the difference either.
It was messy.
Yet the vision my heart held
strongly urged me to continue my journey away from this place of destruction.
I asked, "How do I find my way?"
My therapist advised me to write my feelings
and, since learned behaviors start at home,
I should begin with my parents.

I asked,
"Is it important to send them what I write?"

"No. Just write.
Write a poem, a letter…whatever you like.
Write one to your dad and one to your mom.
But don't expect your change to happen overnight—it can take years."

A Mosaic Poem to Dad

Leaving Your Love

Resurrected from the ashes,
called to life again,
with power to claim my destiny,
I brave each day ahead.

Boldly facing new fears,
I tell them,
"GO AWAY!!!!"
Eyes wide open,
I can see,
life demands it be this way.

It is this newfound confidence
that disturbs Dad the most.
He does not face his fears.
He hides from them instead,
claiming nonexistent reasons
that nail him to his bed.

I have to leave his confines;
his constructs are ill-fated.
His love requires I be like him,
but he is just too jaded.

Knowing Mom was there for her kids,
he ran and hid from life.
Yet, who would do the same for mine
if I lived his cowardice?

It is apparent my strength to live
reveals his helplessness.
He wants me to own the rift,
but the responsibility is his.

I will not, cannot, be his love,
not in the way he desires.
My independence frightens him
and causes him to bluster.

When he looks at me with complete disdain,
some part of me shrivels.
His caustic disregard
has turned many souls acidic.

So I stand defiantly,
my body language declaring:
you cannot kill me with your looks.
I will not die your death.

His love does not die silently.
Rather, it shrieks and wails as it withers.
It is hard to let it take its course.
It is hard to say good-bye.

Health should not mean the death of love,
if love is really love.

A Letter Never Sent

The Things I Learned From Mom

For a woman, there is no such thing as success; there is only survival. You survived Dad, kids, empty nest, Dad's retirement. You coped, but you never succeeded. Dad wouldn't allow it—he was insecure and jealous—and you didn't brave it. You believed the lie and taught it to me; that women weren't supposed to be stronger than men. So you pretended not to be, and in doing so, you never were yourself.

You listened and yielded to his sickness. I can't blame you; look at your mom and dad, look at society. Women are scripted to be fragile, tender, easily and incurably hurt. But we now know that is not true. We are strong, determined, resolute, and thinking individuals.

You stayed in the relationship and love became corrupted. To you, love is a four-letter word. Often I had the subliminal notion that you resented, even hated me. I couldn't believe that, so I pushed it down, but not away. It's still here only now it is masked and I can't name the behavior or emotions that belong to it. I don't have the slightest notion of what human love is. You didn't love Dad—you tolerated him—now you can't even tolerate him. Your "kick butt therapy" left no room for love and support. Sometimes I wanted you to be tender, but your pride insisted on toughness.

Your armor has gaping holes. A desire for physical amenities keeps you insecure and chained. Those things have no reality. They hold no significance in the art of living. Yet you clutch onto things while your very life is being stripped from you. You have no interest in the intangibles. Instead, you seek deliverance in things of dust. You have eyes, but you cannot see.

I like my independence and no longer want attachments because I suspect the pain will be greater than the reward. I fear being drained, pulled, mulled, wretched, dried, and left a shell. I learned a woman's life is shit. It means pain, suffering, martyrdom, always getting the short end of the stick, and the complete loss of personal freedom.

I deny myself life, even as you do. I keep dragging myself along never knowing what it feels like to be fully alive. I wish you had freed me by demonstrating the path in your own life. It would have been easier. It seems my only recourse is to break the ties that bind me. Losing you feels like a crushing anxiety. I'm afraid. It seems not right because it is too uncomfortable to be good. I don't even know how to communicate this to you. I don't believe you will hear—I don't believe you even want to hear me.

(It wasn't possible to tell my mother these things. It was enough to become aware of the grip she held on my mind and emotions.)

CULMINATING EVENT

It was now March, 1981.
Three grueling years had passed since I filed for divorce.
Still, it would come down to one day:
the final hearing.
I wanted to be articulate for the final court hearing.
Everything in my life hinged on that day.

This time
I had confidence in my attorney.
His calm, confident professionalism was never overstated.
Rather, his consistency and discipline seemed to steady my trembling nerves.
He told me not to worry,
just speak naturally to the judge.

When the time came,
I remembered walking to the stand and sitting to the right of the judge.
That's all I remember.
My mind felt like the site of a traffic wreck of colossal proportion.
A collision involving six lanes and more than 50 cars,
trucks, campers, pickups,
several jackknifed 18-wheelers,
and three motorcycles.
Nothing was moving in either direction.
It was gridlock.
It was pitiful.

My attorney came to my rescue.
He recounted all of the decisive events,
which culminated in only one logical conclusion.

Indeed, I had followed the advice given me by the court,
my therapist and the county-appointed counselors.
I had done all that was required of me.

In the end, I gained full custody;
my ex-husband was given weekly visitation.

Our married indebtedness and assets were split.
His child support payments were set at $100 a month for each child.
Within 60 days of the final hearing,
I was given the lien amount of $4,300;
my equity from the marriage.

Immediately, I expressed my appreciation to those who were waiting.

Writing a check for the $100 my mother had loaned me,
I slipped it into a card and asked the florist to deliver the card
with the bouquet of flowers.

The hospital had been patiently waiting more than three years
to close the account on Andy's birth.
I thanked the receptionist in the accounting office
and paid my portion of the balance.

The amount I paid my lawyer seemed meaningless—
no amount would have been enough for what he had
given us. I sent him flowers and a card as well to express
my deep and lasting gratitude.

I had just enough to cover costs.
My new start meant the surrender of everything material,
but I was happy to pay the price.

Chapter 7

RISKING IT ALL AGAIN

THE RITUAL OF ATTRACTION

I had no use for men anymore,
but I was still attracted to the adventure of dating.
Being a realist,
I knew I would stand a better chance of attracting adventure
if I lost the weight I had regained for the third time since junior high.

Sure enough,
after losing weight,
men noticed.

SPEECHLESS IN ST. PAUL

He was cute,
but not really my type.
Being a hardworking stoic,
I really had no time for guys who wore tight pants and leather jackets—
guys who looked like appearance mattered.
Appearance wasn't my thing.
After all, my total wardrobe consisted of two pairs of work pants
and two work blouses,
all of which still smelled of fish.

The guy in the lab next door,
who was trying to arrange a double date,
assured me the friend with tight pants was a nice guy.
"He's stable and hardworking,
owns his own business.
He's ambitious—he contracted the building of his house.
Two other guys and I live with him in the house.
Bill's a good guy."

"Well, he might be a good guy,
but he's not my type."

My girlfriend, the fourth member of the double date,
urged, "It'll be fun. Let's do it."

That was easy for her to say.
I had to clean two homes that weekend
to afford something to wear on the date,
something that didn't smell like fish and look like work.

But, they were right;
it was fun, and he was nice.

Before the evening was over,
Bill had stopped to pick up enough food to feed the boys for two weeks.

On the third date,
we lingered in a tender, dreamy,
yet sumptuously sensual kiss,
which lasted for hours.
Afterward, I found myself speechless in Bill's presence.

DESIRES OF THE HEART

When I regained speech,
I was determined to be smarter about men in general, and Bill specifically.
I observed that our lives and backgrounds were very different.
That difference both attracted and frightened me.
However, I had learned one lesson:
if I wanted to leave the comfort of past sick relationships,
I must choose differently.
This was not easy because anything healthier felt odd and wrong.

Bill and I talked at length about our differences.
His family was upper income;
father had a college degree and was president of a company;
parents expected their four children would finish college;
children went to proms, built floats,
had fun, went waterskiing and snow skiing, golfed, played instruments;
sister belonged to a sorority;
they valued attractive personal appearance.

I…well, you know.

We told each other every secret.
    Past sexual relationships;
    the state of our individual fertility;
    our sins and errors in judgment;
    the trauma of our respective divorces;
    our dismal financial situations.

He told me his faith was important to him.
He was Missouri Synod Lutheran; what was I?
I confided I had felt the touch of Christ as He held me tenderly, sweetly.
He was intrigued but didn't know what to make of it—
he had never heard of such a thing.

Anything that could be known was now known.

I was undeniably attracted and yet exhausted by his energy.
His boundless stamina seemed a guarantee that life would
never beat him into submission.
(Beaten people frighten me—they reflect my own insecurity to live successfully.)

Equally amazing to me was the fact that he communicated, he talked,
he responded!
I had never before experienced a man who shared
his thoughts on a personal level.
I could know him, know what he was thinking.

It was so unfamiliar.
It was an intimacy I craved.

Then there was his body...
my passion that knew no satiation.
I could gorge myself and not have enough;
to breathe his breath,
or inject myself into his veins
and course through the entirety of his body unencumbered by flesh.
Each kiss released my mind from its captivity,
my thoughts melting in the moistness of his lips.
I was ravenous for the food of life he offered;
warm and vital and life sustaining.

I didn't know if Bill was "Mr. Right,"
but I couldn't say he was wrong.
I knew my heart fluttered when he came into a room,
and, I often felt breathless when near him.
It was exciting.
I knew that with him life would hold possibilities.

Yet, he made comments and demands that made me apprehensive.
   "Why don't you have more plants? My ex-wife had plants all over,"
   he quipped.
   "I raise kids, not plants," I retorted.

   "Why don't you shave there? Women aren't supposed to be hairy there,"
   he argued.
   "Says who! If you grow hair there, it's supposed to be there."

   "You're gaining weight. You should lose it."
   "I was thinking instead, maybe I should lose you!"

Sometimes everything about me seemed so wrong.
Was it my baggage, or his?

DEFEND ME!

I knew I was from the wrong side of the tracks,
but he was divorced too; he just didn't have kids.

His family had to decide if my divorce could be legitimized in the eyes of God.
His older sister reasoned my ex-husband had abandoned us by
not supporting the family;
therefore, divorce could probably be justified.
Still, it was difficult for his parents to agree to meet me.
It took some persuasion.

An upcoming family outing seemed to be an appropriate time for introductions.
Bill's younger brother was graduating from the seminary
and brought his fiancé home for the weekend.
She was the daughter of a minister;
blonde, innocent, no children from a previous marriage,
no ex-husband trying to kill her.
She seemed a perfect fit.
The whole family would spend the day together
celebrating the upcoming graduation and wedding.

"No," his mother told Bill, this event was not the right time to meet me—
my attendance could potentially ruin an otherwise perfect day.

Bill asked me to get together with him in the evening,
after he returned from their flawless day.

The day was unblemished with the exception of one thing—I was mad!
"If you really think I am the one you love,
why didn't you choose to defend me?
It would have told me a lot if you had declined to join them.
Instead, you leave me sitting at a bar waiting for you,
then you show up late besides!
I'm really angry and hurt.
Will there ever be a 'right time' to meet me?"

"You have to understand my family.
They will love you once they get to know you.
It will just take them some time."

"Well, that seems to be the difficult part, doesn't it?!"

My dad wasn't much better.
He decided immediately that he didn't like my potential choice.
"He's too cocky and arrogant."

My mother asked if I was confident he was right for me.
"I don't know for sure—how do you ever know that with certainty?
But I'm willing to take the risk."

162

Prince Charming

I eventually met his parents.
They took us to dinner along the Mississippi
on the Wisconsin side of the river.
We were the last to leave the restaurant,
lost in wine and laughter, feeling the relief of our dissipating fear.

With pride and no excuses,
I told them about my sons.
"They are adorable," I bragged.

They wanted to meet them.

By the time their daughter was married that summer,
we were practically family.

I had nothing to wear to his sister's wedding,
so Bill took me shopping at the mall.
I got turned around and lost inside the mall.
He questioned, "Why don't you know your way around a mall?
Every woman knows a mall!"

"Obviously, you have not been listening when I have counted our differences.
I don't have the money or the time to get to know a mall."

He picked out dresses and asked if I would try them on.
I argued about who would pay for the dress.
I wasn't about to take any charity—I could manage on my own!
I had my determined face on when I came out in the first dress.
"You are so beautiful!" he said, glowing like a prince who found his bride.

I didn't want to admit the fairy-tale feeling inside of me.
I wore a store-bought dress to his sister's wedding.
He paid for it.

He was surreal to me:
good-looking,
ambitious,
hardworking,
dedicated,
passionate,
talkative,
and, he never used abusive language.
He, however, was prone to manipulating to achieve his goal.

When he asked me to marry him,
I responded that there was no hurry, I could wait.
"Either marry me now or I'll start dating other women," he commanded,
radiating energy from his astonishingly intense blue eyes.

"That is manipulative!" I countered, with daring in my eyes.
"Go ahead and date, see if I care.
I'll start dating other men!"

A Knot Tied in Reality

That was the beginning joust between our two very strong personalities.
Twenty-three years later,
neither of us has been knocked from our mount,
although we have both tried.

We agreed our wedding would be small, informal,
and it should stress not only our commitment to each other, but also to the boys.
It was quite acceptable to do everything low budget.
There was no engagement ring.
A friend made my dress.
My mother and grandmother did all the cooking for a reception at Mom's house.
And, as usual, my dad did nothing to support the occasion.

My ex-husband insisted on having visitation the night before the wedding.
He was still spewing threats of kidnapping,
so we hired a security guard
and told him to tail my ex wherever he went with the boys.
"Even if he crosses the state line!
Stay with him," we insisted.

While the boys were gone,
my future in-laws called
and asked to see Bill immediately.
It was urgent!

Now what?

They had overheard my aunt say that I could not have children.
They thought, perhaps, I had not confided this to Bill in my
"eagerness" to get married.
Perhaps my intent was to trap him.
No, he assured them, I had told him a long time ago.
"Why didn't you tell us?" they demanded.

Bill returned hours later to confide his parents' displeasure.
Shortly after, my ex-husband returned the boys.
The guard we had hired waited until he drove away,
then hurried to the door and told us all the details of the night.
Bill and I thanked him and paid him for his service.

After Bill left that night,
I lay exhausted, unable to sleep.

The morning of the wedding,
while waiting to be dressed,
Andy wrote all over himself with green permanent marker.
It took an hour of scrubbing to get him clean again.

The church we were married in held its services in a gymnasium.
The boys joined us on the side line at center court as we said our vows.
Now, at six and three years old,
they were a picture of manliness in their new suits.
Ben carried our rings.
Craig and Mary Ann, the friends who helped during my armed move,
witnessed the marriage and signed the certificate.

Throughout the service,
Bill's parents sat woodenly.
Refusing to watch the ceremony; they looked at the wall instead.
When the reception was over,
they took Bill and me aside,
their emotions bleeding from their bodies.
They had planned on watching the boys during our honeymoon,
yet, explosive confrontation was only a nose distance between me
and his father.

I started.
"It's obvious that you are not happy.
I will not subject my boys to this kind of tension for a week."
Looking at Bill, my new husband, I independently announced my decision,
"I will not go on a honeymoon. I'll take the boys home with me tonight."

I saw panic (lost ecstasy) on Bill's face.

His father declared,
"Obviously, you don't know us very well because we love children and would
do nothing to harm them."

"What is obvious here is that we don't know each other at all!
You certainly don't know me!
I will not compromise my boys—not even for a honeymoon!"

I chose to ignore Bill's growing panic,
and the fact that I had starved myself down to my lowest weight ever,
just to ensure his delight!
I wanted Bill to stand up for us.
(A man shall leave his father and mother…)
My face registered my expectation.
I wasn't bluffing.

Bill's father assured me the boys would be loved and cared for in my absence.
The look of cold indifference left his eyes
as he talked of their desire for grandchildren.
Tensions lessened as we all sought common ground
in the happiness and safety of the boys.

They took the boys that evening,
and we left for our honeymoon.
The boys had a wonderful time with their new grandpa and grandma.
Not a word of the incident was spoken upon our return.
Twenty years later, on my birthday,
his parents explained their emotion on that day.

All in all, the wedding was stunning in its realism.

PERFECT STORM

We didn't have money to spend on a honeymoon,
so we spent the week in a house trailer
parked on a hilltop outside of Duluth.

We didn't care that the trailer was nothing fancy.
We didn't care that the weather was lousy; extremely cold and rainy.
We didn't care about the attractions of Duluth.
We didn't care about time, or breathing or sleeping or eating.
We were lost in a perfect storm of passion.
Lost in a moment that lasted an entire week.

We kissed and were consumed,
drawn inextricably beyond reason;
      wanting more,
      needing desperately,
      starving,
      aching.

We touched,
and our flesh begged for more flesh;
      swollen,
      cupping fullness,
      probing deeper.

We inhaled the smell of love deeply,
tasting the delectable;
      luscious,
      moist,
      drinking love,
      insatiable.

As a fire devours oxygen in a room,
we were left breathless by our consuming appetite.
Our sweat mingled,
evaporated,
and clouded the window;
the gray overcast day obscured from view
as winds and rain rocked the trailer.

Still, we craved more.
We were voracious,
and fed our frenzy shamelessly.
Five days later we paused
and said,
"Surely we should stop."
Yet, when we looked at each other during a hike,
we were overtaken by the urgency of our need—
our hunger demanded immediate indulgence.
Finding a cave,
the heat of our bodies was stark against the cold granite floor.
On our way back
we agreed
there was never enough.

On the sixth day we awoke to realize we had lost a day;
the boys would be waiting for us.
Scurrying, we grabbed our belongings and rushed home.

The next morning, the boys jumped into bed with us,
playful, they were happy to be a family.
Bill and I smiled and kissed each other
and reluctantly stopped there.

TRIAL BY FIRE

After returning from our honeymoon,
we met with the pastor
and went over the results of our marriage compatibility test.
The results showed we viewed most things differently;
finances, sex, child rearing, faith...
The good news was that we were compatible in the area of communication.
Obviously, knowing how to communicate
would help us resolve our differences in all other areas.

Uh-huh.
Why didn't we wait for the results before getting married?

I was proud that I brought no debt forward to our marriage;
I had been encouraged by a friend to save $10 a month—
even if it was a meager amount, it would add up.
We had used my savings to buy our wedding bands.

Bill's situation was not the same.
He brought a large amount of indebtedness from his divorce
and was financially burdened by reinvestment in his company.

Raising a family took more time than Bill expected.
It also took more money than he was able to take out of his business.
He wanted better for his family
and without much discussion of options,
he decided to sell his laboratory to a national environmental testing lab.
They gave him a guaranteed salary, bonus and stock in the company.
He was left to manage his lab, the new branch, and was given
the title of president.
That suited him well—
in his mind, it would always be his lab.

Because of debt,
we stayed in my apartment and rented out his house to gain income.
Six months later, his guy friends moved out leaving their filth behind.
There were rotting, seeping bags full of garbage in the basement
that they had neglected to toss.

The bathroom looked as if it had not been cleaned in years;
mold and grey scum buried the porcelain's shine.
I was indignant!
This wasn't fair!
Why was I cleaning up their mess?
Bill and I discussed the situation and decided on a compromise.
I would quit working to stay home with the boys,
(a luxury by previous standards)
and in exchange, I would clean the mess left behind.

It was summer and the boys wasted no time finding friends
while I started to clean the slime from the basement floor.
As we began to define our new family in our new home,
Andy found what he needed to start talking.
Within a few days of his first word, he was speaking entire sentences.
Everyone marveled.

Bill was working gruelingly long days because the business—
a laboratory—was just moved to a new location.
Since money was tight, I agreed to help paint the walls in the office area.
As I approached the lab
I could see two fire trucks, lights flashing, parked out front.
Startled, I sped to the lab, slammed on the brakes, and ran to the front entry,
stumbling over pieces of broken tiles that had been blown off the ceiling.
Breathless, I shouted to a co-worker, "Where's Bill?"
"He's on his way to the hospital.
We had a solvent explosion.
He was blown out of the back by the force.
I'll warn you; he doesn't look good—he has burns on his arms and face."

When I entered the emergency room,
I saw him holding his arms in the air.
Skin was literally dripping in long tissue sheaths from his elbows.
His eyebrows and lashes were gone.
Second and third degree burns covered most of his chest and arms.

He said, "Thank God I was the only one hurt—
none of my employees were injured."
He complained of horrific pain and was given morphine.
Time passed without his notice.

In preparation for his return home,
a nurse taught me a procedure called debridement;
it is the removal of dead tissue.
She advised that once Bill was released,
he was to bathe twice daily while I scraped the dead skin from his upper body.
I recalled the filthy unsanitary condition of our bathroom,
and asked the nurse, "How long until Bill comes home?"
A week, she guessed.
"Okay," I said.
"I'll start cleaning the bathroom.
A week should allow me enough time to find the white of the tub."
She looked at me quizzically.

While home healing,
Bill was touched by the presence of Christ in a profound and undeniable way.
He began to understand the closeness of which I spoke.

COMMON GROUND

After eight weeks at home, Bill returned to work
and immediately began working 12-hour days again.
The deepest scars remained on his arms,
but the remainder of his body had healed nicely.

Ben went off to school in September
and I volunteered to work the Pumpkin Carnival in October.

So this is the Donna Reed life!
What am I supposed to do with myself, I wondered?
Be a normal wife, I answered.
What does a normal wife do?

I joined the women's Bible study at church.
It met midweek in the morning while the kids were at school.
The women were all stay-at-home moms. [8]
They knew their roles well;
they wore them like old shoes.
I tried on the same shoe and it gave me bunions.
Our church supported the submission of women.
I wanted to quit but I felt guilty, odd.

It grieved me.
The heat of my emotions surprised me.
I suppose I felt the need to justify myself because I didn't fit.
Maybe too much water had gone under the bridge for me to be Donna Reed.

I wanted to discuss a dream I had with Bill.
In the dream the women of the church were like robots.
Faceless or with faces that had no reality—masks—
meaning right,
attempting right,
doing their duty,
their holy mission.
They labored nonstop to carry fish.
The fish they carried were dead,
with bulging eyes,
stinking.

From the mountains in precision they came,
faceless with "thou should" woven into their fabric.
They kept dumping the dead fish into my reservoir.

I must tell them that the reservoir is God's
and he doesn't want slaves carrying dead fish.
I must say, "I forgive you—you know no better.
But I can no longer accept dead fish.
In its place, I must have God's truth.
I must throw these fish away."

I tried discussing it with Bill.
He didn't believe in God communicating directly or through dreams.
He believed without question, as his family did, in the teachings of the church.
Men were the head of the household
and wives should not question their authority to make decisions for the family,
including decisions on behalf of their wives.
Parents should present a united position concerning the church to their kids.
If not, kids get confused.

We got into a huge fight.
I called him a chauvinist pig as we stormed away from each other.

I wasn't in the best of moods when the phone rang.
It was the school.
Ben had fallen during a roller skating party;
they were pretty sure his leg was broken.

I grabbed Andy and flew out the door to the car.
As I sped down the highway significantly over the speed limit,
Andy objected, "Momma, you're driving like a crazy person."
I confessed it was a bad morning, and yes, "I know I should slow down."

The school was right;
Ben had broken his femur near the hip.
Because of the location of the break,
he would be in a body cast for two months.

Bill rushed to the hospital immediately after receiving my call.
We sat by our son's bed throughout the night.
A cast would be put on in the morning,
but until then, we were advised to keep Ben relaxed and still.
That was easy to say and hard to do.
Whenever he was about to doze off,
the muscles in his leg would involuntarily contract
causing the broken bone to jut upward toward the skin's surface.
Each time it looked as if the bone would pierce the skin,
Ben would scream in pain.

It happened repeatedly throughout the night.

After each episode,
Bill and I would look at each other in horror,
our eyes misting while we held back tears;
tears that would only increase our son's distress.

When the morning came and Ben was taken into surgery,
I thanked Bill for being there.
I thought of all the times I had been alone nurturing the boys.
This was so different.
We hugged.
I let the tears fall,
so did he.

WINNING HEARTS

It was Father's Day.

Bill and I argued because he did not want the boys to go with their father;
he wanted them to stay with him.
After all, he reasoned, he was the one acting like a father.

The boys were uncomfortable hearing us,
so they waited outside for their ride.

Hours passed.
No one came for them.

We called the boys in to talk.
In the course of the discussion,
Ben disclosed to Bill something he had been told by his father.
He confided,
"I can't call you Dad
because you aren't my Dad.
You're mom's current husband."

The pain immediately registered in Bill's eyes.

A MOTHER DUCK IN ORGANIC CHEMISTRY

I spent half a year still trying to be domesticated.
I cooked dinners for everyone and their brothers.
I liked the art of cooking,
but cooking wasn't enough.
I still had lingering fears;
fears of being vulnerable again in a hostile world.
I had always wanted to finish my degree;
maybe now was the time.

Bill's parents couldn't understand what drove me.
Why was I so unsettled?
I really couldn't explain it to their satisfaction.
I summarized by saying I wasn't a mother duck
who could be satisfied by watching her ducklings swim happily into adulthood.
They didn't understand.

Although Bill never told me he understood,
he supported the idea of my returning to college.
We discussed which program.
He would not support my desire to finish in biology saying it paid nothing.
I bristled at him for shunning my passion,
but realized he was supporting my two sons
without any help from their biological father.
And, since the tuition costs would come out of the equity loan on his house,
it seemed compromise was in order.

Bill suggested, "Why not something to do with food?
You love to cook.
This is an agricultural state.
Maybe we could use my company stock to open a restaurant."
We had calculated the stock's potential value at $300,000.

It wasn't a bad idea.
I did have a restaurant concept already in mind.

Maybe fortune had turned our way.

Together, we visited a career counselor at the University of Minnesota.
I explained the situation and asked which degree program
would prepare me to open a restaurant,
or, if that failed, would be marketable within the food industry in a
career-level position?
The counselor knew just the program for me: Consumer Food Science.
She said it was their most marketable degree!

I was excited.
Bill was supportive.
I signed up.

My first class, chemistry, was held in an auditorium.
I was one of 350 students,
all of whom looked young enough to be my children.
In their youth, they refused to ask for help.
I, on the other hand, was old and did not care how stupid I looked.
I would hunt down the professor when stuck.
He observed, "Aren't you the one with the two boys?
They sit so quietly putting together atomic models during class.
They are very well behaved."

I responded, "Thank you, they are wonderful boys."

ROOM TO TRUST

Bill had never mentioned his real desire to have a child.
He knew when he married me that he gave up that option.
He did not burden me with his secret feelings.

My heart was taken by his silence on the subject,
touched because he loved the boys as his own.

I could not believe the change in my life,
the sacrifices he made,
or his willingness to protect what was good.

He had moved forward unabashedly into our new future,
while some part of me still loitered in mistrust
thinking everything could fall apart in an instant.

I didn't want to perceive life as perilous anymore.
I wanted desperately to move into the gift,
to experience love shared,
love given.

When I had made up my mind,
I sat down and talked with Bill.
At first he assumed I was toying with him.
I convinced him with the details.
I had already done some checking.
Surgery to reverse my tubal ligation was possible.
The success rate was 80%.
The average cost was about $2,000 - out of pocket - insurance wouldn't cover it.
If the first doctor did what I asked,
I assumed our chances for success would be poor.
There was no guarantee of a baby.
But, I said, "If you are interested,
I am willing."

He was immediately interested!

The surgery was scheduled for the first of December,
ironically, the date of my first wedding.
On the day of the surgery,
Bill got violently ill with stomach flu symptoms
and was given a hospital bed before I was.
My mother picked him up at the hospital
and brought him home to care for him.

There, she and Grandmother watched him lay helplessly on the sofa in torment,
waiting for the hospital to call.
The surgery, already twice as long as expected, caused concern.
Surprisingly, Bill's illness passed
when the hospital called to say the doctor was out of surgery.

Bill rushed to the hospital to hear the prognosis.

Dr. Kadue, the obstetric surgeon, was an introverted guy;
very cerebral,
didn't talk much,
wasn't prone to boasting,
usually didn't look at you when he talked.

Not so that afternoon.
He was a man at the top of his game.

He accounted for the length of time and the more than doubling of cost.

He explained to us both,
"The doctor who did the tubal ligation took you at your word.
Instead of cutting the tubes midpoint on their length,
he cut them off at the uterus.
Usually, this is not done.
It greatly reduced the chance of success."

Dr. Kadue then cocked his head to the side
and with a supreme amount of self-assurance,
went on to say,
"If any other surgeon had done this procedure,
you would have less than a 20% chance of ever becoming pregnant.
I have never had a failure,
so you have a fifty/fifty chance."
He continued,
"I had to cut into the uterus to find the tube ends.
It was a difficult surgery.
Swelling could be a problem.
Scarring is more possible.
We'll have to monitor you closely for tubular pregnancy,
which can be life threatening."

Bill shook his hand and thanked him profusely.

Chapter 8

Moving On

Getting Busy

We waited the recommended time before trying to get pregnant, then,
Bill was all over me like a man with a mission.

Things were different now;
we were living separate fantasies.

I wanted a storybook pregnancy this time.
> I wanted to be courted.
> To feel important enough for prime time.
> "Couldn't we go on a date before we get busy?
> You never lust after me anymore unless it is mid-cycle."

I accused him of wanting to recoup his investment.

He wanted me to be provocative;
> to tantalize him,
> to lure him into excitement.

I knew where that excitement led,
and it wasn't making any sense to me.

In the midst of our diverging fantasies, life never stopped intruding.
> A previous love of Bill's called five times asking if he had ever really loved her.
> She came to the lab to ask in person.
>
> Bill and I stayed up until 2:00 a.m. working on a paper I had due, hoping it would distract us.
>
> I miscarried in February and May. Each time, Dr. Kadue called the house out of concern.
>
> Five months passed without any word from the boys' father. Finally, he called and said he was in treatment at the university for alcoholism and depression. His doctor told him visiting the boys would be too stressful.
>
> The Republicans had moved into the White House. Environmental issues took a nose dive, and with that, so did the environmental company that purchased Bill's lab. Things were beginning to go sour.

This really wasn't what I had in mind.
I told Bill I didn't want to get pregnant until things settled down.

BURIED, BUT NOT FORGOTTEN

The idea of bringing a new life into the world caused Bill no angst.
He reasoned inhabitants of the planet had been giving birth
in the best and worst of circumstances long before us.

I didn't disagree that life was tenacious.
And, I wasn't holding out for prosperity's child.
In my mind,
the issues were more complex and hard to pull apart;
they were embedded deep within my psyche.
It had as much to do with carrying the fetus successfully,
as caring for the child after birth.
Neither event could be predicted with any certainty.
The decision to take the chance again
left me with the sensation that I had opened Pandora's Box.

I talked to a minister about my concerns
and recounted a strange dream.
In the dream,
I was ripping sheetrock off an inside wall of a house.
Behind the sheetrock
there were dead babies;
buried;
wedged between the studs.
The dream horrified me.

The minister told me that in our dreams,
a house can represent ourselves, our psyche.
He asked if I had ever had an abortion.
"No," I answered.

"Have you had miscarriages?" he probed further.
"Yes, several...
two within the past five months, since the surgery."

"How does that make you feel?" he asked.

It made sense.
In my mind I had made myself vulnerable to forces I could not control
with the result that two more babies were buried behind the wall.

I marveled at how the mind can be so strangely complex.

LIFE HAPPENS

The national company that owned Bill's lab
hired new management in from Texas.
They were now single-mindedly focused on cost-cutting measures.

We suspected they intended to bleed assets from Bill's lab
and close it.
He objected.
They asked him to resign.
He refused.
They terminated him with one month's severance.
(As we predicted,
the branch was later closed
and Bill's stock value dwindled to nothing.)

That same afternoon,
we sat silently in Dr. Kadue's office
waiting to hear the results of the blood test.
The hormone levels were high.
Dr. Kadue, now knowing his record of success would not be broken,
told us I was definitely pregnant.
It had been a mere six months since the surgery.

CHOICES

Life happened and I let it.
I should have been kicked.
I could have insisted on practicing birth control,
just as Bill insisted on pregnancy.
I knew he had no context for a reality beyond the immediate goal.
Bill hankered for me to be pregnant. Period.
Looking back on it,
he was unbelievably erotic the night of Lori's wedding.
It happened that night, I'm sure.
We made love until morning and missed breakfast.
    Still numb and weak from passion, knees buckling,
    I fell down the church stairs.
    We bandaged my wounds and ate Big Macs while sitting in the sun.

The reality is, I didn't take charge of my life.
I let him decide for us.

Mom suggested an abortion.
"You could try again later."

"No. I just couldn't do that."

"It's your life to screw up.
Now you'll never finish college," she said, with her usual encouraging attitude.

For the first half of my pregnancy, Bill was out of work.

The restaurant idea dissipated with the stock value.

I quit college—
again—
and started working part time at the bank
where my mother worked.
It seemed I couldn't leave my mother's footsteps
no matter how hard I tried.

Soul Sweeping

No doubt about it,
I was heading for a new low.

There could only be one reason that my life continuously took wrong turns.
I was guilty and getting my just rewards.
It appeared everyone around me was receiving fallout as well.
My mind went back in time searching for my most flagrant errors.

I was sure my baby would be an alien.
The exposure I had to radioactive isotopes while working at the university
would make this baby a mutant.
I should have thought of that before I became pregnant.
The doctor said, "No, it will have no effect on the baby."

I thought back further to something that was festering in my soul.
I had told Bill on our second date of a man;
a man before him,
and during my separation from my ex-husband.
At the time, I didn't care anymore—
everything was so difficult.
The relationship was a selfish attempt to fill unmet needs.
I hurt the man and those close to him.

I was convinced I had brought ruin upon myself and others.

I was losing my mind.

Bill called the man and told him of my distress.
Then…Bill handed the phone to me.
I shook and cried.

I asked Bill why he did that.
"Because you have to move on.
Peter also turned away from the Lord.
We all do grievous things.
Forgiveness means it is forgotten.
We're going to have a baby.
Our life is now.
I love you."

Family Protection Plan

Our family was about to take on a new definition.
Bill and I started thinking of things we had not considered before.
For instance, once the baby was born,
we envisioned the three children would be knit together as one family.
What would happen if I died?
How could the children be kept together?
It was impossible for Bill to adopt the boys without their father's consent,
and that, we were assured, would never happen.
Yet, their father's behavior was erratic, irresponsible, and presumably mentally ill.
We wanted to protect against unforeseen possibilities.

We sought advice from a family law attorney.
"Is there any way to assure Bill will gain custody of the boys should I die?"

The attorney said it would be difficult, at best.
She advised us to keep a journal of all interactions with my ex-husband.

He was a selfish, destabilizing, havoc-producing nightmare
that reintroduced itself into our peace of mind
like a reoccurring migraine headache.
There was no cure.

He had not visited the boys in an entire year;
without a word, he had vanished.
Then, in December, he called to tell us he was stabilized on lithium
and planned on resuming visitation before Christmas.
I disagreed vehemently and called his doctor,
the county case worker, and our lawyer.
I explained it was unreasonable to subject the boys to undue potential harm,
especially after the progress they had made,
particularly the oldest, during their father's absence.
Even the county had advised that visitation be disallowed until he sought treatment,
this to ensure steady emotional development of the boys.

But just like before,
it seemed his rights as a parent superseded our collective
rights for health and stability.
No matter how hard I struggled to preserve our family's security,
it ended the same.
He was allowed back in—nothing could be done.

Special Delivery

The contractions started as expected.
We dropped the boys off at Mom's house on the way to the hospital.

Bill had been busy preparing for delivery.
Because I said the sound of waves were relaxing to me,
he had a friend make tapes of water sounds that I could listen to during labor.
He read books on delivery and attended birthing classes.
As a delivery coach, Bill was a bit energetic.
He really had no control over the process and that troubled him;
he had no idea what to do with all of his energy.
It was funny and I loved him for it.

Unlike my first two deliveries,
what marked this delivery as unusual
was that it was not at all unusual.
It followed the predictable pattern through each phase.

In the transition phase of delivery,
when contractions were one minute apart, Bill followed all the rules.

>Don't leave your wife.
>Use simple and declarative statements.
>Don't ask questions that require more than a yes or no.
>Don't react to any abuse you may take.
>Don't argue with her.
>She's looking to you for support and encouragement.
>Stay close to her.

Dr. Kadue came in often to check progress.
That made Bill less hyper.
During delivery Bill lost a little focus on coaching,
but that was okay—
he was fixated on what was happening—where was his baby?

Bill was surprised at how fast she came after I started pushing;
she came too fast for him to really grasp the reality.
Oh, she was beautiful to him.
He couldn't stop looking at her.
He loved her from the first moment he saw her.
He named her Corissa.

Our daughter's delivery was completely without complications.
What a difference love made.

LIVING THE DREAM

During the early years of our marriage,
my journal was filled with entries stating my confusion.

I felt trapped by the demands and expectations of others,
and by my own fears and choices.

> I wrote:
> *It's too late.*
> *Other people depend on me,*
> *and when they do, I go nuts.*
>
> *Ducks have nests.*
> *Return to yours!*

I didn't know how to say that I couldn't live feeling trapped.
To find freedom would mean
I would compromise the needs of my family.
Their pain would become mine.

I was absorbing a lot of useless guilt,
and wallowing around in it.

Finally, I told Bill I couldn't take it anymore.
I had to go back to college and finish what I had started.

Bill was doing well at his new job and thought it made sense.

I started back as a full-time student;
a dream that had never left my mind.
I studied hard and earned an academic award.

My return was a gift of incalculable value to me.

REAL NEEDS

I was beginning to believe I had left the demon far behind me.
Life was good.
My past, was past.
I asked myself,
"Is it right to just walk away?
Do I owe something to others?"

That's basically what I told the food editor at the city's largest paper;
          I told her I wanted to give back.
My college advisor connected me with the editor knowing that
an internship would look good to a future employer.

The editor was open to suggestions.
"What about food shelves?
I know what it is like to feed a family while living in poverty."
She approved the topic and asked me to check in periodically.

I called the largest food shelf in the city and talked to the director.
He said it would be acceptable if I interviewed recipients.
"Dress down so you fit in," he advised.
I assured him that wouldn't be a problem.

He insisted I come and stay a week.
"Why is it important to stay a week?" I asked.
"You'll be surprised what you learn.
The problem isn't lack of food," he answered.

"What is the problem?"

"Let's talk about that after your week is up," he deferred.

I wrote a survey and interviewed every recipient.
I was truly amazed.
The recipients ate meat three meals a day;
steaks, chop, you name it,
they were into meat in a way considered unhealthy by nutritionists.
They admitted to throwing away hot dogs from the food shelf
because they wanted chops instead.

To think I was prepared to write an article on 101 ways to make bean dishes tasty.

"What is this?" I asked the director.

"That's my point.
Hunger isn't the problem.
Education, nutrition, training in family skills, etcetera.
That's what is really needed.
Food shelves make people feel good.
It makes them feel like they are doing something."

"But what about abuse shelters?
Their food comes from a food shelf."

"Yes, there are specific needs in the community,
but for the most part,
food shelves are not addressing the real need," he insisted.

I met with the food editor at the paper to discuss my findings:
"This is far too controversial for the Food Section," she said with a grimace.

"It's true and it's important. It should be told," I asserted.

"Well, it won't be told in the Food Section.
You'll have to start over on something that pertains to the section,"
she said with a matronly tone.
She directed me,
"Recipes are always good. Our readers love recipes."

"Okay, I will. But can't this research be forwarded to the Metro Section?"

"Sure, give it to me. I'll take care of it."

I started researching small local growers
where readers could purchase fresh-grown produce.
I included seasonal recipes.

I don't ever remember seeing anything in the Metro Section on food shelves,
but then again, I was pretty immersed in my life.
I could have missed it.

TIME TO REEVALUATE

All the classmates in my program were female.
It was our senior year and time to start seriously checking out
employment opportunities.
We decided to go as a group to the evening receptions held by
General Mills and Pillsbury.
We put on our conservative blue suits
fully expecting an enthusiastic reception from our future employers.

It didn't happen that way.
They told us they had no use for our degree.
If they wanted a food chemist, they would hire a PhD.
If they wanted business acumen, they would hire an MBA.
"Sorry," they said.

We stood in shock.
The university had promoted our degree as marketable! How could this be?
Our childlike naiveté was exposed.
But I wasn't a child.
How stupid of me to take the academic advisor at her word!
Hadn't I been through enough in my life to know better?

The younger students started crying.
What were they going to do now?
How would they tell their parents they had been robbed?

I couldn't stand to watch them cry.
I rallied them to go to the advisor's office.

The advisor acted shocked!
What?
She had no idea.
After an uncomfortable moment of silence,
she told us to put our collective chins up;
she was sure we would find something.

Sorry, but that wasn't good enough for me.
I had come too far;
this had taken too long;

I had overcome too many obstacles to have her be that cavalier.
I went straight to the dean's office.
I told him the issues at hand and proposed action.
If he would support my efforts,
I would conduct a study of the marketability of our degree program.
He mused for a minute and then agreed.
He cautioned that I would run into some staff that may feel
threatened by my efforts.

I really didn't care.
I was mad—
at myself and them.

My research was closely governed by an advisor.
When completed,
the results indicated the degree program was outdated;
industry had moved on.

I was later told the college changed the program.

I received a letter from the dean after graduation.
> "It was a pleasure having you as a student here in the College of
> Agriculture. I greatly admired your persistence and skill in working
> through some difficult situations."

To its credit, the institution had the courage and wisdom to change.

IF YOU'RE SANE, RAISE YOUR HAND

A black hole in the universe
occurred my last and final quarter of college.
Everything was pulling, spiraling downward out of control.

Bill was going to the doctor regularly with chest pains;
occasionally, he went to the hospital by ambulance.
He was absolutely convinced he was having a heart attack.
The doctors did every conceivable test, including an angiogram.
His heart was fine.
They suggested he was having panic attacks.
This was excruciatingly difficult for him to come to grips with because
emotionally induced disorders were not talked about in his family.
Bill did not believe in the medicine of psychotherapy.
I, on the other hand,
had lived my entire life surrounded by the emotionally distressed.
They were falling from the family tree like ripe coconuts.
Three first cousins committed suicide, one attempted,
and others lived quietly with chronic depression.
I believed in addressing such problems.
It was a difficult time for Bill
and resulted in many painful discussions between us.

At the same time,
my parents, after years of unabashed hatred for each other,
were talking divorce.
Mom saw an attorney and threatened Dad with papers.
Dad curled up into a fetal position.
It was ugly.
> (Mom just threatened;
> she never filed.)

My grandmother was dying of congenital heart disease.

I admitted going crazy trying to deal with everything;
all household chores (Bill didn't believe they were in his job description),
kids,
internships,
work at the bank,
classes,
Dad whining,
Mom blustering,
Grandma dying,
Bill denying.

I went to the emergency ward with severe stomach pains.
The doctor said it was stress related.
I believed him,
and immediately started an internal dialogue on how to solve the problem.
    What to do next?
        Drop something.
    What?
        I don't care, anything!
    Work?
        No, we need the money.
    The internship at the paper?
        I can't. It would look so bad, especially after the food shelf debacle.
    Don't be a putz! You're going to have to give up something.
        My stomach hurts worse now.
    Get over it!
        I'll feel humiliated.
    Tough.

When I called the editor, she accepted without fanfare.
I gave her my research notes and someone else wrote the article that was
later published;
it included recipes.

ANNULMENT

My ex-husband was planning to remarry in the Catholic church.
There was a problem;
his first marriage to me must be annulled.
The same priest that had tried to "comfort" me
phoned me at home one evening.
He asked me a series of questions,
"In which church were you married?" the priest inquired.

     "Lutheran," I answered.

"Oh, that's good."

     "Why is that good?"

"Because your marriage will not be recognized by the church."

     "What happens if I was baptized Catholic?"

"Oh, that might present a problem,"
he said and paused to think.
"What church were the children baptized in?"

     "Lutheran."

"Thank God! That means the boys don't exist
in the eyes of the church."

     "Excuse me!
     They exist in the eyes of God!"

"Well, the annulment will still go through.
That is what I am interested in."

     "This conversation is over!"

ANTICLIMAX

Eighteen years after starting,
and three years after the birth of my daughter,
I finally graduated from college. [9]

Although in moments of fantasy
I had envisioned a ticker tape parade,
there was no party.
Bill gave me a rose and we kissed on the stairs of the auditorium.
The kids cheered for me.
My mother-in-law came to the ceremony;
        my father-in-law played golf with customers.
Mom and Dad argued all the way to the ceremony
and were not speaking to each other when they arrived.

I wished my classmates well as we hugged each other.
Bill took pictures of us together, smiling.

It was a good day—
the sun rose and the sun set.

If nothing else,
I had demonstrated a message to my kids:
NEVER GIVE UP!

CLOSE ENCOUNTER

After graduation
I earnestly sought to know God's will for my life.
I spent several hours every day reading the Bible, praying and meditating.
Although nothing was coming to me,
I delighted in the knowledge I was gaining and the closeness I felt.
I wondered when something would be revealed.

Oddly, a revelation came at night,
as the Psalmist wrote,
"(Lord) if you visit me by night…"

It started as a dream that was
so vivid,
so intense,
so continuous,
it seemed to take on tangible form.
Upon entering the room,
the vision invited me to rise from my sleep and follow.

In the dream,
I knew the body I was bathing was dead.
But,
the skin felt fleshy
and supple;
it possessed the fullness of life.

With each stroke of the dampened cloth against the body,
my hands recorded the tactile sensation of flesh touching flesh.

I heard the water drip into the bowl as I wrung the cloth between each rinse;
the droplets fell in slow motion, leaving ringlets in the basin.

Other than water sounds,
the room was without sound;
still.

The monotone palette of the room
was interrupted only by a lengthening shadow
that inched across the floor,
synchronized with the slow creep of light through an adjacent window.
The shadow seemed a messenger of light diminished,
yet light undoubtedly present.

I realized washing this body was a sacred act,
not meant to clean,
but to express love—

a soft, caressing, lingering communication—
intimate,
yet…reverent.

Alone in this solitude,
I understood serenity;
each touch consecrated abundant peace.

As I finished washing the left hand,
I placed it gently beside the body.
After rinsing the cloth, I turned again toward the body
and found the hand had raised itself, unaided,
with palm extended up.
Its composed posture seemed to suggest an invitation;
an entreaty to accept and follow.

Startled and confused,
I questioned death,
"Who has such power?
Who are you, that you should be alive?"

Still, the outstretched hand beckoned.

As I tentatively reached for the hand,
our two bodies were both instantly transported into my bedroom.
Oddly, the dream still continued.
I became aware the body was male.
He was standing beside my bed.

Everything in the dream now mirrored what would be my waking reality;
my bed—how it was positioned in the room,
the color of the walls,
the shades on the window,
even my husband sleeping next to me.
I knew it would all be identical when I awoke.
Yet, I was still asleep.

The man's outstretched hand continued to implore me to rise from my sleep
and follow.

"How can this be?
How can you be in my bedroom?"

He spoke no words in response;
the manner by which he beseeched me to follow required no words—
words have limits—this, I knew in my dream, was eternal.

With trepidation,
I made the decision to follow.
As I stood to be led,
I immediately awoke.
I was standing next to my bed.

Like a mist in the room,
the visitor's presence was tangible,
yet not evident.
I had a palpable, heart-pounding sense of his nearness.

I became frightened by a sudden revelation:
could the vision I am seeking—
the man who rose from the dead—
be Christ?
Trembling, I felt unworthy to receive such a daunting guest.

I pondered,
"Could it be…
would he come to me at night like this?"

Stunned, breathless and bewildered,
I searched every room,
afraid I would find him,
yet completely expecting to do so.

When I find him,
what will I say?

As if he had morphed into the walls,
he was everywhere,
yet nowhere to be found.

I lay awake the remainder of the night,
unable to sleep—
thinking, praying.

That night,
Christ became unquestionably real to me;
        real flesh,
        real spirit.

It was a soul-altering experience that left me uncertain:
        Why did it happen?
What was I to take from the experience?

Reconstruction

One thing was for certain,
I had to move forward.

I asked the Lord for a new vision.

I recalled what the minister had told me about dream states and
the symbolism of a house.
Without a moment's hesitation,
I saw a vision of a bombed-out cathedral.

Once upon a time,
I felt precious, noble, strong;
set apart to fulfill the Lord's work.

Now, my body, this temple of God,
lay in a heap.
My clerestory, nave, cloisters and crypt
were nothing more than rubble.

I was tired.
It had been a long struggle.
      Sad that the war of life should cause destruction.

I started thinking;
      cathedrals are rebuilt after wars.
      They are rebuilt as a testimony to life.

      Everyone knows they are not the same;
      they are replicas of the original work.

      But that is better than leaving them lay in a heap.

In my mind,
I visualized the reconstruction of my cathedral.
      It would have an expansive interior,
      reaching high,
      soaring on belief,
      the sounds of beauty resonating within.

      The cathedral that God gave me would be spectacular;
      inspiring,
      aspiring.
      All would be possible in this holy place.
      It would be a sanctuary and I would be fed from the table of the Lord.

I decided to keep that vision in front of me to guide me.

Second Awakening

MY STRENGTH

At last, when I found my own voice,
I had confidence it would be heard;
although I suspected some would not like what I said.

It was a time of further testing
and a call to even greater endurance.

Yet I was encouraged by the promise
that once endurance had accomplished its full effect,
I would become mature and complete,
lacking in nothing.

My hope grew imperturbable.

Chapter **9**

Introduction to Corporate America

When Given Lemons, Make Lemonade

So,
I had earned a "lemon" degree.

That happens to a lot of people.

I could be creative.
I could make this work.

I had plenty of incentive.
    One, the tuition was paid for by money borrowed on our home equity loan;
    Two, it had to be paid back.

My steps would include:
    identifying industrial companies that are secondary suppliers to the
    food industry;
    creating a plausible fit between my credentials and their needs;
    communicating the value I could bring their organization;
    and,
    asking for the job.

        EASY!
        FUN!
        A LOT OF WORK!
        It was a full-time job
        finding a full-time job,
        but I loved every minute of the search!

Believing God was with me,
I decided to set my sights high.
I started networking within "THE COMPANY."
This company was everyone's dream of a safe passage to retirement;
it was known to protect its own.

I networked my way in through one contact,
which led to another,
and another,
until
finally,

I was in their atrium waiting for my first interview.
The interviewer was an eclectic woman;
> mid-thirties,
> creative,
> bold,
> a gambler, of sorts.
> It was hard to imagine her in a corporate environment
> yet there she was.

I presented my package;
> a well-prepared candidate,
> and a hard-to-resist story.

That is, an opportunity with minimal risk and a great potential return on investment.

She followed my logic and agreed I should be hired.

Next,
her manager,
a male, dark blue suited type,
very conservative.
This proved more difficult.

He agreed, as long as someone else took the risk of hiring me.

Six months passed before we found a risk taker
who was an innovative free spirit.
He easily bought the package.

Up to this point it was easy…
no problem…a cakewalk.

I was getting closer.
Only one thing stood in the way;
the company wasn't hiring—
there were no open requisitions.

Friends and relatives considered me presumptuous.
People with the right, advanced degrees
weren't getting in.
How would I?
Simple.
The world is full of possibilities,
assuming they can be imagined and faith sets your course.
I just kept imagining and praying
until one day the phone rang with my offer.

It was a newly-created position
in the product development lab,
a liaison between marketing and engineering.
The position had never before existed.
It was created to fit my qualifications.

Although I had a vision that God wanted me here,
I was, nonetheless, in shock.
I was hired and I couldn't believe it.
I kept asking myself,
"Do you believe it?"

I have to admit I felt vindicated...finally.
After all of the years of giving up on myself,
of others judging and discounting me,
of the nay-sayers and dooms-day-sayers,
I had achieved what others I knew only dreamt about.

I felt vibrant and hopeful.

ABSURDITY

For the first few months on the job,
I was convinced I was an impostor.
How could I possibly keep pace
with the education and experience of the people around me?
The terror of being found out
sent tremors through my body,
causing my heart to quake.
It took an inordinate amount of time
for the fear to subside.

I was aided in my adjustment
by the realization of the peculiarities surrounding me.
Like living with my father,
this organization evoked a clear understanding;
abhorrent male behaviors will be tolerated,
regardless of how I might feel.

Immediately I was confronted with numerous potentially explosive situations.
I hoped I was capable of negotiating the mine fields.

Land Mine Number One
    I declined a lunch invitation with an elderly engineer.
    Not to be detoured by my refusal
    he began to tell me stories
    of pornographic movies received through the mail.
    He explained that his wife,
    who never wanted relations,
    had forced him into living fantasies.
    Some of which he shared in great detail;
    number of partners, number of times, his stamina and prowess, etc.

He continued to talk while I edged my way out of his cubicle.

I asked my colleagues,
all of whom were male,
"Is he dangerous?"
They responded,
"No, everyone just tolerates him."
The solution, I was told, is to develop thick skin.

Land Mine Number Two
    I was stopped in the hall by an inventor
    who confided,
    "Whenever I am around you,
    I have a hard time keeping my hands off you."
    It was five o'clock,
    yet there is not another soul in the hall.
    Internal alarms sounded within my head,
    notifying me to beat a hasty retreat.

    The next morning I told my supervisor of the encounter.
    He advised,
    "Never be in a secluded place with him.
    He has a history of such problems."

Land Mine Number Three
    Dave, a man from South America,
    liked to think of women in terms of sex.
    His reputation as a purveyor of computer pornography preceded him.

    One day, he shared a premonition with me,
    "You're good-looking and intelligent.
    You're gonna have a difficult time here."

    Several months later,
    Dave downloaded onto my computer
    an orgy of female bodies
    posed seductively,
    nude.
    One body in full frontal view,
    one reclining behind the first,
    one lying on her side.

    Replete with sound effects,
    one could assume from listening,
    these women were making love in my cubicle.
    In fact, their risqué sounds drew a lot of attention.
    The moment I turned on my computer,
    there they were,

filling the screen with their naked noises.
I could not remove the graphic, nor the sound.
I immediately asked Dave to "take it off."
He laughed as he headed for my cube.

Sitting at my computer,
Dave was surrounded by male colleagues and managers,
all of them laughing.
An hour was required to retract the "gift."

Later that afternoon
I asked Dave to meet me alone.
I expressed my anger and
confided my sense of helplessness—of being out of control.
He offered,
"I caused you to feel violated."

I assumed he understood.

After that incident,
Dave reacted to me with cold indifference.
I solicited feedback on my observation.
"No," he said, "nothing is wrong."

Land Mine Number Four
    George, a supervisor in the lab,
had a tallow complexion—
with skin like the rind of a pork belly.
His face was completely absent of notable features.
Except for his behavior, you'd never notice him.

George never sat straight
but always reclined in chairs,
lying prone,
as if waiting for bedtime and his favorite activity.

George liked to tell stories of
      showers taken with another;
      soap-dropping schemes;
      the enormous size of his penis;
      the pleasures he imparted.

It was typical of him to show a complete lack of discretion in his choice of words.
A friend who worked in another department was amazed to hear him tell her,
"Just throw your tits on the table."
And, "Don't worry, I don't want to go to bed with you."

One morning,
while reclining in my cube,
George became upset.
"Go back to the kitchen where you belong!" he sputtered.
I didn't see the connection to our business update discussion,
so I called him on his statement,
which I found to be rude and disrespectful.
As he stood up to leave,
his pasty face flushed,
and he told me he meant to say,
"You have other options."

        ...REALLY!...

My supervisor felt sorry for George.
"George can't help himself.
He's been through a very difficult divorce."
He suggested I should just leave it alone.

As I moved through each of these personal affronts,
something became clear in my mind;
the difficult part of this job would be avoiding the land mines.
One wrong move and I could kiss my career good-bye.

Something else became equally clear;
I knew I had more than enough capability to do my job as a marketer—
that would be the easy part.
The challenge would be to remain focused on my work.
I did not want to be sidelined by senseless, destructive things.

I was now confident I was qualified for the position.
I was ready to get started.
My impostor feelings vanished.

I'M READY! I'M ABLE!

I was ready to roll up my sleeves and dig in.
I had heard many complaints about the way we did business.
I was anxious to be part of the solution.

With the support of my supervisor,
I compared and contrasted our division to others.
There was definitely room for improvement.

Based on what I had learned,
I proposed the development of a new function in the lab.
Basically, it defined my job.
The proposal was accepted at all levels.

With this new job definition,
my work became fun and challenging.
I was like a racehorse just out of the gate,
eager to work to my capabilities.
I demanded much from myself;
my work had to exhibit the highest level of integrity and objectivity.
Yet I was very comfortable being judged on my work.

Months of focused effort showed results.
People, grateful for help on their programs,
granted me numerous professional awards,
both at divisional and corporate levels.
Acclaim came from marketing and engineering alike.
As a liaison between the two groups,
this surprised and delighted me.

I was especially proud of the character description my supervisor had given me:
> "She is respectful of everyone's input and diligently tries to understand
> their position before making conclusions. Her objectivity and freedom of
> defensiveness convinces people that she is fair, honest and open;
> therefore, they listen to her."

I could not believe they were talking about me.
I reeled from the attention.

Things began happening very fast.
Identified as a high potential candidate,
I was put on the corporation's "Fast Track" and assigned a mentor.
My assessment described me as:
    "objective,
    analytical,
    detail-oriented,
    customer-focused,
    quality-focused,
    forward thinking."

My mentor developed a plan for the next 10 years of my career.
It was written on paper.
Time allocation in each promotional grade was defined.
It included movement into marketing,
an international assignment,
and the assumption of a global market manager position.
It seemed so irrefutable, concrete,
as if it could not be taken away.

I had always believed hard work paid off.

DEFINITION OF SELF WORTH

All of the attention was difficult to deal with,
especially because it was coming from authority figures.
Was I investing too much in their evaluation?
It felt good, yet it suffocated me.

I wrestled with the idea of self worth.
By definition, aren't I the one who defines my worth?

As if to add to my state of confusion
even my dad mailed a note:
> *"The tenth step says when wrong, promptly admit it. Well, Deb, I
> was wrong on giving you a bad time on your education, etc. You had
> to work real hard for it and I admire you for doing it. It must have been
> hard. You now have a good job and I'm sure you will advance rapidly.
> I know you are a hard worker. So what I'm saying is I'm proud of your
> accomplishment. I just wish I'd had the gumption to do it."*

It was a nice note, but I didn't want to invest in it emotionally.
My experience with Dad cautioned me;
the next day he could just as easily call me a quitter or loser.

I decided it would be wise
to keep the evaluation of my worth within my boundaries.
I would seek an understanding from God, not others—
people can be fickle.

DIVIDE AND CONQUER

Julie was a young engineer,
capable and career driven.
She jumped into the project with both feet.
Assigned to work together,
we instituted a methodology new to our division.
Our work received visibility and support from high-level management.
It appeared an excellent avenue for her career growth.

Julie was caught by complete surprise
when first warned by Dave and George,
"Don't get involved with Debra, it will hurt your career."
"Why?" she asked.
"What does she do?"
"She's a 'Ms.' person," came their epithet.
Confused, she probed,
"What does a 'Ms.' person do?"
They had no specifics,
only, "You know, that woman's thing."

Julie felt my behavior appropriate.
She lauded my professionalism.
Despite the warning from her supervisor, George,
she maintained involvement with me
and disclosed to me all they had told her.

I confronted Dave who bragged,
"Yes, I told Julie not to work with you.
Yes, I told her it would hurt her career."

"Dave, why did you tell her that?"
"Because you are a 'Ms.' person," he needled.

"What behaviors comprise the label?" I asked.
Dave remarked, "Your response to the computer incident.
I can't treat you the same anymore because you don't like to be violated."

In my disbelief I challenged,
"Do you hear how ridiculous that sounds?
Unless I am willing to be violated, you are uncomfortable with me."
He didn't think his position was bizarre.

Things escalated.
George and Dave conspired together,
practicing all forms of manipulation and destructive behavior.
Their goal was to make me ineffective.

As the team leader
it was easy for George to keep me uninformed and excluded.
He would schedule team meetings and consistently and intentionally
neglect to invite me.
I would confront him on his intent to exclude me,
and then invite myself.
This would really provoke his ire.
His only remaining course of action
was to completely ignore my presence.
With adolescent antics,
he would literally turn his back to me,
pouting.
It was the equivalent of saying,
"If I can't see you,
you are not there."

If I dared to speak,
George would not respond
or acknowledge my words were ever spoken.
Nor would he allow others to acknowledge my words.
George rode roughshod over others.
Through coercion, many acquiesced to his plan to ignore me.

Julie confronted George on his behavior.
He boasted,
"I intentionally exclude Debra.
And, that's the way I want it to remain."
George also confided,
"The fun and challenge of coming to work
is to see how far you can push people."

Questions that should have been directed to me,
he addressed to Julie.

She was not prepared to answer them.
If she tried to bring me in,
he performed his now normal
ritual of ignoring my presence.

I found his behavior reprehensible.
Our business opportunity was being compromised
by the egocentric games
of one misplaced despot.

Every meeting and interaction followed the same course.

As time progressed
Julie became more trapped.
Her anxiety level increased proportionately
to George's level of hostility toward me.
The mere mention of my name
triggered George's maniacal response.
This went on for months.
The tension was affecting Julie's health and marriage.
Her husband would not tolerate any more discussions on the topic.

When it came time for her performance appraisal,
Julie received the lowest rating of her career from George.
It was a rating which required a corrective action program be established.
His rationale: a management guideline, which he invented.
It was bogus and indefensible.

Julie was devastated, sick and afraid.
Her tears seemed to suffocate my heart.
I felt an urgent need to act.
I had seen this pain before…
in other women who felt trapped.
I could not watch her agony anymore.
I could not bear to see this.

To Go, or Not to Go?

"No, I don't want to go to human resources—
I don't trust them," Julie stated in a trembling voice.
She added, "They're not here for the employees.
They are here to protect the corporation."
I had to admit it was a valid concern.

My new supervisor suggested becoming team insurrectionists, ousting George,
and appointing a new leader.
We ruled that out because George was a manager and friends with the lab
director.
Team members cowered because George's dementia
was made powerful by his organizational status.
They feared negative ramifications to their careers.

We toyed with the idea of exposing George's malignant
behaviors to the department head.
That thought was quickly ruled out.

Running out of options,
I offered to call a friend from my church.
Nearing retirement,
this man had been with the company in HR for many years.
Surely he would know the best approach!
Julie was still reluctant.
To bolster her confidence in this option I provided further details:
"My husband grew up next door to him.
Their families have known each other for years."
She still looked skeptical.
Almost as if offering collateral on a loan,
I stated, " I would trust this guy with my kids' lives."
She looked at me to check my sincerity, and then agreed I should call him.

I called him from home that evening.
He sized up the situation pretty quickly:
George and Dave's behaviors were wrong.
The allegations are serious.
There should be an investigation.
Our confidentiality during the investigation must be maintained.

I could visualize my career blowing up in my face.
I offered another option:
"This is a pivotal point in my career.
If I went forward now, I could lose everything.

The 'Good Old Boy' stuff is too entrenched here.
Wouldn't it be better to just leave and start over in another division?"
As a friend, I expected him to be honest and have my best interest at heart.

He assured me,
"People in upper management have a good, sound value system.
They are spiritual people.
For the good of the company, you should go to HR."

Driven by the injustice,
I decided to go forward.

Julie made the decision to leave the division.

I drafted a letter to HR
and requested Julie's name be kept in absolute confidence;
she had not given me permission to involve her.
Her hope was to get her performance appraisal changed
and slip out quietly.

GOING FORWARD

I didn't go to HR alone.
Other women who had experienced George's behavior,
and who were plenty tired of putting up with him,
joined my cause.

Everything was documented before approaching HR.

Nigel, the HR manager, was soft-spoken and small in stature.
On tour from England, he was learning about cultural differences.
After listening to our account,
he told us he would conduct an investigation.

A month later Nigel informed us that George, Dave and Larry, the lab manager,
had been confronted with the allegations.
Our names had been given out.
The existence of our written documentation was shared.
This was done despite our assurance of anonymity.
His rationale,
"They had the right to know their accusers."

After we dropped from the ceiling, and composed ourselves,
we asked Nigel about his plan for resolution.
He assured us George's boss, Larry, would take care of the situation.
However, I believed Larry was a culturally-challenged man.
It was as if the world went forward in time
and left him behind.
He wasn't aware that women could have aspirations—
other than being subservient to men.
Larry summed up the entire situation as "good natured bantering"
or, "a difference in style."

Yikes! We could almost see the looming disaster unfold before our eyes.

News of our allegations spread like wildfire.
Managers told rumors of a lawsuit.
Everyone was talking, although they had no knowledge of the details.
We, on the other hand, were asked to remain quiet;
it was an issue of not defaming their characters!

And...so...
we remained quiet.
Yet no one worried about our character.

Another month had passed.
Julie was now gone from the division.
I remained behind because I stood to lose significantly by leaving.
I had established my credibility here.
My work had proven my capabilities.
If I left, I would be starting over.
Also, somewhere deep within the recesses of my heart,
I believed change was possible.

It was management's expectation that I continue working with George.
His behavior toward me continued undaunted.
Seen as the victim by others, he felt justified in attacking me.
I was the one he aimed for.
It seemed to be a crusade for him.

I reported the continued destructive behaviors of George
and his cohort in crime, Dave.
Each time HR gave me a new remedy:
    reinforce George's positive behavior,
    develop a thicker skin,
    be more resilient,
    realize the world is not perfect and there are people like George and Dave in it,
    your professionalism puts you on a higher level
    that makes them want to bring you down,
    so just show a little anger,
    and don't get paranoid.

Their remedies left me cold and angry.
I countered these by asserting the real issue,
"I do not own the inappropriate behavior—
it belongs to George and Dave—
and the behavior should stop."

But nothing stopped the flame from spreading.
It raced through every function,
borne on the wind of rumor and innuendo.
It burned the ears of a marketing manager
who had offered me a position in his group.
In haste, he withdrew his previous offer.
I questioned him, "How can this be?
I was your number one candidate!
You designed the job specifically for me!
Upper management supports my assuming the position!"
Once again I asked,
"HOW CAN THIS BE?"

The marketing manager confided that George
had warned him not to work with me.

I was effectively shut down.

LOOKING FOR HELP IN ALL THE WRONG PLACES

I sought the help of a woman in marketing.
She backed away as if I had the plague;
"I don't want to get labeled an Amazon," she said, her arms gesturing,
NO....BACK OFF......DANGER, DANGER!

In some regards, I understood.
She had been trying for years,
without success,
to get an international position.
Although well qualified, they would not give her the thing she desired most.
She suspected it was because she was a woman.

I next turned to corporate employee relations.
A representative there knew our division
and she confided the limitations of our HR staff.
Her recommendation: read a book.
She said, "It's a very good book describing male
response to the erosion of their power."
I told her the world was changing,
and it was not my responsibility to shelter them.

The head of my functional area, a very kindly man,
shook his head, saying,
"It's a shame what has happened to you.
It's more than a shame!"
I heard the words, but couldn't believe them.
I envisioned him waving the surrender flag.

Even my mentor misunderstood.
He saw it as a limitation of my ability to lead difficult people.
I could not make him understand:
There is a difference between difficult people and illegal behavior!
I wanted to scream, "Just stop their illegal behavior!"

My immediate supervisor wrote a letter stating I was an agent of change.
I saw it as a brave act (documenting corporate indiscretion is considered political folly),
but the letter was never followed up with action.
Its impact was felt only by me.

I was alone—helpless.
The sense of extreme isolation and hopelessness edged me toward depression.
Whenever I sense depression's dark, brooding face turn my way,
I have no choice but to fight;
I see my dad's body gripped by its ugliness,
and I become determined to avoid the snare.

REASONABLE STANDARD

Not being the kind to give up easily,
I studied the topic at a law library.
My suspicions were confirmed and my eyes opened.
Even if the system did not understand, I finally did.
Although they would not act on my behalf, I certainly would.

Scheduling a meeting with Jerry, the divisional head of HR,
I informed him that my grievances had not been addressed.
His response was rigid and defensive.
He immediately expressed his concern for Nigel.
After all, if I was correct in my assertions,
it meant he was not doing his job adequately.
Of course, as a result, my allegations "would cause Nigel hurt feelings."

Rather than dialogue
about hurt feelings,
I focused on the issues:
The problem was pervasive.
I had experienced ongoing harassment and retaliation since the beginning of
the investigation.
The impact had directly and negatively impacted me and my career.
There was a cloud hanging over my head, and I wanted it removed.
People with the bad behavior should take responsibility for their behavior.
Managers and supervisors were ill-equipped to deal with the subject.

Jerry argued every point I made.
I substantiated every point with evidence.
He became quiet and sullen.
(I was told later by my supervisor that I had also hurt his feelings.)

It was now time for a meeting with the department head,
the person who had been assigned as my "mentor."
My manager and Nigel were also present.

Before the meeting I prayed,
"Lord please give me courage, wisdom, and the right words.
Be my sword and shield."

Nigel began by reading the
corporate policy statement on harassment and discrimination.
He inferred it was somewhat a matter of sensitivity,
"That is, I could say something to Harry that would just roll off his back,
while another person may be terribly offended."

I requested permission to speak.

Before beginning my explanation of harassment,
I sought to confirm what I heard Nigel say.
He said I had heard him correctly.

I asked if I might expand upon his understanding.
He agreed.
And, so I did.
"In order for a charge of harassment to be made within the law,
the behavior must be pervasive, ongoing, unwelcome and
meet what is called a 'reasonable person' standard.
This means any objective person could look at the situation
and say what has happened is not reasonable.
Any of you gentlemen could look at it and say that it is not reasonable.
This protects companies from being charged by
'oversensitive' people.
In the situation we are addressing today,
the two behaviors acted out against me
that have the greatest impact on business are:
One, exclusion from orientation or teamwork because of sex, and
two, sabotage of an employee's character, reputation, work efforts or property
because of sex."

I continued,
"Specifically, I was told I am a 'Ms.' person and have been intentionally
excluded from participating in business because of it.
Julie was warned not to work with me because it would damage her career.
I have been defamed and my credibility stripped away.
Yet, no one has found my behavior to be inappropriate—
it is said to be beyond reproach.

I ask you to consider the reasonable standard criteria.
You are paying me a salary to contribute to business,
but I am being shut out because of gender.
Any objective person would look at this and say it isn't reasonable.
This isn't a matter of sensitivity,
it is a matter of good business and the law."

The department manager listened attentively but with a great deal of reservation.
He wanted evidence of the pervasive nature.
I gave it to him.
He wanted evidence of my defamation of character.
I gave it to him.
He wanted evidence of my exclusion from activities.
I gave it to him.

Nigel could do nothing but support my claims.

They asked what would be required to resolve the situation?
I requested:
direct, honest communications;
education for the department;
ownership of the problem be placed where it belonged;
and the cloud of defamation over my head be dispelled.
That is to say,
"I must not be labeled a troublemaker because I cared enough to come forward."

I summarized, "This is the 1990s!
I shouldn't have to fight just to be given the privilege to work." [10]

The department manager would have George and Dave apologize to me.

No Regrets

The apologies were botched.
Both men trivialized the situation
and denied any wrongdoing.
As I sat and listened to them
I wondered;
how could something so simple,
be so difficult to understand and enforce?

That evening I shut myself in an empty office,
alone.
The futility and frustration of the battle was wearing on me.
No matter how well I communicated,
or how professional my conduct continued to be,
I could not get through.
No one understood.

I felt like crying.
When I tried to suppress it,
I felt my stomach lurch upward,
as if to express something burning within it.
My throat painfully constricted
around the emotions that were trying to escape.

I was acutely aware that my emotion wouldn't solve the problem—
appropriate action might.
I asked the Holy Spirit for wisdom and guidance.
I picked up the phone
and went straight to the top,
to the man in corporate HR responsible for policy enforcement for the
entire company.

After explaining the situation,
I was advised to go home and not return for several days.
He would take over—
the potential liability to the company was too great.

Anita Hill had just testified against Clarence Thomas,
putting a national spotlight on issues of sexual harassment.
I knew the mission of corporate HR was to protect the company's image
from allegations such as mine.

I stayed home until I was told to return to work.

ALLIED REINFORCEMENTS

While they worked on their end to resolve the situation,
corporate HR suggested I contact employee assistance for support.

I met with Beth, a woman in employee assistance,
who, although paid by the corporation,
immediately elicited my trust.
She reminded me of Meg Ryan;
she had a buoyant, youthful energy that radiated life.

She listened for more than an hour
as I described the events that had brought me to her office.
Whenever I cried, the brilliant sparkle of her blue eyes faded to a mere flicker.

After I finished, Beth said,
"Deb, I feel a great deal for the struggle you have been through,
and I would like to help you, but you would be better served by seeing a
counselor outside of the organization. We do some counseling here,
but nothing on issues as complex and far-reaching as yours.
We deal with issues like how to manage your finances.
I do however, know a woman I would like to refer you to.
Her name is Alletta and she is very good. I think you will like her.
But please stop by from time to time and let me know how things are going.
I want to be a support to you if I can."

Beth was right.
I did like Alletta.
Alletta was an older woman who understood wisdom was a blessing of age.
Comfortable in her skin, she wore it well
and made no excuses for her age or the figure God gave her,
being happy with both.
To me,
she became a spiritual godmother sent from heaven, I was sure.
More than any other person,
she taught me what love is,
and what it isn't.
In the time I spent with her,
she blessed me with an inheritance of wisdom that I will always treasure.

With the support of Beth and Alletta, I found the courage to start over.

RENEWED EFFORT

Upon my return,
several things had been put in order.
Appropriate apologies were made—assured by corporate oversight.
A division-wide education program on harassment and tolerance was initiated.
I was given the marketing job previously taken from me.

I was assigned to work closely with two salesmen,
Ted and Jeff.
Together we developed a combined marketing/sales plan;
the first of its kind for the department.
Because of their physical distance from headquarters,
leading the process was difficult.
Nonetheless, under my leadership, we produced a comprehensive,
well thought-out plan.

Immediately following distribution of our plan,
Ted wrote an e-mail to my boss
applauding my skills and contributions to our team,
    "Her leadership made all the difference in the planning process."
He said he was delighted to be working with me.

NORMALIZING THE ABNORMAL

Jeff and I attended a trade show in Chicago.
Trade shows always made me uncomfortable,
but this one was especially difficult.
Sitting very close to me on a sofa,
Jeff began to make suggestive statements.
"I suppose you could never go for me. I'm too short."
"Don't you think people are looking at us and saying,
'Why aren't they dancing together?
Why aren't they excited about each other?'"
"You know how body language is?"
"You can tell when people are attracted to each other."
"It's okay when we're married to be attracted to each other—it's chemistry."

I ignored Jeff's behavior and expressed my sincere
and lasting intentions toward my husband.

That evening, my husband flew to Chicago
to celebrate our tenth wedding anniversary.
Eleven years earlier, Bill could not afford an engagement ring.
Now, an hour before we were due for dinner,
he surprised me with a carat diamond ring.
Professional etiquette dictated we have dinner with Jeff and his wife.
Although I had no desire to do so, I agreed with Bill that we should attend.

I sat across the table from Jeff's wife and watched
her as the waiter poured wine.
Watching her face, I wondered:
Why would he disrespect her?
Does she know?
If she does, why does she put up with it?

Two days after returning to the office,
my phone rang.
It was Jeff.
He had talked to someone in the lab.
"I found out you are a very dangerous person," he disclosed,
as if he was finally in the know.
His closing comment, "I will no longer say anything to you."

I reported this.
I saw it as continued defamation of my character by lab personnel.

My report was discounted.
I was told by an engineer in the lab
that I could not facilitate meetings with lab personnel.
His commentary,
"You have lost your credibility with the lab.
They won't listen to you."
I asked, "Where is this coming from?"
He filled in the blank,
"Larry, (the lab director who is George's boss and friend) does not respect you.
He is really hostile toward you.
If I mention your name, he gets enraged.
He even warned me not to support your efforts because it would ruin
my career."

Over and over I was confronted by similar stories with the same theme;
Larry wanted to shut me down.

I reported this.
I saw it as continued defamation of my character and retaliation.
I was discounted.

Another trade show was scheduled.
This time I was to attend with Ted.
I expected it to be fun—
Ted and I had worked well as a team.
But dinner the first evening proved differently.

Ted's sister joined us.
The restaurant was posh;
white linens, soft lights, orchestrated music—
a very calm and serene atmosphere.
His sister was warm, friendly and talkative.
Although I had never met her before,
I felt as if I had known her all my life.

Eager for the three of us to bond,
his sister started to share stories of their childhood.
Ted forcefully interrupted her:
"Don't tell her anything!!!
She'll write it down.
I don't trust her."
She looked at him in disbelief.
His insolence was visible.
His dictatorial tone, escalating.
"I'm serious.
Don't tell her anything!"
"Don't be such a jerk," she retorted, disapprovingly.

He continued his assault on me,
"You're nothing but dead weight on the program.
You add nothing!
You're only overhead.
We all think that. After all, you didn't come out of sales.
So how did you get that job?" he said tauntingly.
I responded calmly,
"Because I was best qualified for the position."

My response ignited an explosion of animosity.
"We know you had to get out of the lab.
That's why you got the job."
He tossed the words at me as if they were a hand grenade,
and then he waited for the destruction.

"TED! Quit being a jerk!" exclaimed his sister.

As his voice became louder,
the room became smaller.
People at nearby tables
seemed to be sitting at ours.
Their expressions spoke compassion and concern.
Everyone seemed aware of his noxious behavior.

I asked,
"You keep saying 'We' as if there are many people who feel as you do.
Who are these people?"
He wouldn't answer.
Feeling he was being cornered, he attacked with greater ferocity.
His words chosen to damnify,
"Your performance is poor,
and it wasn't anyone's choice for you to go to marketing. It was forced."

The gates of hell felt like they opened on me.

"How can you be such a jerk?" his sister said,
this time her voice was more determined, yet frustrated.
He justified his actions,
"She's not HUMAN!" he hissed.

As these last words spewed from his mouth,
he became an apparition to me;
an evil specter with mammoth jaws
that opened to expose a cavernous pit.
I feared I would be swallowed whole.

I prayed,
"Jesus, I am sinking into an abyss.
It's so deep, I can't see.
I am afraid.
Hold me up.
You are my rock.
Hold me up.
Deliver me."

The next morning,
I was assigned to work with Ted in the trade show booth.
I arrived before the show doors opened.
He came late and acknowledged nothing.

As a professional, I was expected to promote the company and its products.
But I looked at the products displayed,
and I saw the evil that supported Ted's arrogance.
The products became vile,
just as his behavior was vile.

When I returned to the office,
I was asked by management to forgive Ted's behavior.
Evidently he had already confessed to management
and gave them a list of excuses which they in turn rattled off to me:
"He is under a lot of pressure."
"He has been away from home too long."
"He fears he will be out of a job if his sales don't increase."
Blah, blah, blah…
Also, "That 'women's thing' is getting to him."

I responded by saying,
"I am extremely tired of having the inappropriate and retaliatory behaviors of
others dumped in my lap."

They didn't care.
From management's perspective, there was no problem.
They said it was all over. "The problem is resolved.
You need to get over your anger."
I was told to get used to it.

Later that day I heard from friends.
"Julie is living the life of Riley.
She regularly leaves work by mid-afternoon
and drinks beer at a bar with the guys in her new division."

I never heard from her.
I wondered about Julie.
Her behavior told me she was trying to fit in…to deny.

POWER WITHOUT WISDOM

Sick and emotionally exhausted,
I spent the weekend in tearful prayer and meditation.
Kneeling on the floor
and bowing my head,
I made supplication:
>   What is going on here?
>   Am I going crazy?
>   Am I just so weird I cannot fit in anywhere?
>   Is there no justice?
>   Please help me! Please Help Me!
>   I DON'T UNDERSTAND.

I stood up and paced around the room,
trying to make sense of the senseless:
>   My motivation was pure.
>   My actions beyond reproach.
>   Is this just?
>   Is this reasonable?
>   What is going on?

And, for the first time,
I clearly understood
the loneliness of Jesus on the cross.
I could see him and almost touch him.

I paced around the room,
and spoke aloud to him.

>   "I understand why you remained silent—
>   why speak, if they are not ready to hear?
>   Words,
>   no matter how profoundly stated,
>   cannot guarantee hearing.

>   There is no justice
>   where hearts are not inclined to understand.

>   Mercy cannot be given
>   when power grasps hungrily,
>   feeding itself like a hideous gorging monster.

I am so angry at them—those who hung you.
How dare they think their power
granted them wisdom?
What made them assume they were right?"

Seething with anger,
I screamed out loud,
　　"They were all so senseless!
　　I now understand so well, I see so clearly.
　　I'm sorry!
　　I'm sorry!
　　I'm sorry!"
I couldn't seem to stop saying it.
I could not control my tears or the horror I felt for Him.
I was in his pain and it was terrifying.
I could not bear to see it.
I wanted to make it go away.

　　"If I had been there,
　　would I stand against the powers that killed you?" I asked.
　　"Or, would I be a coward and hide like the rest?

　　I love you, Lord. I love you more than life itself."

I took several deep breaths,
and released them slowly.
I was aware of the silence—it filled me.
I saw myself, as if standing on air;
all of time and space were open to me.
Although no windows were open in the room,
I felt wind blow on my skin.
I was light, unfettered, free from the insanity.

In that moment of grace,
I understood the context of the struggle
and the probable outcome.

It is in the nature of our humanity.

PRESENTING MY CASE

Reinvigorated, I stated my case to corporate:

> "I initiated what was to become an investigation of
> harassment and discrimination in the department. I came
> forward based on the advice of an HR manager, a personal
> friend, even though I knew the consequences to me could
> be personally devastating. There was an investigation.
> Nearly one year later, I feel I have to fight a shadow,
> something lingering which takes the form of covert
> actions and statements nearly impossible to fight. As an
> outcome, I perceive the need to protect myself daily in
> an environment that feels hostile and intimidating. I feel
> discounted and devalued and no longer capable of reaching
> my full creative potential. My character has been defamed
> and my reputation damaged. For health and personal
> reasons, I feel I have no other alternative but to leave the
> department. I am requesting a transfer to another division.
> As I endeavor to make this transition happen, I must
> insist that the cloud lingering over my head remain in the
> department from which I am transferring."

CHANGE FOR THE GOOD

All parties agreed to the move.
Corporate management insisted the move be handled by HR.
I was assured nothing would follow me.
The corporation would give it top priority—
all stops would be pulled out.

They told me how the process would work.
    HR would identify open positions in other divisions
    and then forward my packet.
    I would interview for the new position along with other candidates,
    thereby making it look less conspicuous.
    HR would let me know when they found something.
    Until then, I should be patient and wait.

Two months passed.
I had heard nothing.
Jerry, my division's HR manager whose feelings I had previously hurt,
said, "I suppose you feel like you've been operating in a vacuum?"

The first interview occurred three months after "all stops had been pulled out."
It was a disaster.
Someone in HR had left "evidence" in the information packet
sent to the hiring supervisor.
"Tell them to take this out of the packet," the interviewer advised,
as she pointed to the evidence.
She offered, "The company is a Good Old Boy place, especially the old divisions.
But they can't keep funneling women here because it is friendlier to women.
The others have to get on board."

She had no interest in hiring me—
her candidate had already been decided.
The interview was a waste of time and an exercise in futility.

As I left her office, I felt angry and humiliated.
I questioned how there could be such incompetence thriving in the company.
I fired off an angry letter to HR.
An apology came back
by e-mail.

We tried again.

I was finally moved to a new division six and a half months after my request.
My female supervisor was very young.

She had the perfect corporate profile—
MBA, unmarried, no children, dedicated completely to her career.

She treated me with cold indifference.

To me, she was a woman without eyebrows.
More than eight months earlier, I had a dream that warned me of this type.
    The corporation had removed their eyebrows.
    the expressive part of facial anatomy.
    These women blended into the male corporate body,
    inexpressive of any other reality.
    They were clones of the corporate male.[11]

Her face was mostly expressionless.
She would not let her heart—her more personal convictions—
derail her career.
She was too smart for that nonsense.
She would play by the corporate rules.

I was leery of her.

By then I had become a different person.
My naiveté was gone.
The desire to feel the joy of being creatively productive had left me.
What little energy I had
was spent in a determined effort to give management
no cause to doubt my capabilities.
I could envision them saying I didn't "make it"
because I didn't perform to their standards.
I would not give them an excuse to get rid of me.
I performed.

Something else began to stir within me;
a single-minded purpose directed at changing the corporate mindset
about equality.
I couldn't believe God would have brought me here for nothing.
Something good had to come out of it.

I knew I had the capability of communicating the need for change,
if for no other reason than my experience.
The desire to do so drove me.
I wanted a forum where concerns could be voiced,
rather than hushed.
I fought to be heard.

Impassioned Entreaty

I was "granted" a hearing before the vice president of HR for the entire corporation.
    I had hoped for the CEO.
The meeting was scheduled, and I was escorted to the executive offices.
As the elevator ascended the tower,
I was aware I was riding to the pinnacle of power.
Few employees had ever seen these floors.

The accommodations in the tower were drastically different than our cubes.
The VP's receptionist offered me a glass of water.
There was ice in the glass—I wondered how she could get ice so fast.
I was impressed with the civility in which they worked.

We were seated at a handsome, polished table.
The vice president sat directly across from me.
As one might expect, he was a white, elderly male;[12]
his presence like that of a grandfather.
On one side, a black man, whom I had grown to respect and admire.
On the other side, a white, middle-aged woman
        (Internally, I questioned the existence of her eyebrows).

I had spent countless late-night hours in preparation for the meeting.
I had no reservations, only determination.
Although I had clear presence of mind,
I was a mix of emotions and physical responses.
My right knee shook continuously, almost violently.
In syncopation with my knee,
my heart began beating an exceedingly wild rhythm.
I hoped no one would notice.

I began by stating my desire for the meeting.
    That we would approach each other as human beings,
    not corporate cogs.

    Rather than with intent to conceal,
    could we speak openly
    and from the heart?

    Instead of either side defending
    or explaining,
    was it possible to share what had been learned?

I told them what I had learned about equality:
"People cannot be separate, yet equal.
Thurgood Marshall argued this before the Supreme Court concerning
segregation.

When I am separated,
ostracized,
defamed,
told I am not HUMAN,
I will not be regarded as equal.

Marshall also pointed out the psychological damage;
shame,
fear,
humiliation,
self-doubt.

I can testify to that truth;
it has been my emotional experience.

I sense there is no consensus for change here, because there is fear.
The power base fears an equalizing of power between genders
will be a loss of power—to them it is a zero-sum game.

Discomfort results because there is a fear of the unknown;
they cannot see that a truly diverse workforce is not a scary concept.

You fear an attempt to bring gender equity would result in chaos,
which loosely translated means slowed productivity.
There is no realization of the untapped potential of 50% of the work force.

Without change, the company can expect a continuation of what I have seen:
a loss of creative potential,
reduced productivity,
damaged lives,
potential for lawsuits." [13]

I continued to explain:
"I came forward because I believed the company was run by spiritual people.
I contend it is not only smart to promote equality in the workplace,
it is an ethical imperative."

I then reviewed my 16 points for change, [14]
leaving copies for everyone.

I shared from the depths of my heart
my conviction to the truth of equality.
In return, I asked where the company stood on the topic of equality.

I was not surprised by the answer—
it was manifested everywhere.
The CEO didn't want to get bogged down in diversity issues.
Feelings and beliefs of others were all over the board.
There was no consensus.

The problem, the VP stated, is that society is falling apart outside of the corporation;
there is too much violence on TV.

To me, this was an excuse...a cop-out.

As the meeting came to a close,
I told him,
 "This struggle has taken a toll on my wellness.
 My focus now will be on regaining it,
 and knowing when to quit believing and leave the company."

A Place without Sustenance

It had followed me again,
into my new division.
The reality of my "separate" identity was known.
Opportunities once given,
were taken away.
I felt the isolation.
I was back to arguing my case,
but I didn't want to anymore.

Alletta, my counselor, probed,
"When is it time to quit?
What images come to mind?"

I told her,
    "I see myself in the bottom of a very deep well.
    The well is dry.
    It has been dry for a long time.
    There is no food or water in the well.
    The floor of the well
    is loose dirt with small pebbles.
    I can kick the pebbles with my foot.
    I kick them a lot.

    I have been in the bottom of this well too long.
    When I look up,
    I can barely see daylight.
    I don't know what is on the outside of the well.

    Standing with my back against the stone wall,
    I slowly slide down the wall until I'm seated in the dirt.
    I look next to me.
    I see my Lord.
    'What are you doing here?' I ask.

    'I am here because you are here,' he answers.
    'And, I will stay here
    —right next to you—
    until you decide to get out of the well.
    I will not, I cannot, leave you.'

'I can't have you stay in this well.
That's dumb.
I can see me being here,
but I can't see you staying here,' I respond.

'It's your choice.
But, as long as you are here,
I will be here,' he says, with a completely peaceful expression.

I am frustrated
and mad at myself.

'Okay, I guess that means I need to climb out of here!'"

Aletta asked what the image meant to me?

I sighed, "I have to leave the company."

"Good," she said.

I Quit!

During the five years I was with the company,
for fully half of my stay,
I was harassed and discriminated against.
The last half I spent protecting myself in a hostile environment,
arguing my case,
and seeking change,
all the while enduring continuous retaliation and defamation.
Throwing pebbles at this corporate Goliath
was only hurting me.

Chapter 10

Time for Emotional Healing and Family Issues

FRIENDS OF JOB

Several people who fancied themselves psychologists offered me advice:
>"People who had parents with addictive personalities
>or who were cold and uncaring,
>have distorted images of themselves and reality.
>They end up projecting their expectations of worthlessness outward,
>and naturally, the world responds accordingly.
>What you experienced was merely a result of what you expected."

To me, their advice sounded a lot like "blame the victim."

I didn't disagree that my background taught me little about caring for myself first.
I did disagree with the notion that people with healthy self-images
would not find themselves experiencing trauma.

I responded to their argument:
>"It isn't a poor self-image that causes a person to stand up
>when few others will.
>Their understanding of reality, in fact, warns them they will take a beating.
>However, to them avoidance behavior isn't an option.
>
>Using your logic, I would have to say Christ had a low self-image.
>He stood,
>and they killed him.
>
>So if I am understanding you correctly,
>people with healthy self-images never fight injustice
>because it is not in their best interest.
>They sail through life obtaining everything
>they project to be due themselves;
>fancy cars, clothes, big houses, great careers.
>Only in America could we think such a thing.
>The vast majority of the world struggles daily.
>
>Let's say you are correct.
>Perhaps I did project my own worthlessness.
>Even if I accept that to be true today,
>I would still stand again,
>because it isn't right to ignore what will harm or destroy us."

I knew deep down that I had a lot of issues from childhood to overcome;
I had been battling them for years.
But I didn't need "well-meaning" people telling me I brought the injustice
onto myself.

ROOM TO HEAL

To understand my reality,
Alletta suggested I paint what I couldn't say,
to unleash feelings locked far beneath my consciousness
and inaccessible by other means.

I rented a small office space;
inner hall,
no windows,
fluorescent lights,
and draped a huge plastic blue tarp from wall to wall
to protect the cheap industrial grade carpet from my oil paints.

Saturdays were spent entombed in my grief room,
alone.
I cried.
Talked aloud.
Paced.
Spattered paint on the canvas
as well as the walls.

There was nothing planned about the madness I practiced in that room.
I simply allowed myself to be mad.
No judgments on the right or wrong way to paint.
No preordained notions of correct subject matter.
No desire to demonstrate technical aptitudes.
I was without explanation or apology.

Time became enmeshed and lost in each stroke of the brush.
The feverish working of the paint
seemed to spiral the hour hand of my life backward in time.
I was living past moments in the present,
acutely aware of things formerly hidden.

Oils by nature are intense, yet forgiving.
They allow time to explore every emotion buried;
to unearth it, think it, give it life,
and finally let it be.

The unrestrained experience was cathartic,
liberating,
empowering,
and healing.

JOY IN SHARING

My entangled emotions were no longer spinning in frantic circles within my soul.
They were defined in my paintings.
I could see them.
Explain their origin.
I no longer felt the dread of their unnamed nature.
It was powerful and worthy of celebrating.

The process was a curiosity to many.
I wondered too,
what gives women strength and courage?
Many women I knew
had a reserve of strength that was hidden
and never celebrated.
They were each unique and beautiful in their own right.
Why not celebrate together?

The art guild I had joined agreed celebration was in order.
We decided on a showing.
The guild would provide the hors d'oeuvres.
They also knew a woman with space in an old warehouse;
we could use her space for a small fee.

Those who would attend
wanted to know what I was thinking as I painted.
Therefore, to enhance their experience,
I wrote my thoughts in verse
and mounted them alongside their respective painting.

Something was missing however.

This celebration was not about me.
It was about us;
a means to rejoice in our individual character and collective beauty.
I wanted them to know the gratitude my heart felt
as I pondered the strength, resiliency, beauty, intelligence, grace,
and love of each.
An ode to each seemed appropriate.
As I wrote the collection of odes,
my heart warmed with gratitude and appreciation.
Each ode was rolled up like a scroll and tied with a ribbon.

The attendees would be given their personal ode
and a tapered candle as they entered.
I placed a white plastic disk, measuring three feet in diameter,
in the center of the room and filled it with sand.
A pillar candle would be lit and placed in the center of the sand.

The attendees would be asked to read their ode privately,
light their tapered candle from the flame of the pillar candle
and place it within the sand.
I liked the symbolism,
but didn't know if it would communicate as intended.

As the day drew near,
Bill and Andy
installed temporary spot lights and directed them at the paintings and
attendant verse.
It was unbelievable and exhilarating to see it come together.

The evening of the showing,
I watched as attendees read their odes.
Some cried.
Some became flushed.
The stoics said "oomph" or "pshaw" while their eyes glistened.

My eight-year-old daughter enjoyed watching the surprise and delight on
their faces.
Running back to me frequently,
she'd grab my arm and share something she had overheard.

I enjoyed the metamorphosis of the great sand disk.
A single flame,
joined by many flames,
extended its light and warmth into the room.
People sat around the flame-filled disk
as if warming themselves about a campfire.
The hum of their combined voices and the light of multiple flames
filled the room,
reaching a zenith by mid-evening.
Then, one by one as people departed,
the hum subsided and the tapered candles diminished,
dissolving into a luminous pool of wax.

A few flames refused to die and flickered while floating on the pool's surface,
tenacious reminders of their bearer's presence meant to linger longer.
Eventually, all that remained was the lone light of the pillar candle
adrift in a great pool of wax.

I sat on a sofa and stroked my daughter's long auburn hair
as she lay with her head in my lap.
Bill asked, "How do you feel?"
I responded, "This has been one of the happiest days of my life.
Thanks for being here with me."

PAINTING # 1

DEATH OF A MARKETER

Once there was a marketer who died.

There was no funeral.

No people gathered.

No kind words were spoken.

There were no hot-dishes, Jell-O salads or
buttered rolls served.

There was only aloneness.

And the knowledge that others, who must remain silent,
had experienced this also.

Painting # 2

Burning Guts

ANGER!!!!

ANGER!!!! hits my gut

ANGER!!!! causes a burn...
twisted,
tangled
and
aching.

PAINTING # 3

COLD

A deep, dead, coldness
lies over my heart.
Like a blanket of ice,
it covers me.

My naive beliefs of
right and wrong,
justice,
love and mercy,
equality,
are gone.

Living in a perpetual frost,
I fear the creeping silence
heralding the death of my soul.

DARKNESS

Darkness is what happens when you live other people's
agendas, not your own.
Darkness is the feeling that captures a person without
defense mechanisms.
Darkness is a scary place the soul must
explore alone.

PAINTING # 4

BRAIN WAVES WHEN DEPRESSED

Depression grips my forehead
making it hard to see, hear and feel.
I perceive my despair as blackness.

I cannot make sense of this…
it all seems hopeless.

In an instinctual response,
my brain shunts all activity inward;
a self-preservation technique,
leaving little spark for normal functioning.

Painting # 5

Bad Men in a Blender

PULSE ON:

Chop, chop.

Parts ripping.

Guts flying.

Blood splattering.

PULSE OFF.

PAINTING # 6

YOU DON'T DESERVE TO EXIST

I left the comfort of past definitions;

definitions given by others,

to journey to a place of my own making.

I asked: Who am I?

Answer: I don't know.

And then that voice—the voice that hurts—
it said:

"You're not going to journey anywhere.

You don't deserve to exist.

You're nothing."

Painting # 7

My Mother the Wrecking Ball

I feel small relative to my mother's
psychic power…

her size much larger than myself
like the moon orbits the earth,

I feel forever pulled by her magnetic field.

She cannot be diminished.

Pain only increases her power to claim me.

I am sorry…

for her

and for me.

PAINTING # 8

BLINDING RAGE

I am encircled by a blinding rage.

Like an electron cloud spinning around
a nucleus,
my negative charge is apparent.

Negative thought patterns were formed
before I was cognizant.

The voice inside of me lashes out
without mercy.
Roaring at me, it says:
You're not worthy of love.

Nurturing is for wimps.

You don't have the right to be beautiful
or peaceful.

If you take care of yourself, you can't be taking care of
more important things.

Life is tough, and then you die.

So get on with it—be tough.

Painting on display in the virtual gallery at www.setfree.biz

PAINTING #9

I'M OUT OF HERE!!!

I'm tired of all the confines:

the expectations,
(be a good girl)

the definitions,
(women don't get angry)

the repression of self.
(people won't like who I really am)

I'm tired of living in the shadow.

I want out of here.

To thrive—not survive.

I'VE HAD IT!

I'M OUT OF HERE!

Painting on display in the virtual gallery at www.setfree.biz

PAINTING #10

IN GOD'S WOMB

I need time:
time to heal,

time to reflect,

time to cry,

time to bleed,

time to discover a new me.

No place on earth feels safe.

I will hide in God's womb.

There I will have time,
time to be created anew.

PAINTING #11

ALLOWING THE PROCESS

As the earth was formed

pulled from a vapor ball,

slowly defining itself—
water from land,
soft from hard,

so I want to re-form myself—
to claim my softness,
to admit my hardness.

ERRONEOUS DEFINITIONS

I wanted to live forever in that night of celebration
with hope that the last flame in the great sand disk would burn
with everlasting warmth—
a reminder that we are not alone in our struggle for soul.
Unfortunately, morning came, causing me to grieve
the loss of family I felt that night.
Left alone, I felt broken.

Although painting helped me acknowledge my anger and see its origins,
now it was out in the open—I could no longer hide from my scorched soul.

I tried to collect my fragmented pieces
and found I could not put them back together in a manner
that convinced me I was whole and worthy.
I could not pretend when I was dying inside.
I had acted with good intentions—now I was left with the injustice.
What could I do with my anger?

I was completely aware of the insidious nature of unattended anger.
When anger has nowhere to go,
it turns its anguine head inward,
and takes up residence in the deepest recesses of the body
poisoning the well from which the soul drinks.
And, if one isn't careful,
it can stay for a lifetime.
I would become just another member of the walking wounded.
Life is full of them.
I did not want to join the legion of those traveling that soulless void.

In an attempt to understand how to form myself anew,
I read books, talked to friends, journalized my dreams
and prayed.
But the prayers traveled fruitlessly into a void as immense as my anger.

Entwined in my confusion
was the notion of being female
in a male dominated world—
a foreign land in which I would always be an alien.
I could attempt to learn the language—to look and act the part—
yet I felt I could not thrive as Joseph did in Egypt.
I was a woman.
There was no getting around the obvious.

The negative ramifications of being female in a male world
had fueled a voice of evil within me.
The voice had grown brazen and grotesquely confident.
Smug because the world had collaborated with its intent to destroy,
it chose words that lacerated with the surety of a sword
attempting to mortally wound its crippled prey.

That evil voice, previously hidden deep within my soul,
had operated with stealth and cunning as an unknown enemy.

Now its insidious nature was out in the open,
blatant and obnoxious.
Counseling and the process of painting had opened the vault
and there was no putting the demon back in.

My mind was beset with agony on hearing its words of destruction
as they tumbled forward;
specters unearthed to deliver immortal fury,
hideous and frightful.

I was overcome by an urge to run as fast as possible
away from the menacing voice storming inside my head.
But there was no running from my own mind.
I must fight back.
I must claim myself anew by undoing a lifetime of negative messages.
This would be no small task.
It could conceivably take more than my lifetime.

Yet I clutched onto the idea of rooting out the cause
and finding the remedy.
I wanted something concrete, something I could act on.

Just like counselors before,
Alletta thought it was an issue of lessons I had learned from my parents,
mostly because I did not know how be to be a good parent to myself.

I decided to take an emotional journey backward in time
where negative messages first took root—
to dig them up—
and look at them with a new eye.
I would redefine myself today,
with the hope that past demons would no longer follow me.

INSIDE THE BEDROOM WINDOW

I drove back to the neighborhood where I grew up,
and parked the car alongside the curb.
As I sat looking at my childhood home,
a consuming fear gripped my chest.
Rather than fight the impulse to ignore my body's signal,
I let it tell me the story I had come to hear.

> I envision myself going to prom in a store-bought dress.
> I am a vision of beauty.
> My father is watchful, yet happy with my date.
> My mother tells me I am beautiful and kisses me at the door.

I am aware the fantasy did not fit reality.
I never dated.
I never went to prom.
I never had a store-bought dress.
And beauty only caused problems.

> I run to the mailbox every day,
> anxious for a letter from the man I am to marry.
> There is no letter...ever.
> He explains he is not a letter writer.

How do I package that?
Why didn't I say, "I don't deserve this!"?

> I am in junior high.
> A fat, clumsy girl.
> I feel inadequate and ugly.
> The neighbor lady's clothes I am wearing attract attention,
> as do the high heels bought at Bakers on closeout.
> They are not ballet slippers, the fad at the time,
> but my mother tells me they are better for my feet.
> Although I don't understand why corn-forming shoes are healthy,
> I understand the high heels are cheaper.

I believe I can overcome all of this oddness
by being sturdy and hardworking.
I am a stoic survivor.
My strength of character is derived from the hard knocks of life.

I pause again to think about that precious little girl.
I can see her standing inside the bedroom window,
and I don't want to tell her she is strong or hardworking.
Those words are meaningless to me now.

I want to tell her she is precious and beautiful;
that I am so glad she is my daughter.
She would have hugs and kisses every day,
as many as she needed, as often as she wanted.
I would tell her she doesn't have to be strong all the time.
And life is more than survival.

When I realize I cannot hold that little girl,
I am enveloped by a sense of isolation and grief.
Her time is past.
It is as if death has stolen her from me.

I see little joy and happiness in her face.
I want so badly to tell her I love her,
to find a way to start her life over again.

I want to capture her essence and carry her forward.
I will give her new descriptors;
    beautiful,
    healthy,
    fit,
    confident,
    self-assured,
    spiritual,
    human,
    smart,
    creative,
    interdependent,
    loved.
And, I will cherish her all the days of her life.

A NECESSITY OF LIFE

I didn't understand how to love the little girl within me.
I had no understanding of love.

I closed my eyes and searched out images of my mother's love.

My mother's love was
        without arms,
        without lips,
        without the soft fullness of flesh.

She could not hug me.
She could not say, "I love you," or
kiss me good night.
There was no softness of embrace,
no warmth of her presence.

She later admitted love's absence in her care for me,
and explained the cause:
She was crippled by her past,
        a fallow place devoid of love.
She never learned love's face,
        to recognize its look and feel.
She could not pass love along.

Could love's absence create a void in me?
        Am I worthy?
        Do I deserve to exist?

Although afraid of this void,
I realized I must invite this shadow in,
and acknowledge its various forms;
        manipulative,
        destructive,
        sick,
        unloving,
        frustrating,
        entrapping,
        repulsive,
        win or lose,
        pass or fail,
        controlling.

I acknowledged having many of these characteristics myself.
Would I ever learn love's true nature?

To start anew today,
speaking the words the little one inside of me longs to hear.
> You are precious,
> loved,
> beautiful,
> worthy.
> You deserve life,
> > happiness,
> > wholeness,
> > respect.
> My greatest desire is to be there for you,
> and delight in your new beginnings.
> You are flesh of my flesh.

Learning love was odd and very foreign to me.
The difficulty alarmed me,
causing me to fear that perhaps love's time had passed me by.
I became determined to pass a different legacy to my daughter.
I would speak to her with a different voice;
the voice of love.

HO, HO, HO, MERRY CHRISTMAS

Overcoming my negative voice meant challenging some assumptions,
separating myself from ideas and norms that were not healthy
and developing my own healthy voice.
     It seemed I had been working at this for years
     and getting nowhere fast.
     It was frustrating.
     Yet vigilance demands energy.

To be expected,
the most difficult place to start
was with my mother.

It was impossible to tell my mother what she didn't want to hear.
But sometimes defending love's intent must begin with small steps.
For instance, with a decision on how to celebrate Christmas.

My mother had a strong belief in tradition.
That meant you celebrated Christmas with her family.
This was nonnegotiable, unless you didn't care about her feelings.

Mom had two brothers and five sisters
who prided themselves on being "lively;"
unlike my father's side,
who were condemned for being very Lutheran.

Well, I had to agree with my husband.
This particular Christmas got out of hand;
unless, of course,
you were looking for the entertainment of an adult-rated, three-ring circus.

There was something going on in every room.

In the kitchen
two aunts had begun to fight.
The mean one punched the youngest,
who ran out of the house without her jacket in below-freezing weather.

My husband and I quietly took our daughter downstairs,
excusing ourselves by saying we would look for Grandma.

We found my mother playing poker in the basement.
She was a serious gambler, as were her sisters.
They did not coddle those who interrupted during their game,
especially for such frivolities as small children.

However, they did make exceptions for kids who were old enough to
play poker,
and had money to lose.
Then they were welcomed to the ranks.
(Our daughter was not of that age or financial stature.)

The three of us stood there for a while,
watching the game.
After hearing the "F" word used one too many times,
we decided to leave that room also,
which really didn't matter because mom never stopped long enough to notice.

We moseyed down to the TV room.
OOPS!
The guys, along with my dad, were watching XX rated movies.
We quickly backed out of that room,
closing the door behind us.

The only room remaining was the living room.
We sat in there alone, waiting for the "white elephant" gift exchange.
White elephants are things of little value you have lying around the house.
With the roll of the dice,
the exchange began.
It became competitive and combative,
as it usually did.
The vulgarities started flying,
and continued unabated.
Mom's family prides itself on their use of vulgarity.
It's considered good humor.

The evening finally ended.

I shook my head as we drove home in the car that night.
Maybe I was changing.
It all seemed too far over the edge.
My husband, meanwhile, was having an emotional hemorrhage.

I wanted to make a break from her tradition.
But I could hear my mother's arguments already,
"What? Are you holier than thou?
You Christians are all alike—judgmental!
It's my family, that's the way they act!
You goody-two-shoes!"
Mom would go on and on.

I knew my decision to make a break
would be seen as a judgment;
a condemnation on them.

I knew I had the right to choose differently,
to have my own feelings and needs.
There were no judgments intended.

We made the break that year.

THE DANGER OF SELF-EXPRESSION

I still feared my mother's reaction.
I couldn't explain why she loomed larger than life to me.
Nonetheless, I suspected she could scare the devil himself,
so that left me feeling pretty vulnerable.

It may have been the coward's way out,
but I decided to voice our position in a letter.
I stated our intention to no longer celebrate the holidays with her family.
I also wanted to clarify my feelings regarding
what appeared to be a disparity in her treatment of my children.
    For Christmas presents,
    Mom made my daughter a dress from remnants in the basement,
    while the boys were each given a sizeable amount of money.
    The boys were ecstatic and didn't notice the look on their sister's face;
    she was bewildered.
    As I watched her grapple with her feelings,
    the despondency of my youth was rekindled.
    The "gifting" smacked of the same unequal treatment I had
    received growing up.
    I wanted to deal with the issue,
    to tell Mom it is the disparity of love, not the size of the gift
    that communicates a message.
    I didn't want my daughter being given a message that she was worth less.

Well, just as I expected,
my mother received my letter as a death knell.
She wrote back that our relationship had changed;
we could never be close again.
I had hurt her very much
and turning the kids against her had been the final blow.

After two more letters
it appeared a pointless struggle.
Our distance grew greater.

I was now completely isolated from all family relations.
I became a woman without family,
without heritage.

What I gained was peace
and room for health.

Chapter 11

RECONCILING WITH DAD

DESTABILIZING INFLUENCE

More than a year had passed without one word from my mother.
When she called to say Dad was in the hospital,
I felt simultaneously numb and tingly.
I arrived at the hospital and asked to see Dad's doctor
to get firsthand information.
The doctor told me Dad's condition was serious.
He had a toxic level of antidepressants in his blood
that were causing him to hallucinate.
His diabetes was out of control.
His kidneys were not fully functioning,
and there was fluid building up in his lungs.
The doctor recommended bypass surgery
but wanted to wait until Dad was stabilized.

Because I feared my presence might destabilize Dad further,
I waited outside the nurses' station
while his nurse asked if he wanted to see me.
She returned and said, "It's fine. Go on in."

In the years since the demise of our relationship,
I had not experienced anything closely resembling a normal conversation with Dad.
When I married Bill, Dad had once again withdrawn from me,
isolating himself in anger.
As I neared his bed,
I braced myself knowing I could never predict his moods.
However, I was different now—
I could choose to block his harmful poisons.
I could protect myself.

To my surprise he was cordial.
He was never affable except to strangers and fellow alcoholics;
he reserved his hostility for family members.
I wondered if death's appearance at the threshold
had made an impact on his personality.
He asked about the kids and inquired as to Bill's whereabouts.
Normally, he pretended none of us existed.
He seemed coherent, congenial and human;
almost approachable.
He was a different person.

Two hours later,
when I said good-bye,
I kissed him twice and told him I loved him.
He confessed, "I love you, too."

MOOD SWINGS

On my next visit,
Dad was stabilized and ready for surgery.

This time,
his black, thunderous mood was back—
the mood that always scared me.
 I remembered the time he told Mom to hide all the knives in the house.
 He feared he would go ape,
 and in a moment of homicidal passion,
 use them to slice us up.
 At the dinner table,
 he told us he could commit murder
 and hide the body deep in the swamps of northern Minnesota.
 No one would ever find a body there
 and he would never get caught.

I really hated the unpredictable nature of his moods.

This day, madness cloaked his face;
 he looked like a deep, dark, muddy bog
 capable of decomposing the unfortunate who became entrapped
 in his emotional morass.
 A mire that smoldered and belched a vaporous fog,
 the by-product of decaying love.

This day, he would neither look at me,
nor acknowledge my presence in the room.
This day,
I didn't exist.

I decided I liked his personality better
when he was hallucinating from an overdose of antidepressants.

ACRIMONY DAMAGES THE SOUL

Dad had his bypass surgery and went home within the week.
He was readmitted later when he appeared to be losing blood.

Mom called and reported,
"Your father has lost his mind.
He doesn't know who people are.
He won't eat,
and he doesn't know where he is."

I was cautious about Mom's assessment—
I suspected extreme resentment clouded her vision.

Mom and I talked outside Dad's room before I entered.
She stated her position on his ailing health;
"I don't want him in a nursing home."
She explained her motivation;
"I stayed with the bastard so I could spend all of his money when he's gone.
If he goes into a nursing home,
they'll take all his money!"

I couldn't help but think her solution was to have Dad die quickly,
before the money was gone.

For years she had been saying,
"When he dies,
I'm going to take his money and do everything first class.
I'll buy what I want, when I want."

Instead of wishing him dead,
I wished she had the guts, determination, or principle to divorce him years ago.
She reasoned, "Why should I divorce him and have to work that hard?
I deserve his pension.
He keeps stashing his pension,
but I'm going to get it."

The doctor came by while Mom and I were talking.
He had the impression from Mom
that they should do nothing to extend Dad's life;
they should not even give him blood, although he was continuing to lose it.
In amazement I said, "No, I don't think you mean that, do you?"
"I want no heroic measures," she insisted.

"What are heroic measures?" I persisted.

I was about to learn.

The conversation with Mom was more than I could take for one day,
so I said, "I'm going to stop in and see Dad for a minute."
I expected to find an incoherent person,
but to my surprise, he seemed connected with reality.
I watched and listened to substantiate Mom's evaluation.
I couldn't figure it out—I didn't see it.
He seemed quite glib to me.
> Dad muttered something that Mom couldn't hear.
> She said, "Robert, what do you want?
> Do you want me to crawl into bed with you?"
> "No," he replied, "we stopped doing that years ago."

> That was a very true statement—very connected with reality.

> Well...Mom never took a slam without returning the volley.
> She started back at him, and her sister joined the cause.
> Dad moaned, "Stop picking on me.
> Leave me alone."

To me, Dad seemed capable of making accurate statements
and expressing his needs.
It didn't seem like dementia to me.
However, my emotional distance was bound to make my view different than hers.
I knew the reality of my dad's miserable existence;
still, I felt it important to separate emotions from life and death decisions,
decisions she was about to make on his behalf.

It's Difficult to Know the Truth

It was no secret,
Mom had grown to hate Dad.
Their relationship was toxic,
and both suffered the consequence.
Because of his failing health,
Mom was now in the driver's seat.
It was difficult to know what was true within their relationship,
or what was the truth of his condition.
I followed Dad's condition hoping something would become clear.

Dad was given a scopic exam to determine the cause of bleeding.
They discovered a large bleeding ulcer and administered blood immediately.
To me he seemed to be improving.
To my mother, he was still on the precipice of death.

I started visiting regularly.
Perhaps, I inadvertently put myself in the role of guardian.
I remained perplexed by such different perceptions of Dad's condition.

During each of my visits, Dad would eat well.
One day he told the nurse, as he patted my hand,
"This is my daughter.
Isn't she good-looking?" he said with pride.
"Dad, don't say that!" I muttered, becoming embarrassed.
"Why not?" he said. "I'm proud of you," he added and kissed my hand.

Maybe he was hallucinating again.
I couldn't tell.
But, I didn't want to reject his love as delusional.

The next day when I arrived
it was obvious the doctor was not happy with Dad's condition.
I asked the doctor, "What's wrong?"

"Your father's respiration is too slow.
It's critical we get his respiration up or his heart will stop."

"Do you want me to leave?"

"No, stay here and keep him alert.
Keep him talking until we can get a drug injected to stabilize his rate."

The nurse suggested I talk to him about football.
Dad said he didn't care for football.

I started on the topic of hunting,
directing the discussion to both Dad and his nurse.
"He used to hunt pheasant, duck and deer.
One year he got a nice sized buck,
but mom hated the smell and taste of venison so she refused to cook it.
I think you gave it to the soup kitchen, didn't you?"
The nurse offered, "I heard venison tastes like chicken."
Dad said, "No," shaking his head in disgust.
"What does it taste like?" she asked.
"Horseshit," he responded.
She laughed.
He laughed and his eyes twinkled.

By the time lunch rolled around,
he was ready to eat everything in sight.
Of course, someone had to feed him cause he couldn't see the tray
while lying flat.

After I fed Dad,
I went to the bathroom.
While I was gone
the doctor stopped by and told Dad I had saved his life
by keeping him talking.
Dad shared the doctor's comments with me.
"I love you, Dad."
"I love you, too," he said.

It was surreal.

Stabilized with fluids by IV, his blood count holding constant,
Dad told me what was happening to him seemed unfair.
He thought he should be getting well.
"I don't want to die," he protested.

LEFT FOR DEAD

After conferring with my mother,
the doctor called a family conference.
We all pulled our chairs into a semicircle around the doctor.
The doctor and my mother had decided to pull Dad's IV.
The doctor explained that the only way my father would survive
would be to start eating and drinking on his own.
If he didn't eat, he would die.
If he did eat, he would go to a nursing home.
I objected.
I was told to support my mother's decision.
Helpless,
I felt completely helpless.
My mother declared,
"This isn't a democracy and we aren't voting.
The decision had been made."

At the close of the conference,
my mother immediately left with her sister to get Chinese food—
they were starving.
Dad's sisters stopped in to say good-bye to Dad and then left.
My brother and I stayed.
I ordered a lunch tray for Dad and fed him.
His appetite was good.
"Can I come to feed you every day?" I asked.
"Brownnoser," he quipped. It was one of his favorite expressions for me.

The next day
he had already been transferred to Hospice Care.
His IV had been removed.
I immediately tried to get him to drink,
but the nurse cautioned me not to do that because he might aspirate the fluid.

Feeling the hopelessness,
I cried.
Dad's face flashed desperation when he saw my tears.
I stopped crying and turned my head away
telling him everything would be okay.

Sitting on the edge of his bed,
I started reading aloud from my Bible.

Tears slid from the corners of his eyes as he faintly moaned, "Pray, pray."
Those were words I never expected to hear from Dad.
I felt an urgency and an immediacy that went beyond my understanding.
I ran down the hall to find a minister.

When I returned, Mom was in the room.
She brought out the scripture card Dad had been given
the night he stopped drinking.
She started to read it aloud but couldn't continue because she got teary.
I finished reading it for her.

Dad closed his eyes and never spoke again.
"Pray" was the last word he ever spoke.

My mother and I prayed with the minister.
I don't know if Dad heard our prayers,
but I do know that moment with Dad replaced all the hurt that had existed
between us.

He died in the middle of the night, less than a week later.
I rushed to the hospital, knelt by his bed,
and prayed alone in the silence of the dimly lit room.
He wasn't cold yet.

Mom came later.
We hugged.

DIVERGENT INTENTS

"What do you mean Dad wanted to be cremated?
He hated the idea of being burned whole—
it reminded him of the Nazis.
He was a veteran.
I thought he wanted to be buried at Fort Snelling."

The mortuary director heaved a languid look across his desk at my mother
and me.

"Well, he changed his mind," Mom asserted with her jaw set.
"Besides, why put all that money in the ground?"
Mom was following the philosophy passed down by her mother:
"Outlive the bastard and spend all his money!"
She would have just as easily left Dad's ashes in the trash can at the mortuary.
Anything spent on a funeral would be that much less for her to spend.
She had serious spending plans of her own
and no desire to waste time or money grieving Dad.

The big question was what to do with Dad's ashes.
The director offered a selection of urns.
"How much do they cost?" she quibbled.
He told her.
"Is there any law against putting his ashes in a cardboard box?"
she wondered aloud.
"No, that is perfectly acceptable.
We have a box for $10.95," he responded.
"That's fine.
You and your brother can decide who wants the box," she said crisply.

"What about a funeral service?" I asked her.
"I am not planning one.
You kids can if you want."
I was perplexed and inquired,
"You have no interest in any kind of funeral?
Don't you remember Dad saying he wanted the bagpipes played at his funeral?"
Her response was short and tight-lipped, "Nope."
"I can't let Dad go that way!" I exclaimed.
"Fine, do whatever you want. It's your decision. It's your money."

I cast a furtive look at the director,
who in turn offered the use of the mortuary for the service.
"Okay, let's set a date for the announcement in the paper
and I'll take care of everything," I told the director.

I found the bagpiper in the Yellow Pages
and asked my pastor to conduct the service.
I told the florist to design something whimsical, yet earthy.
No carnations, please.

The night of the service
Mom was her perky, social self,
meeting and greeting all of the alkies
(as my father affectionately called them)
from Dad's AA group.

Dad lay in his brown cardboard box, on a small table
next to the lectern from which the pastor conducted the service.
The box was no larger than a hardbound college dictionary.

Earlier, my brother had indicated a desire to speak before the gathering,
so when the time came,
the pastor turned the lectern over to him.

My brother had disowned Dad several years earlier,
and wasn't around much while he was dying.
Now he felt shameful
and suddenly, in his mind,
Dad took on heroic proportions.
When my brother stood up to speak,
he cried instead.

It was hard to watch.
As a matter of fact,
I couldn't watch.
I stood beside him,
hugged him,
and spoke for him.
Soon all of the alkies were offering stories of Dad's selflessness in saving lost drunks.
In their recollections, he was a very noble guy.

When the evening was over,
Mom commented how great it was to see old friends.

I put up my emotional shields,
took Dad home and laid him under the Christmas tree,
turned on its lights, drank a cup of tea and felt numb.

Frigid Cold

A month later,
my mother, brother and I
agreed to drive Dad's ashes to his childhood home,
which was a four-hour drive north.
The temperature had dipped to minus 15 degrees that day,
and the wind slapped my face leaving it to ache in warning;
only fools have no respect for the winter cold.

I offered to drive our minivan
which began acting up 70 miles outside of the city.
"I really don't feel comfortable taking this van up north in this weather,"
I said, as we slowed for a stop sign in a small rural town.
"That's those fucking Dodge vans—they're pieces of shit,"
my brother spewed.
"Just pull over at the diner up there and we can decide over breakfast,"
Mom suggested.

It was a typical small town diner.
All of the locals stopped and looked as we entered,
returning to their business only when we had settled in a booth.
My brother and I sat across from Mom and sipped our black coffee.

Mom wasted no time making things clear;
"I am going to spend every last penny Dad saved.
Even reverse-mortgage the house and spend all that too!
I outlived the son of a bitch, and now,
I am going to do whatever makes me happy,
whatever makes me feel good.
When I'm dead there won't be a penny left for you guys.
I'm going to spend it all," she said defiantly, with her chin jutting forward.
"I'm going to buy new furniture and drapes.
I'll take a couple of trips—first class all the way!"

Not wishing to engage emotionally,
and trying desperately to keep my shield up,
I responded, "That's fine. It's your money. Do as you wish."

The subject turned to medical and funeral expenses.
Mom thought the cardboard box was plenty good enough and asserted,
"I'd be damned if I'd give any of that money to a nursing home

just so the bastard's life could be prolonged, leaving me with nothing."
To which my brother sarcastically replied,
"Well, we took care of that—we pulled his plug so
he died before they could get it!"

Feeling my shield was quickly disintegrating,
I left for the bathroom.

After breakfast,
we returned home agreeing to make the trip in the spring.

During the winter,
Mom sold everything that was Dad's;
his truck, trailer, guns…everything.
We were never informed of the sale;
we were never given the opportunity to have anything of Dad's—
even if we paid for it.
Mom spent all the proceeds on whatever made her happy.

I resented Mom's hard and callous heart,
even if I did understand where it came from.

A Cardboard Box Riding in a Black Limousine

Spring finally came.
Mom's heart thawed slightly.
It was again time to attempt to deliver Dad to his final resting place—
Penguilly, Minnesota.

Mom rented a stretch limousine,
invited her youngest sister to join us,
fried some chicken,
and packed a lunch.

My brother came,
minus his wife.
(Smart woman—she had no stomach for our family's sickness.)
Bill, Andy and Corissa joined me—as support.
Ben was away at college and could not make it home.

We all piled into the back of the limousine.
It was tense, very tense.
Mom and I had not spoken more than a handful of words since our falling-out,
and recent dispiriting interactions did nothing to bring us closer.
My aunt had a very short fuse on her anger that was easily ignited.
My brother, with a similar personality,
at 6'9" tall, presented a frightening spectacle when enraged.
Explosive interactions were not uncommon at gatherings.

Bill came along to protect his family from injury.

Bill really hated—could not abide—hostile and foul language,
especially the "F" word.
This posed a problem since my mother, brother and aunt
all thought it a customary and usual way of communicating.

It would be an eight-hour day,
cooped up together in a confined space.
We brought the game Trivial Pursuit to help pass time.
Mom brought food to help pass time.

The limousine driver, supposedly diabetic,
stopped every 35 minutes to urinate.
Grateful, my aunt exited the limo before it came to a
complete stop for a smoke.

No one had thought through what to do with Dad's ashes
once we arrived in Penguilly.

So when we arrived in town, Mom suggested we throw them in the lake.
That wasn't a bad idea because Dad had loved fishing on northern lakes.
We all agreed that would be appropriate.
To be expected, the driver could not find a public access to the lake.
Mom and my aunt suggested we pull over on the bridge
and dump him overboard—
quickly—since there was traffic behind us.

I was repulsed by that idea, so I asserted,
"No, that is not a good idea!
Where is the reverence in that?"
"Reverence, schmeverence." Mom was opting for the expedient.

"Well, if we are okay with stopping every 35 minutes on the way up and back,
the least we can do is stop now and do it right," Bill suggested.
"That's well and fine, but where do you suggest we do that?" my aunt snipped.
"Pull into that driveway," Bill directed the driver.
"What are you going to do?" Mom questioned, with a confused look on her face.
"I'm going up to that house to ask the owners
if we can access the lake through their property," he said firmly.
"You can't do that!"
Everyone thought that was bold.
"Sure I can."
Out he flew before anyone could argue.
"He's not really going to do that, is he?" my aunt asked.
"Yep, he is. That's the way he is," the kids and I assured her.

We waited fifteen minutes. Still he had not returned.
"Should someone go get him?" my brother asked, growing impatient.
"No, he's the social type. It'll take him awhile." The kids nodded in agreement.

He returned.
"Well she was a very nice lady.
Her husband is dying.
She's been home nursing him for over a year.
She completely understands that we want to make the moment special.
She expressed her sympathies and said she'll pray that our time is meaningful."
Bill resumed his spot in the back of the limo.

"Oh, good God. She's one of those types!" fumed my mother.

Bill gave the directions to the driver.
We pulled down a gravel road stopping 10 feet from the lake.
A small dock sat off to the side.
It was a beautiful sunny day.
The lake shone with diamond reflections of the sun.
Dad would have thought the spot perfect.

While we conducted our ceremony on the dock,
my aunt sat on an abandoned clothes washer that was
overgrown with weeds, and watched.
We brought tapes, a boom box and our Bible.
While music played in the background,
we read aloud chosen verses and talked of memories of Dad.
Mom didn't say much, but she was there and seemingly okay with things.

Eventually, we each, with the exception of Mom,
took handfuls of Dad out of the cardboard box
and scattered him into the lake.
He wasn't completely powdered—some small bone chunks remained.
I saved one of the larger ones—it was the only physical
thing remaining of him.
The kids thought me weird. Bill understood my weirdness.

Mom laid out the picnic lunch she had brought.
It was the lunch my father customarily demanded
on our first day traveling during summer vacations:
fried chicken, hard-boiled eggs and potato salad.
He liked graveyards, so he would find one in the middle of nowhere.
We would park the car and eat our chicken
while leaning up against tombstones of people unknown to us.
Ironically, this time it was his graveyard.

We played a tape of bagpipe music in his honor,
as we ate our chicken under the shade of a nearby tree.

DUST ON THE BOTTOM

I later recalled that day on the dock.
It lived within the vivid pictures my memory had captured.
I can see Dad's ashes floating in streams of gray dust,
carried by the wind blowing across the lake.
And slowly, very slowly,
the water pulls his dust translucently downward
to his final resting spot at the bottom of the lake.
As I look through the clear water,
I see him on the sand bottom.
A fine dust over sand and pebbles,
it is all that remains of him.

I allow my memory to take me further back in time,
to go fishing with Dad one last time.
I am six on a brilliant sunny day.
My hair is white blonde.
The sun's reflection off my head, I am told, could blind a person.
My bare feet feel the heat of the sun as it warms the bottom of his aluminum boat.
There is the smell of gasoline from his Johnson motor.
Gasoline forms a rainbow-colored glaze over the water.
Immersing my hand in the minnow bucket,
I recall the way the minnows feel as they dart to escape my hand.
I love the way the boat rocks gently in the waves.
Dad and I eat our catch of sunfish until we think we'll bust open.
I am his "little herring choker."
He pats me on the head, and I am full of scampering delight because he loves me.

And then I return—the irreversible procession of time
prohibits loitering in the past.

I wondered where his anger came from. Why did he hate me so?
Why was he mentally ill?

As I became a woman,
I wanted to be sure in his love and confident he would be there for me.
I longed to be happy in the assurance we would spend endless years
choking down sunfish together
while sharing our love of the north woods.

I still love the north woods and beautiful sunny days.

I miss the dad I knew only for a short while in my youth—
the dad I wished for.
Now, he is dust on the bottom of a lake.

Chapter 12

RETURN TO THE WORK WORLD

GET BACK ON THE HORSE

It had been three months since I left Goliath,
and I still had no idea how I would survive my return to the work world.
Despite learning a few tricks from Alletta about maintaining my boundaries,
I felt inadequately prepared.

Bill and I argued incessantly about my return.
He wanted me to get a good paying marketing job just like the one I left at Goliath.
I wanted to find a dark closet and curl up in the back corner of it—alone—
and stay there until it felt safe to come out.

He insisted, "You can't stay at home.
You're good at what you do.
If you hide, they've won."

"I frankly don't care who 'wins.'
I don't want to play the game anymore.
How can you push me to do what you know will hurt me?"

"You'll never get a job earning what they paid you and that means our family loses.
Male dominated industries pay more,
and we need the money."

"How can you be so thoughtless?
Why can't you hear me say it will kill me?
I don't want to be forced to earn the same salary.
I want to become an artist."

That idea really sent him around the bend.
"Give me a break!
That's like your brother wanting to be an actor.
Get real! Dreams don't pay. Jobs do.
You'd never make a living as an artist.
That's why they call them starving artists."

What I saw in the male dominated world of business
were behaviors that frightened and sickened me.
I saw a world where gaining control and maintaining power
were sufficient and laudable life goals.
This belief system served men well in corporate America.
Many women bought into the power model,
and it served them well also.
I, however, had no desire to conform myself to that world view.
I sought to understand how to claim my own place in the world.

Role Models

Some psychologists say that women learn nurturance from their mothers.
It isn't because we can't learn nurturing from our fathers,
but most of us had mothers who stayed home and cared for us,
while our dads went off to work.
In theory, therefore, men represent our ability to negotiate the world,
while woman represent our ability to nurture ourselves.

The process of reclaiming myself was not about blaming my mother.
It was about claiming and growing myself from the reference point of love.
I accepted that my mother acted out her victim status,
and over time,
it looked and felt like hardness on her.
Because of that,
I understood there could be no "victim" in the lexicon of my reclamation.
I would be responsible for my decisions.

That being the case,
I looked next at attributes normally assigned to males,
characteristics considered helpful in negotiating the larger world.

It became immediately obvious;
I learned nothing from my father about negotiating the world—
he hid from the world.

I had used Old Testament biblical characters as role models.
I assumed if we were to model the faith of Abraham, for instance,
it should work equally well for a woman and a man.
Or one could model the warrior in David, or the intelligence of Joseph.
However, my experience taught me men much preferred
Mother Mary or Mary the prostitute as role models for women.

I was at a loss to understand my purpose and place in the
whole cosmic mess called life.

INSULT TO INJURY

I stalled out;
not knowing how to move forward,
not wanting to remain where I was.
My husband and children did not understand,
nor accept the reality of my trepidation.
There was no hiding.
I had to face the world.

I had assumed the world would be better once I divorced my first husband;
after all, one bad decision didn't make the world a dark place.
Now, however, the world did look dark to me.
No matter how much I tried to psyche myself up,
everything looked terrifying and worthless.
What was the point of all this anyway?

I gained weight.
Again.

Then,
one Saturday morning,
everything that had been building
unexpectedly erupted in an argument of cataclysmic
proportions between Bill and me.
Chores and responsibilities stacked up.
We argued feverishly
about who had lost more during my battle with the corporate Goliath.
I wanted Bill to understand what he was asking of me.
He wanted me to be healed and whole
and go slay the dragon.
I wanted to hide.
I wanted him to take care of me,
to protect me and give me space to heal.
I wanted him to shoulder the burden of the financial needs of our family until
I felt better,
then I would return to work.

He wanted a fully functioning wife who would help pay the bills.
He wanted me to lose weight so he would find me sexually attractive again.
He wanted things to return to normal.

Unexpectedly he exclaimed, "Maybe the only solution is a divorce."

The knockout punch landed squarely.
My darkness became darker.

We talked only sparingly for weeks
while we both wrestled with our separate feelings.

Later, I told Bill his love felt cheap and conditional.
I advised him to never use my weight again to injure me;
I would not tolerate nor accept such behavior.

He apologized and explained that feelings of helplessness
had caused him to lash out.
He asked me to forgive him.
We cried in each other's arms realizing we had both experienced loss.

SMALL TOWN FEELING

Well, if I had to return to work,
I would look for a place that was safer,
more caring than business.

I had the greatest affection for the hospital where Dad had died.
Maybe it was because it was so familiar.
As a candy striper, I had roamed the entire place.
Two of my children were born there.

When I saw the hospital's ad in the paper, I jumped at the chance to apply.
I didn't grow up in a small town,
but that place was close to what I imagined one would feel like.

After three rigorous interviews, I was given the job.

During the interviews
I was troubled by the manager's attitude toward her staff,
but chose to ignore my instincts because of the fondness I felt for the hospital.
It seemed she agreed with the power model of management.
Regrettably, I should have listened to my instincts.
She immediately positioned the job as "we against them."
"Them" (the staff) did not understand that health care was business.
She had confidence I was on her team though, stating,
"You come from business—you understand."

She said the budget numbers were abysmal
and if something didn't change,
the department would be folded.
She was looking for drastic measures.

I suggested we hold strategic planning sessions
and involve everyone in the solution.
Eighteen staff voices rang out in unison, "Good idea!"

Heather, Karen and Gary,
volunteered to cut back on hours to address financial concerns
and protect from layoffs.

The remaining staff joined them in willingness to sacrifice for the good of all.

We finished and submitted our plan.
The staff felt the joy of team involvement and shared responsibility.
We were riding high on team spirit.

The next day the manager called me into her office and shut the door behind me.
She started by confiding she had no intention of using the plan developed by
the staff
because she had her own;
it had already been approved by upper management.
Tomorrow, she would announce layoffs.

Tomorrow, would be Heather's fourteenth anniversary with the hospital.

I felt duped—
as if we were merely pawns to management.

Heather expected a homemade cake to celebrate;
Instead, she got her walking papers.
Her face lost color.
She sat and stared at the letter in her hand.
Staff came by her cube to hug her,
and cried.
When the manager walked in,
they quickly returned to their desks,
heads bent to the floor.
They would have gladly sacrificed for Heather.

Heads shook in disbelief.

Our team spirit died.
To resuscitate it, the hospital hired a consultant
to evaluate the cause of our poor morale.
We were interviewed separately,
but upon exiting the interview we immediately compared notes.
The overwhelming majority had clearly communicated disappointment
with the manager's style of leadership.

The conference room was filled the day
we were to hear the consultant's report.
To our surprise, we were all asked to support the manager.

In a matter of months many had left, including Bruce, Karen and me.
We all kept in touch and mourned the loss.
Still, the grief seemed to follow us long after we went our separate ways.

Bruce was killed when a ladder he was standing on fell and hit an electric wire.
He was a beautiful person who never suspected he would be leaving
a wife and small children behind.
Stunned and shocked,
each of us fell silent on the phone when we were told of his death.

Karen, diagnosed with cancer,
battled with everything she had rather than leave her daughter.
We gathered outside the church on a beautiful summer day
and wondered why she was taken so young.
We whispered our concern for the daughter she left behind.

Heather discovered she had cancer during surgery for another matter.
She was told,
"You are fortunate we accidentally found the tumor while it was still small.
Of course, you will not be able to have children, but you are alive."
She now gets scans twice a year.

Bruce, Karen and Heather,
all in their thirties.
Each expected long lives.
None of us know.

Time lost in a compromise of truth
cannot be brought back.

Eventually, the hospital announced the manager was
"leaving for another opportunity."
It was too late—our small town had been ripped apart.
The manager admitted, "I am just not good with people.
Managing people has always been difficult for me.
I think my new job will be a better fit."

We all see more clearly in retrospect.

The manager,
who with passion had originally established the department,
was hired back to rebuild it.
I met her at a reunion several years after my departure.
She apologized for what we had all experienced.
"It was unfortunate," she sighed.
She described the joy her work gave her.
"I know that as a manager I can positively impact the lives of so many people.
It can be a great opportunity to leave something worthwhile for others
because the people who come behind you, inherit what you leave."

RISKY BUSINESS

I assumed the same power paradigm I witnessed in male dominated environments
would not be present in health care. [15]
The experience was unfortunate.

I had to move on.

Was it dangerous to consider employment
in an engineering company
controlled by men?
Some assured me not all were the same.
I was told it really boils down to being a savvy interviewee;
    ask all the right questions,
    and be assertive.

Ned, the hiring manager, was VP of marketing and fairly new to the company.
He appeared to be a man without pretense, intelligent, and well intentioned.
He realized the company's disparity in gender representation
and was determined to start the remedy process.
I would be the first female in their business management ranks.

During further interviews with males in like positions to mine,
I was encouraged by their allied desire to see a gender diversified company.

Dan, the president and majority owner,
was traveling and not available for an interview.
I was told he dressed well in hand-tailored suits and monogrammed shirts.
Begrudgingly,
male managers described him as attractive and European in style and manner.
I thought it important to interview Dan,
but I let it go because I suspected a small company desirous of growth
would have little time or interest in participating in deliberate discrimination.
I accepted the offer in Dan's absence.

Only a few months into the job,
I wanted to quit.

I should have quit.

Instead, everything I thought I had learned about upholding myself—
balance,
health,
soul—
I was allowing to blow out the window on the winds of work overload.

All of the other business managers were:
hard driven males,
always working,
never home,
willing to commit 210% to the job.

I didn't want that life.
Yet I found myself pulled into 60-hour work weeks
with an ever-increasing workload.

We all agreed the expectations were insane,
but the guys refused to say anything—it wasn't politically smart.
They would play the game by the rules.
Even if the rules stunk.

I confided to Jim, a colleague whom I quickly learned to trust,
that I wanted to quit.
Confessing my fear I told him,
"I just don't know how to tell a prospective employer
that I left one of the 'best' companies in Minnesota after five years,
the hospital one year later,
and now, merely one month into this job, I've had enough!
I'll look like a quitter.
Nobody likes excuses."
He admitted companies are cautious of people who jump jobs.

Trapped by my own insecurities,
I stayed and exceeded my manager's expectations,
and was rewarded with even more responsibilities.

Difficult Behavior to Explain

Although I still had a dearth of product knowledge,
my boss, Ned, signed me up to do distributor training
saying, "It's a great way to learn."

On my first trip out,
after my presentation was over,
one of the distributor reps asked me to swim naked with him in the pool.

On the second trip out,
another business manager and I were to meet up with Paul,
a salesman on the west coast.
I was warned by several employees not to trust Paul. "He's a snake," they said.
"He'll stab you in the back and you'll never know what hit you."
Paul happened to be the budding protégé of Jack, the VP of sales.

Paul picked us up at LAX in his
new, gold-trimmed Lexus—
the executive model with leather seats.

As he sped down the six-lane freeway,
he made mention of the money in LA,
noting the black BMWs, Mercedes and various foreign cars,
all driven by the new wealthy who were finding gold in the dot-com boom.

For most of the trip,
the other business manager and I sat in the back seat of the Lexus
talking to each other about our respective programs.

After our day ended,
Paul dropped us off at the airport to board a plane to San Francisco.
I took my voicemail messages when we landed.
There was one from Ned asking me to call him as soon as possible—
he had something to discuss with me.

I called Ned from a nearby phone booth at the corner of a busy intersection.
Finding it difficult to hear, I nearly shouted,

"You have something important to share?"
Whenever my boss was perturbed, his voice had a special quality.
Despite the noise, I could hear it had that quality now.
"Jack called me while you were in flight.
He said Paul told him your conduct was unprofessional.
Supposedly you made negative and disparaging comments about Dick."
Dick was another salesman who also reported to Jack.

    Dick had a nervous tick.
    A high strung, high maintenance individual,
    he certainly generated plenty of comical things to talk about,
    but I knew better.

Ned, being a fair-minded individual,
told Jack he would check into it and get back to him.
He was familiar with Jack's destructive tactics,
and was not about to give him a pint of blood so quickly.

As Ned listened patiently,
I told him my account of the discussion in the back seat,
all of which was positive and supportive of Dick.
He then asked me to put the other business manager on the phone.
Our stories matched.
Absolutely nothing negative was said about any salesmen.

Although Jack was part owner in the company,
and prone to making mountains out of molehills if it suited him,
I didn't believe my boss would cower,
or play politics—
it just wasn't his style.

I prayed,
"Lord, please don't let this be the same nightmare starting all over again."
My guts began to ache from a very familiar pain.

A Test of Capability

The next morning we met to train a large distributor
who had recently won our company's contest
for sales in excess of a million dollars.
The reward was a one year lease on a brand-new Mercedes.
They were an important distributor;
the type we were to impress.

As the reps took their seats around the conference table,
I cringed, noting they were all male, every last one of them!
More than 30 men.
One woman—me.

Hotel conference rooms filled with business men,
cheap commercial furniture,
and the dank smell of air-conditioning,
had grown repulsive to me.

Reignited by the events of the day before,
my mind hearkened back to another hell I had recently left.
My body began sending a very strong signal;
leave or heave!

As my mind was thinking of a response to the signal,
the 30 reps had started introductions around the table.
I came out of my fear-induced fog to hear one of the reps challenge me:
"Debra, do you remember my name?
Do you remember his name?" he said pointing to another rep.
"Or his name?" he added, as he went around the table.
"The point of introductions is to remember,"
he smugly asserted.
While the air-conditioner clattered noisily in the corner of the room,
their laughter rattled inside my brain.

I wondered to myself, "Why had he singled me out?"
No men in my group were similarly tested.
If they had been,
they would have failed as well.

I knew there would be no point in challenging them—
Jack would use it against me,
especially since the distributor was so important to the company.
So, I apologized for being distracted.

DANDY PICTURES

After we finished distributor training,
we spent the remainder of the day making account calls.

The salesman in San Francisco drove an older SUV.
I, thankfully, had the backseat to myself this time.

The first stop was basically a garage shop with an office on the front.
The employees were all male, with the exception of the female receptionist.
Every workbench assigned to a male employee
had a calendar of female nudes proudly displayed above it.
Each calendar demonstrated a different style of nude shot.
I likened it to dogs and their owners;
every owner will select and defend his chosen breed.
(It somehow adds to the definition of the owner.)
I tried hard not to notice the calendars,
but they were literally above every workbench.
If a male employee's eyes met mine as I deflected my view from his
prize calendar,
he would stand straight, shoulders back and beam,
like a proud owner of a pedigree.

It felt like a bad '50s movie;
cigarettes rolled up in sleeves,
hair combed back,
and nudities everywhere!
This, however, was the '90s!!!
Maybe this was a horror flick.

Certainly, this place had to be an exception.

Again, I was glad to have the backseat to myself
as we drove to the next account.

At the next account,
the receptionist was the owner's wife.
She cordially offered us coffee or water to drink,
and quickly returned with our requests neatly arranged on a tray.
She was a woman in her early fifties,

diminutive and docile in appearance.
She seemed bewildered by my presence
and watched me as if I were an odd animal.
Her husband came out of the back to greet us.
I knew beyond any doubt that he was the head primate at this zoo.
His bravado immediately filled the room
like the smell of crap in an outhouse.
Propelled by arrogance,
he personally guided our tour,
stopping to point out his accomplishments along the way,
always allowing sufficient time for our obligatory admiration
to be spilled at his feet.

It was no big surprise,
there were female nude posters everywhere in the plant.

When we finished the tour,
the owner led us into his office which doubled as the conference room.
The walls were lined with old, cheap, dark wood paneling,
and the floor with dingy green shag carpet.
The dim light futilely cast from two old dusty table lamps
barely illuminated the room.
We were directed to sit on the three chairs
facing the owner's antiquated mahogany desk.
Behind the desk,
a life-size painting of a reclining nude hung in an elaborate, gold-gilded frame.
She was definitely meant to be the focal point of the room.
(The two smaller nudes hanging opposite her presented little competition.)

The owner's wife entered the room to check on drinks again.
As she stood waiting for our replies,
her husband laid his hand on the gold-gilded frame,
and while looking lustfully at the nude said,
"Isn't she something?"

I wondered how his wife felt.

From her position of sumptuous reverence,
the nude appeared to watch us the entire meeting.
I, personally, couldn't escape her dispassionate gaze
(an elephant in the room would have been easier for me to ignore).

I didn't participate in the meeting;
I sat back and watched the guys with me who seemed unaffected
by her carnal presence.

During the meeting
a difference of opinion erupted on a recently placed order
at which point, the owner commanded his wife to bring in the disputed order.

Having found it,
his wife slipped in and out of the room delivering it to him
without ever appearing distinguishable from the paneled walls;
her marginalized stature was perfected to the point of invisibility.

Her body spoke of resignation.
My soul reverberated her message.

Dead air filled the SUV as we drove back to our hotel.
The salesman offered, "It must be uncomfortable...being a woman."

BLOODY AWARENESS

I wanted nothing more than to find solitude in my hotel room that evening.

I would always be a foreigner
in this foreign world of men.
Their inhabitable land had become my desert experience.

I shouted at the Lord,
"I hate their world.
I hate everything about it."

"How could I have done this to myself again?
Am I a moron, or what?" I asked.

The Lord didn't answer.

I took a shower.

As if to accentuate the point of difference between men and women,
I began to bleed profusely in the shower.
The blood ran down my legs,
choking the drain
and filling the tub with the sanguine fluid.
The white porcelain quickly became glazed over with warm ruddy blood.

Like a clip from the movie, Psycho,
it was an eerie sight.
As if third person,
I watched mystified and horrified
as my toes disappeared beneath the rising pool of blood.

I wondered if a woman could die from her period while showering?
I asked myself, "Should I go to the hospital?"

It wasn't until I became woozy
that I stopped asking questions and got out of the shower.
In my light-headed state I quickly drifted off to sleep.

Political Limb

When I arrived back at work,
Ned called me into his office and shut the door behind me.
He showed me an e-mail he had sent to Jack.
It appeared my boss was willing to go out on a limb for this one.

The e-mail read:
Subsequent to our discussion, I have had an opportunity to discuss, in greater
detail, the reported conversations and comments with all three parties involved.
Two of the three—(the two business managers)—have a total and complete
agreement and understanding of what was said, and more importantly, what
was not said. They both were flabbergasted, amazed, incredulous, and
absolutely contradicted Paul's version of the communications that took place.
According to both of them—and I discussed it with them separately—
the only reference made at all to Dick was in the context of praising his
knowledge of the market, and the invaluable assistance he had given both
business managers on many occasions. Nothing more.

I, and everyone else who knows her, consider Deb to be a person of
highest integrity, professionalism, good judgment, a team player, responsible,
considerate of others, wanting to be tactful, yet prepared to be direct if
necessary. If you would read the psychological evaluation done when
she came on board, you would find all of those descriptors and many more
like them.

In short, I believe the business managers' version of what happened, without
any reservations. Furthermore, I do not want to drop this. Paul's comments
have maligned and slurred Deb's character and her reputation. Therefore,
when Paul is up here for the Xmas party, I am scheduling a meeting with (the
three involved parties), you and me, and we will put this incident to rest, one
way or another. I will not tolerate innuendo, slander, or disrespect to become a
part of the way we operate. Whatever happened will not happen again."

I liked my boss.
He had guts.

When they didn't show for the meeting,
Ned clearly stated his disappointment
and asked Jack to take responsibility for setting another meeting date.

No other meeting date was set.

Ned apologized to me.
He explained he was at the end of his political rope.
If the majority owner was not going to confront the situation,
he alone had no power to hold a minority owner accountable for a remedy.

Pranks

Jack, invigorated by his apparent freedom to create mischief,
found it difficult to restrain himself.
Again, I was his target.

It appeared an errant memo was sent out by mistake.
I had issued the infamous memo and had given it to marketing services for mailing.
This meant I was ultimately responsible for the mishap.

Jack sent a copy of the memo to Ned.
He had scribbled across the top,
"More mistakes from the Clown Carnival!"

I checked with marketing services
whose trail of documentation indicated there had been no error.
They were befuddled by the accusation.

When I offered this evidence to Jack,
he called in Dick, the salesman with the tick,
to support his accusation and testify against me;
that I had indeed committed the ultimate blunder.

I knew Jack had already notified Dan, the president,
so I immediately sought to address the issue and explain the situation to him.
On my way to his office,
I requested that marketing services begin calling the mailing list;
first to discern the degree of error,
and, where a mistake had taken place,
to quickly and professionally deal with any concerns.

As I stood before Dan's desk,
he acknowledged that he had seen the "Clown Carnival" memo.
I assured him I took full responsibility and that the cause was being investigated.
Apologizing, I promised to remedy the situation.

After leaving Dan's office,
I hurried over to the marketing services group.
They discovered that not one memo had been incorrectly sent.
Not one!
We had made no mistake!
Jack had created an imaginary "Clown Carnival" event.

So what was that all about?
Why did he invent the story?

Pinocchio

Following several foiled attempts to use his destructive power against me,
Jack turned his attention directly on Ned.
Pulling me aside at a trade show,
Jack launched into an inflammatory tirade against Ned
detailing alleged sexual harassing behaviors, incompetence and malfeasance.
I could not substantiate, nor would I support any of Jack's claims,
all of which seemed outrageous to me.
Nevertheless, shortly after initiating his campaign,
Ned was mysteriously dismissed from the company.
The standard political explanation was announced,
"The VP of marketing has left the company to pursue other interests."

I missed Ned.
He was a sane man in our insane world of work.
After his departure, I felt unprotected.

An upcoming sales meeting promised to be fertile ground for Jack's bedevilment.
Emotionally arming myself, I was determined to be polished, confident
and professional.

The meeting was held in southern California at a beachfront hotel.
When Jack entered the conference room,
it felt as if the room sealed shut
and his presence filled it like water fills a confined space;
I hoped someone would open the door before I drowned.

Jack was an obtrusive man,
with a bawdy sense of humor.
The protuberance of his midsection
was accentuated by his tie and suspenders
that scarcely stretched across the curvature of his large form.

The conference room was long and narrow
with one table spanning the length of the room.
I, the only woman, sat surrounded by men.

While waiting to present,
I fortified my mental shield
and did a systems check on my emotional security alerts.
Alarms were going off in my head and stomach as I started my presentation.

Jack's mouth began to move as soon as I spoke my first sentence.
His eyes rolled back.
He laughed at my numbers,
and choked on the stated possibility.
Yawned, drummed his fingers and drew pictures.
He passed one of the pictures around the table while I was presenting.
It was a picture of me as Pinocchio.
Under the picture the caption read,
"Marketing lies."
The picture was passed around the table until it came to Dan,
who in turn, continued to pass it along.
When it came to me,
I kept it,
explaining to Jack the likeness was not good—I was much cuter.

At noon,
the guys laughed and joked as we all proceeded to the hotel's restaurant.

The waitress commented to me,
"Well, aren't you the lucky one—the only woman with all these handsome men?"
I told her I would be happy to switch places with her.
She laughed.
I swallowed hard.

While we waited for our lunches to be served,
Jack told a joke about a prostitute and substituted my name for the prostitute's.
The men laughed.
I swallowed hard.

After lunch,
Jim and I talked in the hall.
He said, "I have never seen you as animated, passionate or committed as you
were during your presentation. You come ALIVE in those types of sessions,
and all that communication skill and knowledge benefit everyone. I wonder if
the president knows how fortunate he is that you joined us?"

Thanking Jim for the compliment,
I commented,
"I don't think I want to continue to pay the price."

On the way to the airport,
Dan offered, "You handled yourself well today."
I swallowed hard.

DROWNING

During that year I fell progressively further into fear:
>Fear of the irrationality that surrounded me.
>Fear of finding no safe place.
>Fear of losing the war.
>Fear of not loving myself.
>Fear of people who cause hurt.
>Fear of leaving God.
>Fear of the indescribable sort that lingers when others have left and you are alone.

I was lost in fear.
I had compromised my dreams.

I drank to become numb,
to mask the truth,
drown the emotions,
and hush the internal voice crying,
>"Enough!"

My healthy response mechanism was crippled by a world of
bombarding messages:
subliminal and direct,
subtle and intentional.
They poisoned me and confused my reaction.
The messages were encrypted with lies meant to steal and destroy.

The message encoder is insidious and eternally patient.
Meanings became twisted:
>Making a different choice meant admitting defeat.
>Leaving implied loss of house—of stability—of future prosperity and of possibilities.
>A focus on health and soul translated as "LOSER."

So I stayed,
stuck on a moving walkway through a tunnel of deceptions,
a hall of mirrors reflecting only distortions.
It was a labyrinth of exit signs that beguiled me with illusions of escape.

Flames of entrapment seared my stomach as I traveled the tunnel of lies.

Deadened,
options for escape dissolved within my family's financial demands,
or were evaporated by my skepticism.

HOWLING IN THE WILDERNESS

"Lord, I am lost in the wilderness.
I can't find my way.
I have listened to the lie,
and thought it truth.

How could I leave you?
Am I distrustful of you and afraid to admit it?
Maybe that's true.
Please open my mouth to speak what is buried deep within me.
Why didn't you bring me victory against Goliath?
I thought you were a just God.
Why would so many seek to diminish me,
destroy my soul,
and you are silent?
You are silent now.

Why do I doubt you?

I have never experienced you as anything other than love.
Whenever your love came near,
I felt the warmth and closeness of an embrace free of touch.

I have heard your voice in the sweetest and most tender of moments.
When I could no longer bear to be apart from you,
your presence filled me.
In that holy instant,
spoken words lost their meaning
and love was understood as eternal.

Once, I could seek your presence
and be transported spiritually into a safe place
where your nearness healed me.
A haven of incomprehensible bliss in the midst of fear and fatigue.
When weak,
I could hide and come back strong.

Now,
my spirit strains in vain.
I imagine my soul is a telescope scanning the heavens for remote light.
It finds none,
not even the faintest.

As if a great chasm opened in the universe,
I am being swallowed up,
falling endlessly, helpless,
unable to stop my spiraling descent.

Savagery would refuse me my true love.
I feel the panic of an animal ensnared by a trap.
An animal would howl and chew its leg off, rather than stay imprisoned.

Hear me!! Help me!!"

THE BODY SPEAKS

Eventually everything collapsed inward on my body.

As usual,
I didn't listen.
I didn't respect my body's message.
I kept pushing,
driving it against its will.

My body spoke louder,
piercing my consciousness
without respect for my imagined control.

With persistence and clarity
it pointed out my vulnerability,
my fragility.
It had no concern for appearances of strength.
Necessity drives its own will,
and I was its captive.

Like an Achilles' heel,
my lifelong ailment proved to be my weakness.
Seemingly manageable,
albeit uncomfortable,
my chronic condition had now become acute.
I could no longer ignore it as the unexplainable childhood irritant.
Inflamed, it demanded attention.
There were more trips to specialists.
And a warning:
I had to stop driving, demanding, controlling.
It was time to listen.

I felt so stupid.
I was leaving God,
compromising my health,
and losing my mind.

For what?

REFUSAL TO ACCEPT

While the doctor advised me on my physical condition,
Bill advised me of my spiritual condition;
he thought I should start reading my Bible again.

I couldn't.

Once so precious,
like the Velveteen Rabbit worn by love's interest,
my Bible showed wear;
its cover hung by a thread.
When I first met Bill,
its tattered condition
was evidence to him of my true love.
For a wedding gift
he recovered my tattered Bible
and engraved my name and 1981, the year we were wed, on the cover.

It frightened him to see it now lie
gathering dust.

I just couldn't read it any longer without experiencing excruciating pain.
Passages I had previously skipped over, I could no longer ignore.
The questions posed by them hurt too much.
    Am I, as Paul says in Timothy, to learn from men in silence?
    Am I to have no authority to teach men?
    Must I be silent because, like Eve, women cannot be trusted?
    Am I to believe my only salvation as a woman is through childbirth?

It was clearly obvious to me that the work world dominated by men
found power and authority in that notion. [16]

I had stopped attending church with Bill and the kids.
My decision was preceded by years of arguments between Bill and I.
It was heartbreaking for both of us.

In my mind,
continued attendance would only hasten my spiritual death.
I suffered a suffocating sense of worthlessness each Sunday
as I sat silently in the pew.
Our church did not talk about the pain that silence might cause some women
because belonging meant acceptance of your role.
I could not endure the deprivation of spirit any longer.

Bill was helpless to know what to do.
He refused to leave his church,
yet he wanted to fix the situation.
He wished I would put my brain back in order.

It wasn't that simple.
I had been irrevocably changed.

He first noticed why I cried
when he attempted to render an inclusive version of the New Testament for me.
It hurt him to see what I saw.
He agreed the language excluded.
But the task of inclusion proved too large for him,
so he began his search to find an inclusive Bible.

I desperately wanted to feel God's presence again.
I wanted it more than air to breathe,
or water to drink.
I was dying and I knew it.
Just as a person without food in their starvation
hallucinates every delectable dish ever imagined,
I ached for the taste of God.

I needed to be alone and quiet—
to find perspective in stillness.
To me, the North Shore had always been a spiritual lightning rod,
a holy place.
I decided to go there and hike along one of the many
rivers that flow into Lake Superior.

DEVIL'S KETTLE

The river's path splits in two.
A narrow rock outcropping
causes the schism.
River water haplessly flows
toward the rock that cleaves.

One half of the flow
drops over a falls.
The bombardment of droplets
against each other and the descending rocks
cause eruptions of energy.
Water splashes and sprays in every direction
as it tumbles into the pool below.
This basin,
designed by nature to accept the lavish flow,
manifests a never-ending white wave pattern,
> churning,
> erupting,
> rolling.

The water fights to discover its rightful path downstream.
When the flurry of activity is over,
the water quietly returns to the river
and resumes its steady course toward Lake Superior.

The other half of the river
follows a path of unknown fate.
They call it the Devil's Kettle.
Objects dropped into the Kettle
never surface again.
They do not join the river downstream,
but disappear into the black cauldron, forever.
It swallows,
appearing never to give back.

It seems as if the water resists dropping into the abyss;
it lingers over the Kettle,
folding upon itself.
Some of the water attempts to leap across the rock divide.
It is a pathetic and futile fight.
With persistence,
this half claims its own
to some unknown grave.
I stand before the spectacle.
Tears well in my eyes.

Dropping to the ground,
they seek their own path
to join the river.

I speak aloud to the Lord,
 "I am so lonely.
 I hate living apart from the fullness of your love.
 Yet, I am afraid to relinquish my heart fully.
 You know my struggle:
  I was born a woman.
  You are called 'Father',
  Your 'Son' was a man,
  His 12 disciples were men.
  I have lived the consequence of the world's interpretation of your plan.
  It has impacted my soul.
  I cannot resolve this chasm.
  If I pretend it is not there,
  am I a traitor to what I have learned
  as well as to all those who will not persist?
  Am I a coward?"

I wish to say,
 "'Blessed are the weak in spirit,' for I am very weak.
 Please help me to open the doors of my heart fully.
 The doors are made of steel, heavy steel, and they are closing;
 closing more each day.
 I am pushing against the doors—to allow your love access.
 Your love is a torrent:
  never-ending,
  perfect in design,
  bringing peace and joy."

I ask the Lord,
 "What am I to do?
 I am confused and there is no ready answer.
 I have known your love,
 and I crave home,
 where I come before you—
 shed of the world—
 and say, 'I am here wholly.'"

The river is below me.
Standing at the precipice,
eyes closed,
the stillness of the perfect day enters my soul.

In the quiet, I hear:
    "I have created this river—
    designed it to divide.
    Neither half is bad,
    but both are good—
    perfect in my plan.

    So it is with you.
    My love flows into you
    in never-ending torrents.
    I will always give you overflowing love.
    Half drops into an unknown place,
    but that should not frighten you.
    I have created you and destined you to receive my love in this way.

    A portion of my love flowing into you
    follows a visible path.
    It is comfortable because it is known.
    The remaining flow is understood by me, alone.
    It is not of the devil—it is of my design.
    Because you do not understand it—
    nor do those around you—
    does not make it evil.
    My love is still flowing into you with a force and volume you cannot change.
    Steel doors cannot stop my love.
    I am directing some into a deep and unknown place.
    That is my purpose.
    You must trust me."

In my confusion I say to the Lord,
    "Please understand,
    this feels bad.
    I don't understand what you mean.
    I feel fractured.
    Is this unknown place an aquifer?
    A reservoir of clean water?
    I do not know what you want of me.
    Am I safe from destruction?"

In reply:
    "It is enough for you to know
    your path is not evil.
    Trust me.
    Trust my love.
    I have created you,
    just as I have created this river."

Chapter 13

Boundaries Require Defense

Enough!

Still confused,
but now reassured by God's love,
my fears were abated.
I started to reason my situation aloud,
to hear my thoughts:
    "No matter how hard I work,
    I never work hard enough—my best isn't good enough.
    I cannot solve the corporate problem;
    nothing will ever be good enough or fast enough.
    I am working nights and weekends.
    I have no balance and I am compromising my well-being."

Disgruntled for living my old script again,
I wondered why it was so hard to uphold myself.
As I listened to my thoughts again,
I realized it was the voice inside my head that asserted I was not worthy:
    "You don't deserve to exist.
    You're not good enough."

    Elie Wiesel, a survivor of the holocaust and Nobel Peace Prize winner,
    wrote of this condition:
    "...but there is something even more serious—to realize that I am a
    stranger to myself, which means that there is a stranger in me who wants
    to live my life or my death—or even to die by pushing me to my death
    through self-hate. This stranger forces me to look at things, events, and
    myself with his eyes, urging me to give up because of him." [17]

I will not give up!
It may take years to obliterate these thoughts, but on that day I declared aloud,
    "I am doing my best and working fast enough!
    The corporate slavery model is not for me.
    If I am to stay, I must be given distance and a safe place."

I made an appointment with Dan.
Prior to the meeting, I imagined myself standing before the river gorge
and hearing the voice of God's boundless love.
I asked Dan for accommodation to work half days at home
to tend to my health needs.
I was confident it would not compromise my job responsibilities,
yet I was prepared to leave if his answer was no.
He listened, understood and accepted.
He was gracious.
It astounded me.

PRODIGAL DAUGHTER

Seeking freedom from the destructive voice inside my head
seemed to produce correlative effects.
I started working half days from home and found healing for my physical ailment,
and thanks to the love and perseverance of Bill and a family friend,
the path home to faith graciously emerged from the darkness.

Although I had ignored several invitations from Jason to visit his church,
our friend would not be dissuaded.
He avowed a difference.
"You'll love this church; it's different; it's awesome."
Finally I acquiesced knowing he would not give up.

I was surprised and delighted.
Free of liturgical structure, casual in dress and feel,
it was radical in the belief that the church is not a house of judgment,
but a haven for the lost and transforming.
This church boldly presented the truth of our identity in Christ.
The pastor, minus the constraint of vestments,
freely and perpetually bounded across the stage of the public school's auditorium,
which was where the church gathered to hold its services.
When he was excited, he whirled both arms in huge circles.
If ignited, he jumped up and down, his sneakers squeaking on the floor.
The man had a passion for Christ that was as overwhelming
as his own rate of thought and speech.
He headed fearlessly into topics that revived my heart:

The spiritual equality of women and men; one Christ, one body.[18]

All people are important in the battle to bring light to the darkness.

Living in a spiritual war zone means struggle;
it's important to never give up the fight.

The first moment of grace is often followed by years of transformation,
especially if you come from dysfunction.

Each time you fail, grace extends itself anew—
it never grows weary of your journey.

God's love cannot be concealed by fear.

Darkness cannot overcome us.

And Bill, after months of searching,
finally found an inclusive language New Testament. [19]
The minor changes made all the difference in the world.
I could feel the beat of Christ's heart as I held it close to my chest.
Famished, I dove into it face first.
Like a person in a pie-eating contest,
I was mindless of the mess I made scrawling affirmations in the margins.

Christ became a consuming fire that burned away the wall of lies
that had obstructed my vision and kept me bound:
    I am not a daughter of bondage—
    I am a daughter of freedom.
    Christ has set me free to live in freedom.

I suspected I would return to bondage periodically.
    Freedom is not a destination point—
    it is a journey that allows the traveler
    to glimpse the true nature of our eternal form.

I prayed I would now see the demands of the world in the light of truth.

JUGGLING ACT

I was given a new role in the company.
My responsibilities were expanded to include leadership
of a market development team.
I feared being sucked back into work overload.

Dan, having a voracious appetite for growth,
wanted the team to keep eight areas of exploration
moving forward simultaneously.
It felt a lot like juggling eight balls—
I knew it was inevitable that several would fall.
Yet I understood his logic;
until we knew which would drop out,
it was more time efficient to keep all of them moving forward.

To my amazement, the task was manageable.
I loved teaming,
the challenge of exploring things unknown to me,
and the balance I now had in my life.

I no longer had to interface with the male dominated world of
equipment engineers
or their distributors.
I was free from their perversions.
It was as if a new world had opened up to me.
Because of this new sense of balance,
Bill and I allowed ourselves to dream of notions we had long since set aside.

DREAM HOME

Bill yearned to live in the country,
to honor the memory of summers spent on his aunt and uncle's farm.
He admired the simplicity and honesty of their lives.

I didn't care about memories or farms,
and although I did agree with the notion of simplicity and honesty in living,
I heartily disagreed that tying ourselves to a huge mortgage would give us either.

He surmised, "You have lived so many negative experiences,
you're afraid to dream."

"Maybe. Maybe not."

Nonetheless, one evening I did have a dream about building a house in the
country. The house's foundation was set north of a gravel road in the middle
of a field of tall grass. Large oaks lined the road as it curved around an
adjacent lake.

I decided to humor Bill.
"Honey, if you find the lot of my dreams,
I will consider building a house in the country."

Because Bill is a persistent man,
we spent more than a year of Sunday afternoons
driving country roads in search of my dream.

He found the lot on a bright and beautiful fall day.
We sat in a field to the north of the gravel road.
You could see the lake through the oaks;
their leaves fluttering in the breeze.
The shoreline was a bit compromised by the close cut of the gravel road
as it curved around the lake.

It was a dream-like day.
We took off our jackets and used them as a blanket to mat down
the tall prairie grasses undulating gently in the mid-afternoon warmth.
It was hard not to be in love with the day, the place, and the dream
now shared.

After cuddling on the hilltop for a deliciously relaxing period of time,
we ambled down to the lakefront.
Everything in my heart that longed for good
leapt forward into my consciousness and begged me to believe.
We lingered at the lake's edge.

Due to the angle of the sun in the fall,
the water appeared to be a deeper, darker blue.
In contrast to the lake's depth of color,
the sun's rays were scattered brilliantly
with the sharp clarity of cut diamonds across the water's surface.
The reflected sun was blindingly beautiful.
Sharp as a razor's edge,
the rays forced me to shield my eyes from their piercing brilliance.
The look of diamonds on the water always rejuvenates my soul.

At the end of the day,
as we got back into the car to drive home,
I agreed with Bill that it would be a beautiful place to build a home.
But, unlike Bill, I was nervous:
> "What happens if my job goes sour again?
> I am not in the mood to sell my soul for a new house—
> no matter how beautiful the setting."

Bill questioned, "Why do you have such a hard time envisioning the future
and believing good things could happen to us?
Aren't things going better at work now?" he asked.
"What makes you think things will change for the worse?"

"I'm not sure they will.
I'm not sure they won't," I countered.
"I just don't want to wake up one morning, feeling imprisoned
because we have a mortgage payment to make."

There was silence.

"Do you understand what I am saying?" I insisted.
He assured me he did.

Then he reminded me of the dream I had more than a year ago.
In the dream we were building a home
in a field of grass,
up the hill from a gravel road
that curved gently around a lake.

As winter approached, we settled into the idea of building our dream home.
We decided to design it and do much of the work ourselves.
Bill would contract out the big jobs.

Vibes

During the Christmas holiday I received a letter from Dan
stating that he had hired a man to start as director of operations,
and assuming he showed himself competent,
he would quickly be promoted to take over the role of president.
Dan hoped my skills would be fully utilized by his replacement,
and that together, we would build a strong and rapidly growing
company in his absence.

We were introduced to John, the newly hired director of operations,
during a marketing staff meeting held in the big conference room.
I sat with my back to the wall of patent plaques,
a treasury of the inventive intelligence of the all male engineering staff.
At the far end of the room Dan,
effused with pride and confidence,
stood alongside the man he hoped recognized his accomplishments,
and understood the personal impact of this handoff.
Side by side they stood,
Dan and John,
two elderly icons,
stanchions at the gate of commerce.
I had developed an appreciation for Dan
and couldn't help but think this passage must have been incredibly difficult.

After saying a few words,
John sat down at the table.
I studied him as the meeting continued.
His movements were slow, calculated, almost soft.
With rounded shoulders and benign hand gestures,
his hawkish nose alone severely accentuated his otherwise placid presentation.
He wore a consistently detached expression that betrayed no emotion.
His dispassionate demeanor alarmed me;
how could he possibly run the company with the same fervor as Dan?

Midpoint in the meeting,
we locked in on each other's gaze.
It was momentary, probably not noticeable to John,
yet eternally revealing for me.
Spontaneously, a shudder went through my body
and my guts twisted.
It was as if he had been silently communicating in an unknown wavelength
that was amplified within my consciousness.

SUSPICIONS

I wanted to check my intuition.
Why did I respond with such apprehension?

It appeared John and I had something in common,
a previous place of employment.
I left Goliath because of harassment and discrimination.
He left with a sizeable early retirement package.

Females who knew him offered me feedback.
One said John was an excellent mentor.
All others said he had an aversion to strong women,
to the extent that he tried desperately to get rid of them.
A distinction was made;
he only mentored women who posed no threat to his power or control.

I decided on a preemptive approach
and scheduled an introductory meeting with him.
If we were to begin our working relationship free of suspicions,
a forthright discussion seemed appropriate.

His only comment concerned my accommodation to work half days at home:
"Why is there no paperwork in your file?
There is no doctor's recommendation."

"Dan accepted my request without requiring one," I remarked casually.
He felt differently, "I want a written recommendation from your doctor."
Assuring him that would not be a problem,
I returned two days later with a document
written and signed by my doctor.

TEAM DYNAMICS

John announced that he would be reorganizing the company.
I suspected the team would be kept together,
and I would continue as leader since a change in leadership
always induces a temporary slowing of progress.
The team had finally reached the performing stage of functioning
and was coming closer to the vision Dan had long held for the company.
Everyone understood their role on the team and executed tasks on time.
This did not come without its challenges.

Dick with the tick,
who had twice previously conspired to cast doubt on my competency,
was assigned to the team by Dan,
who didn't want to tell him he required direction;
reigning in, so to speak.
Unknown to Dick,
Dan gave me the role of reign-master and cautioned me,
"Dick has been with the company a long time
and believes he is running the show.
I expect you will be able to work around this.
You're a woman—women are skilled at that kind of stuff."

Any expert in organizational dynamics would say this was a setup for failure.
I knew that and expressed my concern.
My concern was not heard.

Nonetheless, several months later, we seemed to be doing splendidly.
Too splendidly, I discovered during a luncheon meeting that Dick requested.

My teammate quickly got to the reason for inviting me to lunch.
While his face turned the color of a ripe tomato,
he forged ahead, "Would you consider having an affair with me?" [20]

My stomach flipped and then sank.
Where in the world did this come from?
Why would someone just blurt that out?

    I asserted, "I'm married."

    "That's okay," he responded.

Monitoring the quality of my voice,
I stated what was obvious to me,
yet...it evidently escaped him.
    "I love my husband very much and an affair is out of the question."

    "Are you sure?" he asked.

    What a repugnant line of questions!

    "Yes, I am positive."

Not one to give up easily,
Dick came back at it from several different directions.
He applied tactics he must have learned in Sales 101 on handling objections.

I certainly objected!

    "No. Not now. Not anytime in the future. NO."

I remained calm and decisive.
Experience taught me that if someone were to be harmed by this interaction,
it would be me.

I asked him to put this behind and
not let it interfere with our work on the team.

He agreed it would not affect our teaming together.

BANDAGING THE WOUND

It wasn't long
until I was trying to bandage the wound.

The love-smitten team member
became very difficult to deal with.
He was now demanding,
belligerent,
argumentative,
combative,
defensive,
irascible,
and generally a difficult person to work alongside.

He sought to heal his wounds
by talking disparagingly about me to team members.

Our performing team was in chaos.

Due to the nature of things,
I felt it best to call in an outside facilitator.
I discussed it with John who had now become the "acting president."
He recommended a woman facilitator he had worked with previously.
I met with the facilitator first.
John spoke with her independently and also informed Dan of our plan.

Because the facilitator was aware of the igniting incident,
and the complete reversal in team dynamics pursuant to the incident,
I had expected she would approach the issue outside of the team
in a one-on-one meeting with Dick.

She chose to deal with it inside the team.

Much to my chagrin,
she pulled out her whole bag of teaming tricks
and we went through them together—the entire team.
We took personality profiles,
and surveyed each other's strengths and weaknesses.

My spurned teammate scored me off the charts on the negative scale.

It seemed unfair that team members had no idea what created the shift—
I had not spoken of the incident to any of the team members.

Everything the facilitator did led to nothing.
Eventually, she was forced to deal with the incident outside of the team;
actually, inside John's office.
The four of us sat in a circle facing each other on his executive appointed furniture.
John pretended not to know
while the facilitator led Dick down the road to confession.

I sat silently in my discomfort and became increasingly angry.

I have learned when I become angry,
and there are no appropriate ways immediately available to relieve the anger,
I cry.

So I cried.

Dick admitted to his behavior and was told by John,
"You can see the effect that your behavior has had on Debra and the team.
Your behavior could be considered sexual harassment.
We have zero tolerance for that in this company.
Do you understand?"

Dick understood.

I wondered why this meeting was not held at the beginning
instead of dragging me and the entire team through the mud?
After the meeting I expressed my frustration to the facilitator.
She patted my arm
and told me as a woman she understood my frustration—
"It's a male world," she confided.

There are no words to describe how I felt.

THE ANNOUNCEMENT

John was officially promoted to president,
and like a proud turkey that had spread its plumage,
he strutted about acting twice his size.

The week the reorganization was to be announced,
the business managers were individually trotted into John's office
and given notice of our new roles.

With his presidential-sized desk between us,
I sat and listened.
In a cryptic message,
John told me he was stripping me of my previous responsibility and authority.

Deposed from my team leadership position,
all direct reports were removed.
I was assigned to work on one product only;
to be clear, it wasn't one product line, it was only one product.

I asked John to explain his reasoning:
    Had my performance been inadequate?
    Were there concerns with my leadership?
Again, I was given an encrypted message,
a message encoded to say nothing,
especially nothing politically dangerous.
(Large corporations are the training ground for such communication,
generally employed to avoid lawsuits.)

I called Dan, who now confined his role to CEO,
and asked if he approved the decision.
He explained,
"Before John would accept the position, I had to agree to let him run the show
and not interfere with his decisions."

In the end,
I had no idea why my leadership role was taken from me.
There was no shared reason, only an expectation of compliance.

Reason is a beautiful thing.
When communicated, it helps thinking people
understand and cooperate for change.
In its absence we are little more than barnyard animals.

PLAYING THE ROLE

John had definitely established himself as the dominant cock in the yard.
I was now a bald fledgling
stripped of all my feathers.

Faced with my diminished role, I decided to make the best of it.
With only one product, for one application,
it wasn't hard to focus.

This new product took the company in an entirely different direction.
I was proud because for the first time in the company's history,
I was able to do what had never been done.
I successfully "sold" the one product I was given
by convincing an entire market chain to buy.
It took a great deal of strategic thinking and excellent communications.

Therefore, when John reviewed my performance a year later,
I was taken aback by his assessment.
He thought my performance was poor and my communications skills
needed improvement.

I felt plucked, again.

Fired Up!

On the first day of the sales meeting
John went over the numbers.
The company was not hitting target
and he was mad.
Although his face remained expressionless,
his words shredded everyone in the room.
He reserved special words for Matt and me;
we were the only two who worked isolated in new market development.
Before the entire group,
John described us as incapable, incompetent
and, bottom line, worthless.

Matt shrugged it off saying
it was the kick-butt kind of coaching he had grown up with in sports.
I found it to be reprehensible "coaching."

We were all to reconvene the following day.
That night I worked feverishly on my presentation.
When I got up to present,
I was fired up!

With my mental and emotional fortressing in place,
I listed all of my program's indisputable accomplishments,
and displayed letters of recognition for my work from customers and suppliers.
I reviewed the method used to project the numbers and answered all questions.
I presented an honest assessment of the program's progress,
its guiding strategies,
completed tactics,
tactics remaining,
things outside of our control,
things we could impact.
And, I told them,
"I have no crystal ball to discern when this market will take off.
I can only share the indicators that say it will.
You assess them for yourself.

It is an entirely reasonable decision to drop this program now
and invest in something with an immediate return.
That, however, is not my decision to make.
What I can say is this;
right now we are perfectly positioned to take advantage
of the market if it moves.
So for as long as the program exists,
you have a choice to participate, or not.
I personally hope you choose to support the program."
When I had finished
there was a line of salesmen who wanted to sign up.

John had been put into a position
where he could do nothing
other than acknowledge my accomplishments,
which he did publicly in front of the group.

I packed up my materials at the end of the day and walked to my car alone.
Before starting the car,
I thanked God that I was still working half days at home
where I could temporarily escape the onslaught.

A Patient's Rights

When I answered the phone
I definitely was not expecting to hear my doctor's voice.
I had not seen him in months,
so why would he be calling?

"Hey, kiddo, how 'ya doing?" he said with his customary casualness.

"I'm doin' fine, but I have to admit I am surprised it's you on the line."

"Yeah, well that makes sense.
I was surprised to get a call from some guy who says he's the president of the
company where you work.
Some guy…let me see…what's his name?"
he said, fumbling for the paper on which the name was written.

I offered John's name and the name of the company.

"Yup, that's him.
What's the deal with that guy?
He wanted to know if I had really written the note recommending flexibility.
Did he tell you he was going to call me?" my doctor asked.

"No, he has not said a word to me."

"Is he some kind of creep?
Doesn't he know he has to have a signed release from you to get
that information?
The least he could do is talk to you."

"Well, that would be nice, but…"

"I told him nothing," my doctor scoffed.
"If he wants that information, he'll have to go through you to get it.
I won't divulge patient information—that's between you and me and
nobody else.
It is unethical for him to suggest I should."

I appreciated the "family doctor" style of medicine he practiced.

"How's it going otherwise?" he asked.

"Well, if you want my honest answer,
I think work is a toxic activity that no one should be forced to do."

He chortled.

MISTRUST

I wanted to discuss my doctor's call with my new boss, Karl,
so I scheduled time on his calendar.

I asked him if he knew anything about the call.

He did.

"What are the issues here?" I inquired.

(What I appreciated most about my new boss
is that he didn't play the political game of speaking in cryptic messages—
he just spoke.)

"John doesn't trust you.
He thinks you're home doing other things.
He doesn't believe you need the flexibility to work at home half days.
He also thinks you've been loafing for two to three months."

I informed Karl of my doctor's position on ethical behavior,
and added,
"If there is an issue of trust,
I think it needs to be dealt with now.
What do you propose is the best way to address it?"

He had no viable solutions.

To clarify, I told Karl that if I were not allowed to work half days at home,
I would have no choice other than to leave the company.

He understood he was a man stuck in the middle of a difficult situation.

LOVE IS A DECISION

The next day I had to travel to the west coast to visit an equipment manufacturer.
While on the plane, I ran all the scenarios and options through my mind.
Most of them meant losing our new dream home.
I could see my family's faces when I confessed to them I just couldn't do it anymore.
I made a commitment not to lose my soul for a home, and now look at me.
Why was it so difficult to assert my own needs regardless of their response?
Why, if they loved me, did they not actively encourage me to leave my job?

I felt I had no choice other than to leave the company.
But the idea of leaving all I had gained to start over—
again—
exhausted me.

How often would I be forced to give up and leave unconscionable situations?
I just couldn't tolerate the injustice.

I had built wonderful relationships with my customers and suppliers in the market.
So much was in place for success.
If I left, it would be as much the company's loss as mine.
It didn't make sense.

My mind kept playing old tapes—
all the hurt, disappointment and futility.

That night, I called my mother from the hotel to check on her health.
We had a distant relationship since I started expressing my needs and wants,
yet I felt a responsibility toward her.

She was surprised I was calling from California.

After 30 minutes of a nonstop monologue about herself, which was the norm,
I interrupted to say it would feel good if she asked about me,
or the kids, or Bill.
I inquired if she had any interest in knowing how we were.
One remark led successively to the next until she admitted to herself and to me:
"Okay…I don't love you.
I have never loved you.
I don't know how to love—
I never learned."

Whoa, the sting of the slap hurt.
I had always suspected she felt no love for me,
but knowing it was another thing.

Chapter 14

BREAKING FREE

Status Check

It was time to regroup and count the losses and gains.
Evidently my subconscious knew that as well
because that night I had a dream,
a dream that the minister would say was very revealing.

In the dream I stumbled into each of the darkened rooms of my mind.
I found no answers, purpose, or reason for my life.
Deep within the shadows everything seemed like the same shade of abstraction.
Fumbling, I found a knob to open the door to a library.
As I stood on the threshold, an insatiable hunger, a craving to learn came over me,
but the bookshelves were empty.
Feeling blindly the length and depth of every shelf,
panic and desperation filled me.
The only thing disturbed on each shelf was a thick layer of dust
that bellowed up into menacing clouds of allergen-emboldened monsters.
Choking, gasping, sneezing, I was forced to retreat from the library.

The swimming pool made with colorful mosaic tiles was empty.
Its cracked bottom and sides were lined with a film of gray sludge;
bio-remains, like dried milk film on an empty glass.

There were no pretty dresses hanging in the closet.

The grass out front was overgrown.

The refrigerator empty.

With the drapes pulled shut,
the sunrise of each new day did not fill the gloomy corners of the rooms.

The furnace was not working and the lights were out.

An alarm system installed a few years back was the only thing working.
In my dream, I lamented,
"Wouldn't it figure? Now that there is nothing in the house worth stealing,
the alarm system is the only thing that works!"

The house still stood, simply because it was built too strong to fall.
Oddly, there was a sweet aroma wafting through the house,
visible like a vapor cloud drawn in cartoons to tickle the nose and entice.

If the minister was right about the psychological meaning of homes in
our dreams,
I had become empty.

CRIES OF WOMEN

It seemed that darkness followed me wherever I went.
I had no belief that things would ever be different.
My gut was telling me John would wreak havoc in my life.

I had learned that when feelings of dread crawl up my pant legs like cockroaches,
it is time to be alone with God.

Feeling tired, lonely and scared,
I wanted to hide from the world,
pull the blanket over my head,
and tell everyone to go away.

I searched to find safe harbor in the Lord's presence
and started by explaining my distractions aloud:
"I am tired of being strong.
Tired of others telling me I am strong.
Tired of the expectation that I should be strong.
Tired of providing at the cost of my soul.
I want to quit."

I asked:
"Can't somebody take care of me for a change?"

I pleaded:
"I am wasted,
exhausted.
The dogs of hell are at my feet.
I'm scared.
Can't I come home?
I want to come home.

I want you to care,
and it feels like you don't.

Look, a lot of people are stupid,
and you rescue them.

I feel like I am talking to myself here."

I stopped to listen.
The hearing is not of words.
The response comes like energy,
a signal.
I quiet further and listen for the Holy Spirit.

I am aware the words my brain uses are entirely inadequate
and cannot grasp the fullness of the message.
Nonetheless, the message is not dependent on words.

It was conveyed that I must be strong.

I repeated:
"I am exceedingly weary of being strong."

You must be strong and this is why:
Immediately within my spirit
I heard the sound of hundreds of women crying.
All the cries were different, each layered on top of each other.
They were women, not men.

I raised my hands to cover my ears:
"Please, I don't want to hear this.
I am telling you I can't.
I have nothing to give.
I am a wasted human being.
Dried up.
Dust.
Empty."

Again, there is silence.
I couldn't hear the voices crying any longer,
but I remembered them.

I wanted to cry.

"You know I can't just ignore this.
Can't we reach a compromise?

Can I be taken care of for a while?
I need rest.
I don't have the strength.
I can't find it.
I need shelter for a while."

I listened.

I was aware the Holy Spirit conferred with another entity—
a moment passed while my request was considered.

My request was granted;
I would be given rest, time and space to heal.

The communication wasn't in the form of a demand,
just a shared understanding.
The choice was mine to make.

"When will I know who these women are?
What am I supposed to do about it?
There are a lot of women who cry for all kinds of reasons.
Are you sure I am not psychotic?
Maybe those voices are just my cries for help."

STAND UP AND WALK

Months went by while I wrestled with uncertainty.
Feelings of inadequacy stymied my ability to see my way out.

Trying to free my mind of restraints,
I let my gaze wander past the living room window,
beyond the trees lining the road,
all the way to the edge of the perfectly blue sky.
I wanted to see into eternity if I could,
where I was sure all things would finally become clear.
I asked the Lord, "What's wrong with me?
Why do I keep getting myself into these situations
and then stay feeling discounted?
I'm fed up with other people's definitions,
their judgments and imposed limitations.
Life beats me down.
I try, but never quite succeed in claiming my place.

Help me—I know I own part of this. What is it I should do?"

I used my Bible as a field manual, keeping notes in the margins.
Sitting in the middle of a sunlit square on the carpet,
I prayed for guidance and picked it up.
I read and perceived what I had previously not been able to see.
The words were once spoken to a lame man, who try as he might, never
succeeded in walking. Then one day, he was challenged to have faith.

Here was the challenge given me:
    "You have to overcome this inertia.
    You've been sitting in that spot for too long.
    Show an input of energy—stand up!
    You must stop abiding in your fear.

    Don't assume you'll be leaving the memory of that grubby mess you've
    been lying on;
    it will go with you.
    It will remind you of the past,
    of lessons not fully learned.
    But that can be a good thing—
    You'll see my grace when you look back.

    Now, you must get your faith moving.
    Claim the victory—
    it will give you confidence.
    And always remember,
    where you go,
    my love goes also."

IMAGINING THE FUTURE

It was too easy to get lost in the demands of the world,
to forget everything I had learned.

Resisting the onslaught required constant vigilance.
It was amazing that what I did not learn as a child
had created an enormous vulnerability in me.
I could see it as if standing outside of myself,
yet day-to-day I lived without awareness,
often finding myself surprised.

It was easy to understand
I should stand up and walk—
I should get out of there.
But where would I go?
Was there a mystical place where things are different?

I wondered if faith could birth the reality I craved
a situation so sublime only a miracle could cause its existence.
The fantasy appeared as a mirage.

I confronted my disbelief in context to the challenge I was given:
    The lame man could only dream of walking,
        yet faith made the lame man walk.

I asked the Lord what I should do about the burden of financial responsibility
I had to my family.
The same principle applied;
    I could stay in fear,
        or walk in faith.
        It was my choice.

I took my first step by surrendering my family's fears and needs to God.
Then I set my mind on identifying a win/win scenario
for both myself and my employer.
If they were to buy in and financially support my transition,
they would have to gain something.

I formulated the logic that supported the creation of my new company,
and made a luncheon appointment to test the concept on a key salesman.
He cautioned,
"Your business rationale is sound and the benefit to both parties is obvious,
but John's decision won't be based on sound business judgment,
or on overcoming rational objections.
It'll probably be based on hidden issues that won't be revealed to you."
I probed, "Why do you say that?"
He shrugged his shoulders and didn't elaborate.

Next, I phoned Dan.
He was enthusiastic and boldly asserted,
"If John doesn't support your business idea,
I'll personally start a separate company to champion your efforts."

My confidence was buoyed.

Now it was time to take the idea to Karl.
To him, it appeared I had achieved a win/win scenario.
"Write up the proposal and I'll take it to John.
I'll personally communicate my support," he said confidently,
nodding his head in agreement.

THE GENERAL'S ARMY

I wrote the proposal and gave it to Karl by the close of the week.
I copied Dan, the owner,
and waited...
waited to hear how John would receive the idea.

It didn't take long.
The answer was an unequivocal "NO."
A "NO" with no discussion necessary.

I appealed to Karl to try again.

Each time Karl came back more frustrated.
He confided,
"I have never experienced this kind of difficulty with John.
Usually we think the same,
or I can get him to go along with me.
Somehow this is different."

I continued to badger Karl
because I wanted to know how John would respond to a certain line of reasoning.

"He won't respond to my straight line logic," Karl lamented.
"He keeps circling around,
diverting the discussion,
never stating his concern.
As it relates to your proposal,
his behavior is irrational.
It's the only thing he is irrational about."

I implored Karl to try once more.
"Deb, I'm really feeling trapped in the middle.
John won't be rational on this and it is going nowhere.
From now on, I suggest you go directly to him yourself.
I am going to stay out of it."

I stood up to leave his office.
As I grabbed the handle of the door,
he added,
"If it were up to me, I'd just say yes and get moving."
His tone was conciliatory,
yet defeated.

That evening, I phoned Dan and updated him on the struggle;
John's supposed irrational and intransigent position,
and Karl's inability to discern the cause or issues involved.
I asked Dan, "How do you interpret John's rigidity?"

"He is probably having difficulty because generals
are not accustomed to privates arguing back."

I asked his advice for the meeting.

He suggested, "He doesn't like emotions.
See if you can get him to disclose his feelings."

Right...
simple, a general confiding feelings with a seditious private.
Will it work?
Not a chance!

Still, it was my battle to win,
or lose.

END OF DISCUSSION

The meeting was held in John's office,
which immediately took me out of neutral territory
and gave the comfort advantage to him.

This wasn't looking good.

Although I wished to repudiate his evaluation,
I felt maimed and crippled.
I tried to pick my mutilated self-concept off the floor,
but it resisted and laid lame in a puddle.

John's posture was defined by harsh restraint.
His hands, folded over each other,
were resting imperturbably atop my proposal.

I sat across from him at the conference table
and placed my hands in my lap
where he would not see them shake.

I had come to recognize his various methods of control.
Facial expression,
or more precisely,
lack of expression,
was paramount to control.
After all, any slip of expression could be interpreted wrongly.
He had confided to another that he prided himself
on the equanimity of his temper,
the discipline of his emotions,
his habitual self-possession in the face of excitement.
Today, he had everything under control,
foremost, his facial muscles.

He began by acknowledging he had read my proposal
and since he had already clearly communicated his position through Karl,
he expected the meeting would be short.

Wasting no time, I quickly began by stating,
"Yes, I was told of your position.
As president of the company,
I acknowledge that you are the captain of this ship

and your authority rules.
I accept that you are in the position to say "No" to my proposal.

It would, however, help me if I understood your objections.
Perhaps there are ways to overcome your concerns.
I don't desire to take an intractable position,
but rather, I'd like to learn."

He began to shake his head in disagreement,
so I decided to launch into the logic and benefits of the proposal.
He remained silent,
neither agreeing nor disagreeing.

His hands still lay inanimately atop my proposal.

I then led the discussion through what I understood to be his objections.
His face turned stone and developed a greater degree of severity.
I went through the list of objections,
all of which could be overcome.
I stated that his last objection was open to speculation.
He flushed as he said,
"If I let you do this, then all the marketers will want to start their own businesses."
I listed each marketer and the reasons why each would not take such a risk.
My assessment was accurate.
He knew I had evaluated correctly, but it was an issue of perceived control.
His jaw set.

He would not be dissuaded.

I would not concede—
this was my last opportunity for honesty.
I would take the advice of Dan and fight on the battleground of emotion.
I stated what had brought me to this point:
> Continued harassment had
> created a hostile work environment
> that exasperated my medical condition,
> which required me to request flexibility.
> After which, my responsibilities were drastically cut
> even though no evidence was given of my inadequacy.
> I have since been demeaned, mistrusted, maligned and castigated.

Given this disagreeable state of affairs,
I believe it is reasonable to find a mutually productive solution.

He disagreed.
He and the company had no responsibility to remedy my perceived issues.
My choices were two:
Go back to my cube and do my job,
or quit.
He would not approve a severance package.

I had obviously pushed the boundaries.
While his face seemed to convulse and contort in an attempt to remain impassive,
his hand moved off my proposal in a gesture toward the door.

I, in return, attempted to mirror back his same callous countenance
and announced my decision to leave the company;
I would turn in my resignation effective immediately.

This caught him by surprise.
Like my first husband, he, I believe, assumed I would not fight—
I would not leave.

If I left immediately, it would be difficult to manage
the adverse effects on morale.
This created some vulnerability on his part.

He requested I stay two weeks to allow for morale adjustments
and then suggested,
"Karl can decide to hire you on a consulting basis
once you have a legitimate business.
That is his decision."

In response, I offered,
"Regardless, I want you to know I will continue to support the program
and work to assure the product's success in the market."

He led me to his office door,
shutting it behind me.
I am sure he wanted to punch a hole in the wall.

HARDBALL

Karl still approached things with the same degree of honesty.
"Sorry, Deb, there is no reasoning with him.
There will be no negotiating.
I have also been instructed to monitor you more closely
because he doesn't trust you."
Evidently the intensity of his hatred had grown
because now John claimed I was committing "seditious treason!"

The candor of Karl's response amazed me.
"I really shouldn't be this honest with you.
John and the management team directed me to play hardball.
There will be no severance package.
If you're out, you're out.
The role of management is not to be honest or compromising.
I am to force your hand.
Play hard—play to win.
I am not supposed to let you know that I'm willing to move on severance.
I have to tell you, realistically, it will be very hard to get two months,
and don't tell John that I shared this with you."

When I asked how they would fill my spot,
Karl felt the pain personally.
"John instructed me to pick up responsibility for your program."

"Are you telling me they really believe all the relationships
I have established will not be compromised?"

"Yes, John believes anyone can step in and nothing will be lost.
The hard part for me is that I do not have time to take over your program.
In truth, it will just sit idle."

In my mind that demonstrated John's arrogance.
Regardless, they were pushing me out
and they wanted to make it perfectly clear.

It seemed too much like subjugated servitude
to go back to my cube,
with my mouth shut,
while being closely watched,
all for some crime that I never committed.

It was not just!

SOVEREIGNTY

The president lurked within the shadow of his lofty title
spitting venom to destroy me.
He considered me unworthy.
From his mouth he spewed poison.
His intent was to destroy my honor.
His declaration:
>She is an untrustworthy liar,
>inferior in her knowledge
>and she has accomplished nothing.

His edict:
>Go back to your cube
>under close supervision,
>or leave.

His announcement:
>I will tolerate no more of her insurrection.

He exclaimed it was his destiny to win:
>Others have said I must be destroyed if he is to win.
>There is no possibility of a win/win scenario.
>It is a zero-sum game;
>I must lose and he must win.

I visualize him enthroned in his executive chair.
His tongue is a sword intent on maiming.

He is only one of a legion who seek their power at the expense of others.
I would be forced to start over yet again.
I was fatigued from starting over.

I know the evil that causes such destruction.
I can see evil's abhorrent face.
I know its putrid odor.
The sound of its slither is discernible to me.

I was repulsed and proclaimed:
"I have only one God,
and you're not it!
I will not genuflect before your throne.
My destiny is not in your hands."

Standing Tall

A mere nine months earlier,
Karl had stated his desire to resurrect my reputation.
Since I had been treated unfairly
he had wanted to make me a hero.
It would be his mission to bring gender equity and fairness to the company.

He failed.

It didn't matter.
I was standing tall now!
August 14, 1998, was a beautifully clear and breezy day.
As we bounded the stairs to the government building in St. Paul,
Bill and I radiated the confidence of my new beginning.
In line with four other would-be entrepreneurs,
we paid the fee to expedite the registration of my company.
It was official.
I was a member of the growing rank of women entrepreneurs. [21]
It felt delightful!
Of course, my client list was short—none, to be precise—
but there was no turning back;
only forward movement defined by faith.

We grabbed a quick sandwich at the McDonald's by the state capitol,
kissed each other good-bye in the parking lot,
and headed to our respective jobs.

I went straight into Karl's office,
handed him my letter of resignation and explained my reason for leaving.
I had my own business to grow.
I showed him the documentation of my company's existence.

My sudden departure under strained circumstances
would have an effect on morale.
I countered that morale wasn't my problem.
If they wanted my participation in anarchy abatement,
they would have to pay for it.

He struck a deal independent of the opinion of others in management;
a two week notice of departure in exchange for two months of
consulting contract.
It wasn't much, but I took it.

Two and a half years after first asking the Lord for my deliverance,
I was delivered.
The joy was a sweet taste in my mouth.

It's a Jungle out There

During my two-month contract period,
I committed myself to upholding the company and its products.
The output of my efforts, if done with integrity and honor,
would give testimony to the truth of my deliverance.

I was informed my short contract period would
be used to find my replacement,
whom I would train.
The handoff would be made and I was forewarned to exit quietly,
without disturbance.

From what I could piece together,
Dan was not being told the truth;
that efforts were being redirected away from his passion,
the food service program.
In their game of management subterfuge,
the program was gradually slipping away:
    market research reports were missing,
    people reassigned,
    dollars reallocated,
    priorities secretly shifted,
    time lost.

One evening when Dan called
I expressed my concerns for the program.

He investigated.
Over the loud objection of John,
he immediately intervened in the business to reestablish priorities.

This greatly disturbed John.

Karl was angry with me and fumed:
"The president and his staff are competent professionals.
We are being paid to run the business and set priorities.

We take prioritization seriously,
and we should be setting them without interference from Dan."

I couldn't criticize their position.
But they should have clearly communicated their intent,
rather than conceal it from him.
That was fool's play.

Dan expressed his severe disappointment to John,
who passed it downstream to Karl.

In a closed-door meeting alone with me,
Karl, now tense and defensive, argued:
    "I was schooled to follow the chain of command.
    You don't step outside the chain of command—I do as I am told.
    I am a good German soldier.
    I trust the president implicitly.
    I would give up my job before I would compromise that trust relationship.
    That is the way corporations work, you do as you are told."
    (I couldn't help but think good Nazi soldiers did as they were told.)

Funny thing,
John didn't appear to have a problem letting Karl go sometime later
"to pursue other interests."

Time's Up

My two months were up.
Management was walking a bit more tender of foot due to the discovery of
conflicting priorities.

Dan's original assertion to start a separate business
to champion my efforts vanished in the craziness.

The burden was on me to define a contract that was acceptable to John,
who, I might add,
would rather have seen me court-martialed.
The message management was sending was clear:
    I added no value.
    I was dangerous.
    They wanted nothing to do with me.

However, Dan still wanted me around.

I became very creative in putting forth options.
If they were not willing to invest in food service,
I was willing to take the whole thing on the outside.
I even found another cooperative company willing to make the investment
and proposed a final solution.

That was too much!
I was out of control and needed to be brought back under control.
(Control seems to be the first objective of business.)

I was called in for a meeting.

Karl feigned that he had now seen the light,
and finally understood how we could leverage
the company's investment in food service.
It was a moment of sharp clarity for him.
He offered to hire me back as a full-time marketer.

It was insanity of a sort.

I declined his offer.

He looked perturbed.

The Ruler of this World

No doubt about it,
I had become a bitter pill to swallow.
They didn't know what to do with me.

To limit my ability to do harm,
they begrudgingly allowed me to continue my pursuit of
two potential customers, Heinz and McDonald's.
I was to focus my attention on one product in the condiment market only.
There would be no discussion of a comprehensive food service offering.
The contract they signed was miniscule, but it gave me exposure and time.

I had developed a rapport with McDonald's,
and in a manner described by them as "unprecedented,"
had inserted myself within their system and supplier network.
After a great deal of work and applied strategic thinking,
the product was finally approved by McDonald's.

It was a triumphant moment!
Never before in the company's history had something like that been done.
Although the sale of just one product
wouldn't contribute appreciable to sales volume,
it was a notable inroad into food service,
and was therefore amazing to many.
The accomplishment, however, was discounted and ignored by management,
who rewarded my success
by establishing a new order prohibiting my future entrance into the company.
The receptionist was given the task of informing me.
"Sorry, Deb. I am not supposed to let you go past the lobby desk.
You'll have to wait here. New rule from John. What can I say? The guy is weird."

My gut wrenched.

This use of power and authority caused me great angst.

I prayed for enlightenment.

In the book of Matthew it is written that those who abuse power,
do not practice justice, mercy and faith;
rather, they lock people out with their judgment.

FREE-FALL

My miniscule consulting contract was not enough
to cover my portion of the bills.
We were $30,000 in debt
and there was no end in sight.
I had scrambled and re-scrambled my brain trying to find the promised land.
Still, it eluded me.
Maybe there was no justice.
I had stepped out in faith,
but I couldn't go on like this.
We financially couldn't go on like this.

I needed guidance.

I went again to the North Shore,
hiked into the Devil's Kettle,
sat quietly,
and allowed my mind to drift.

I felt as if my life was going over the falls.
Just like the river before the falls,
I had meandered a flat course
never suspecting that just ahead my soul and mind would split in two.
Simultaneously both halves were in free-fall.
One half was pursuing the freedom and independence my soul and body craved.
The other half was dropping into the abyss of how to pay the bills.
I was fractured, split in two, just like the river.
And, like the river, I was lunging bravely forward to an uncertain tomorrow.
There was no turning back.

Funny, my life seemed exactly as it should be;
each facet pursuing its own tomorrow,
each uncertain,
yet determined.

For some unexplainable reason, the direction I was taking felt right.

I had come back to experience something,
although I was not certain what;
    the visual drama,
    urgency,
    the commanding certainty of the flow of things.
There were no alternatives but to follow my decision
and hold on for the ride.

I didn't know what the future held.
I didn't care because I had gained back my assurance.
There is a plan,
and I was part of it.

All things are tested in love.

I knew that I was not alone because God was with me.

I would claim my victory when others expected me to fail,
hide,
or cower.
I had the freedom to choose the power of an eternal God
over the intimidation of man.

I chose God.

Let Go

I had a visceral sense of path and purpose,
but something still lingered.
I wasn't being totally honest.
It was time to confront my feelings with God,
to talk of the fear and anger that bolstered my reluctance to trust fully.

I had never known God's presence to be anything other than loving,
yet here I was, at a fork in the road
and I doubted that my God really loved women equally.

Closing the door to my office,
I asked my family to respect my need for quiet time.
I felt a strange sense of tranquility come over me
as I settled into my chair by the window.
Immediately I was freed from struggle.
That evening I went through every passage that grieved my heart.
In the midst of my struggles and tears my spirit found peace.
I learned to trust fully that women and men are spiritually equal.
I was taught that the battle is not between the sexes,
but against the power of darkness.
Inequality exists to the extent that the culture supports evil's malicious intent.

I felt exhilarated,
yet uncertainty still remained.
Why was my faith walk seemingly leading nowhere?

I petitioned the Lord,
"I stepped out in faith believing there was a promised land.
Surely you would not bring me this far for nothing.
What am I to do?
We can't go on like this financially."

I was told to let go of my concerns for my business.
>My company belonged to God.
>I was now delivered from evil,
>and brought under the authority of God.
>I would walk before the Eternal in the land of the living—
>a place where people would not rob me of worth;
>rather, we would uphold each other in truth.

I asked,
>"How am I to participate with the grace shown me?"

It was revealed,
I had to let go of my anger.
In peace, I was to pray for those who had harmed me.

Salvation came to me anew that night.
I could hear the voice of wisdom and healing, of wholeness and life.
A voice so peaceful and loving it defied description.
Unlike anything on earth, it is recognizable by its tranquility.
>It is constant as if to measure eternity upon it.
>Soft and gentle as a breeze.
>Love without earthly context.

I gazed out the window at the profusion of stars
as they bloomed brightly against the deep navy of the night sky,
and thanked God for my deliverance.

A Time for Every Purpose

Companies the size of H.J. Heinz are hard to penetrate.
Their marketers, overloaded and continually in meetings,
are seldom at their desks to answer the phone.
If you're not on their priority list,
they probably won't respond to your voicemail message.
I had made repeated failed attempts over the past six months
to reach a particular marketer at Heinz.
I was informed a new woman had moved into that position;
perhaps my chances would be better now.

Reaching her would be pivotal to my family's financial future,
yet I had no desire to participate in the endless striving of my past.
Now, I was aware of an alternative reality—
a place of incomparable beauty where I was promised rest—
where my labor would not be in vain.
My heart's desire was to remain focused on the promised land.

I paused before I picked up the phone to call Heinz,
allowing my mind space and time to find God's peace.
As I dialed the phone,
a sense of calm filled me and I drifted euphorically listening to it ring
once,
twice,
three times.
I was jolted when she answered.
"Hello, this is Kim."
I hadn't mentally rehearsed what I would say,
so I quickly sat up in my chair
grasping to find the logic that would convince her to meet with me.
I had a slight rush of adrenaline and then every word fell into place.

My contact had a dual purpose;
to promote my client's product
and to communicate the potential benefit I could bring to her as a consultant.

She was interested in talking further so we set up a meeting in Pittsburgh.

I marveled that the door had finally opened.
Dropping to my knees, I thanked the Lord.
    "Why did I live so long not knowing
        there was a place inside your love this beautiful?

How could it be veiled from my eyes?
You are so beautiful! Thank you.
I don't ever want to leave this place."

As the meeting date approached, Bill was hospitalized;
it was possible his intestines were obstructed due to an earlier surgery.
His temperature shot up and his pain became intolerable.

Given my new state of awareness,
it was obvious to me that I should call Heinz and postpone the meeting.
Bill argued,
    "Deb, it took you six months to get this meeting.
    If you don't go now, there is no guarantee another will be scheduled.
    You should go—there is too much at stake.
    We need money."

Bill hoped our abysmal slide down the financial slope
would soon come to an end,
and in his mind, this was no way to begin the process.

I disagreed and stood fast.
I was living in a different place now,
and I did not want to go back.

Although Bill doubted my worldly judgment,
he trusted my faith and agreed to the postponement.

Five days later Bill was released from the hospital without complications.

Oddly, rescheduling the meeting took only one phone call.

Now, with more time to prepare,
I developed a logo to communicate my role as a contractor for Heinz.
Bill did the graphics.

I researched H.J. Heinz, the company:
their strategic intent,
weaknesses,
strengths.
I knew how I could help them, and I targeted my presentation accordingly.

Several contacts in industry agreed to write endorsements
communicating the value I brought to the marketplace.
With some apprehension, I even called my contact at McDonald's.
He also agreed and sent a wonderful, detailed and specific endorsement.
In all, I had seven recommendations.
I recalled God's promise that I would walk in the land of the living
where my worth would not be diminished, but upheld.

It was all so effortless!
Nothing went wrong:
the computer didn't crash,
the printer didn't break—
it was marvelous!
A compelling presentation was taking shape without the customary angst.
Bill and I were amazed that rescheduling the meeting
actually worked in our favor,
since it allowed sufficient time to develop a convincing proposal.

I felt I was living within the divine plan.
For the first time,
I could step outside of my life and see it from a distance—
as part of an eternal construct for good.
The disassociation gave rise to a liberating and powerful feeling of freedom.

When the big day finally came,
I opened my briefcase on the plane
and found a handwritten note from Corissa, who was 12 at the time.
It read:

Dear Momma,

Go kick some butt, right?
I love you very, very, very much and I hope that you have fun while you are
out because you are Market Connections and we are very proud of you and I
know that you will succeed.

So, I love you again times a billion, million, trillion, infinities and we are
praying for you so have fun.

Love,
Your daughter

THE MOMENT OF CHANGE

I felt the prayers of all those who supported me the day of the big meeting.

When Kim, the marketer, met me in the lobby,
I was caught off guard.
From her phone voice and last name,
I expected someone who would be
tall, dark haired, and look Italian.

She exploded into the reception area,
a red-haired package of enthusiasm and buoyancy.
Just over five feet tall, unpainted fingernails, and pregnant,
she patted her abdomen and explained she was Italian by marriage only.

I apologized for causing the meeting to be rescheduled.
"No problem," she said with the wave of her freckled hand.
"This worked out great.
I actually got one of our vice presidents to attend.
He has a short attention span,
so I hope you talk fast because he won't stay long."

She expressed her regret for holding the meeting
in the "shabby" conference room.
"All the nice ones are taken," she explained, as she crinkled her nose.
The room was small and a tight fit, but that helped reduce my tension.
(I get very uncomfortable in large, pretentious conference rooms
filled with blue-suited men.)

Her casual and earthy approach was refreshing and fueled my confidence.
I knew this would be the moment of change.

Much to Kim's surprise,
the VP stayed for my entire presentation.
It was the McDonald's quote that really tipped the scales in my favor:

> "I have worked with Debra on the development of a
> customer self-serve, bulk condiment dispenser. Debra was
> instrumental in capturing our needs on a very critical component
> (connector) and working with the component OEM to make
> modifications that resulted in a significantly improved design
> that will likely become the standard in the condiment
> dispensing industry.

Debra also coordinated and implemented a retrofit
program for existing equipment currently used in many
of our restaurants. Debra's retrofit plan was crafted around
the needs of McDonald's, the OEM and the integrator
to ensure that the needs of all parties were considered
and that the ultimate benefit was shared by all including
the restaurants.

I would endorse Debra Krueger as a conscientious,
knowledgeable professional who has excellent communication
and team-building skills and a very deep understanding of
market dynamics. She is a true 'can-do' professional."

The VP read it twice, showed it to others
and asked me if the gentleman from McDonald's really wrote it.
With the confidence and pride that can only come from hope,
I answered, "Yes," without elaborating.

Taking Kim aside, the VP encouraged her to get a
signed exclusive contract with me.
Although priced at the low end of the consulting fee schedule,
the contract paid four times the hourly wage I had made as a tortured employee.

It was a day conceived of in heaven.
Kim had no idea what had led to that day,
yet she stood at the critical point where 40-plus years of struggle
changed overnight.

PAY DAY

When I returned home,
I was conscious of a transformation larger than myself.
I was enormously grateful to God for setting me free.

To me, freedom had been synonymous with independence—
an imposed break between myself and others.
I struggled with loving others;
mostly, I feared them.
Yet, love is implicit in movement toward the eternal,
and I didn't want to stay where I was.
The emotional barricade I had constructed
kept me locked in,
more than it kept harm out.

I recognized my indebtedness to the gentleman from McDonald's
who had written the endorsement,
which in turn influenced the VP,
who persuaded Kim to quickly draw up my contract.

As I began working with Kim,
my fear of interdependence began to lessen in our growing friendship.
What she gave me was a gift larger than the paycheck;
it was something a paycheck could never give
because a paycheck is anonymous and impersonal.

I was developing a boldness, born of faith, that was anchored in hope.
So when John, the president of the company I had left,
wanted to meet for lunch,
I accepted.

As one would expect,
we met at the company's country club.
The hallway to the dining room was lined on both sides
with framed photos of old and aging men,
all important members of the golf fraternity.
I felt a foreigner in this strange land.

Reminding myself of my eternal citizenship,
I straightened my back and entered the room.

Karl and John sat stone faced
waiting for me to explain the value I brought to their organization.

This was hard to understand since I was successful
in the only two miniscule consulting projects they had given me:

My trip to Heinz had produced a purchase order for their product.

McDonald's had approved their product for use in their stores,
and I had personally implemented the change-out that made it possible.

I didn't need their insanity anymore.
I had been set free.

I told them my rate had just increased,
and if they wanted me to continue working exclusively for them,
it would cost.
It was their choice.
I explained my new rate (four times higher) was established by my client,
Heinz.

Karl choked on his asparagus
while John perfected his look of habitual self-possession.

I didn't gloat.
I was grateful to God for deliverance.

Dan still wanted me around,
so they paid the price.

Third Awakening

MY PURPOSE

With the eyes of my heart enlightened,
I grew to believe I had been called to a hope beyond myself.
I could imagine it as if seen from a great distance.
But I wasn't certain.

This did not trouble me,
because hope that is seen is not hope.
For who hopes for what is seen?

Rather, I hope for what I have not seen,
and wait for it patiently.

Chapter 15

A JOURNEY INTO SPIRITUAL FREEDOM

POWER STRUGGLE

Aware that I was living in a new place,
I knew it was essential that I transform my mind
and bring it into congruity with the Spirit of God.
Paul wrote of this in a letter to the Romans more than two thousand years ago,
  "Do not be conformed to the world,
  but be transformed by the renewing of your minds
  that you may discern what is the will of God."

Rehabilitating my mind proved to be a difficult task—
it was like grabbing a king cobra
and wrestling it into a gunnysack.

One particular day the contest of wills going on inside my mind
lasted more than an hour.
The sun had not yet come around the side of the house.
As I sat in the loveseat, aware the time was set aside for devotion,
I struggled to subdue the thoughts inside my head that insisted I
"get on with the day."
I gave voice to the opposing thoughts in my mind to clearly
hear what I was battling.

The pugnacious voice of the world was ready to fight for the
right to control the day.
It had tolerated a week of devotions dedicated to something other than its agenda.
Today, it wanted its own way.
Today was planned;
    business in the morning,
    visit my mother in the hospital,
    volunteer at a charity.
All the things on the list were important.
There was no arguing that.
What I argued was control.

That voice, a voice of the world, had run my life onto the path of death.
Everything in the world led to nothing.
Every route was fruitless, futile, devoid of meaning and peace.
Still the voice would not give up.

I told the voice I had listened to it for too long.

Every road of its choosing was a dead end.
I wanted to relinquish control to God,
to say God's name unabashedly.

I knew I avoided doing that
and the voice knew my secret.

It spit out my secret: "God is hokey!"

I was stunned by its brash delivery.
I thought to myself, is this really true?
Do I really believe God is hokey?
Or is this the voice of the lie?

I answered:
 My Lord is the only real thing in my life.
 The only consistent truth.
 I cannot live without that relationship.
 All the things in the world are a hoax.
 Those thoughts try to move me farther from God.

The voice of the world, insidious and clever, responded:
 "I can crawl within dark places of your soul.
 It scares you to think of what I can do.
 I can show you faces of fear.
 I have the power to make you hide.
 I can win."

We argued.

 "No you can't.
 Ultimately, it comes down to this.
 I know the voice of my Lord.
 I hear Him.
 He says, 'My sheep know my voice.'
 That voice is the truth because it is always constant and life-giving.
 It is love without strings.
 It is so much love, I can't figure out how to receive it.
 I put out my hand for a teaspoonful, when I could have a universe full.
 And yet God's voice always comes whispering like the wind,
 gentle and peaceful.

It lands.
It fills me.
Nothing can separate me from this love—nothing on earth—
nothing in death—
NOTHING.
At death I will be carried home.
Like a bride across a threshold,
God will carry me gently, lovingly into eternity.
And I will rest in that love."

I told the voice, "You are nothing, worthless, a liar!"

Now it was even more determined.
"Get up and go write the proposal.
You have wasted enough time.
This is irresponsible.
Do you think people in business would waste a day—a week?
You have responsibilities to your family.
I want you to go upstairs and start working."

I knew I could not give in:
"No, I won't give in to you.
Try as you might,
I am not leaving this couch until you let go. Let go! Let go!"

It retorted:
"The day is slipping away.
People will think you are a loser.
It's slipping away, another day shot!
Do you think everyone in the world can sit around and think about God?
You're not a monk.
You have to bring in money.
You're acting irresponsibly."

This was worth based on doing, not being. I could not give up:
"I am not moving until you let go.
My life is not your agenda anymore.
Let go!
Let go!
I can feel that you have not let go."

Relentless, the voice continued:
>"You know you'll never proclaim the name of the Lord,
>because you never have.
>You think people who run around talking like that are different.
>You feel uncomfortable around them.
>That's not for you.
>You'll never admit your faith boldly.
>You're just wasting time on this 'faith walk.'
>One of these days you are going to wake up
>and your business will be gone."

Satan offered Christ the world if only he would fall down and worship him.
I resisted:
>"I told you I am not moving until you let go.
>You are a spirit of control.
>I recognize you now and I won't live your meaningless agenda anymore.
>When you let go, I can turn my life over
>and the Spirit will help me boldly tell of God's goodness.
>I trust that will be true.
>My life will be changed.
>I want the change.
>I want you to let go."

It appeared we had reached loggerheads.
I knew if I got up, the next time the voice would be more insistent.
I had to be firm in my resolve.
For a breath of time I questioned my sanity.
No, I answered my doubt, I knew what was going on.

I turned for help.
>"Holy Spirit, please help me."

I listened and heard nothing.
There was only silence except for the noise of the bulldozer next door.

I asked the Holy Spirit again:
>"There is so much noise I can't hear you.
>I am distracted.
>Andy is up.

What do I do if he comes down and sees me wrestling with this spirit?
How do I explain that I am not crazy?
Help me hear you instead of it."
I waited for guidance.
I heard nothing.

I restated my position.
"I can't go on with my life in endless pursuit of garbage.
It is all so meaningless. It comes to nothing.
If I get up, I'm back on that bus.
Help me.
Guide me."

Opening the Bible,
half blinded by tears,
I blinked and saw:
I will give you wisdom and revelation.
I will make the eyes of your heart enlightened.

Then, within my spirit I heard:
"I will show you why you should refrain from listening to that spirit.
Draw a line down the middle of the paper on the table.
On one side write what the spirit of the world would have you do today."

I obediently wrote the list of things to do.
"If you listen with your heart, this is what God will give you today.
Write this on the other half of the paper.
He will give you:
Knowledge of the hope to which you have been called;
all the riches of God's glorious inheritance;
and the immeasurable greatness of God's power if you believe.
The choice is distinct. God wants to give you all good things:
hope, riches, power.

If you listen to the spirit of control,
you can have three tasks done with no assurance of the end result.
No confidence you will share love with your mother

because you are not motivated by love.
No guarantee your business efforts would prosper.
No grace surrounding your good deed.
Your heart would not be in the right place to prosper your efforts.
They would just be efforts."

I asked the Holy Spirit what I should do.

I heard love respond,
"Receive these gifts in your heart: hope, riches, power.
Hold them in your heart.
They are yours.
Repeat them to yourself until they are etched in your heart."

The sun had come around the side of the house.
Its warmth cupped my face in a tender caress.
I thanked God for the sun.

Later that morning I received news that a woman
who once called me a failure unworthy of Bill's love,
had been promoted to VP of marketing at her company.
The world tugged at my sleeve.

I called my mother who had recently had a stroke.
With a slurred voice,
she protested the move from hospital to nursing home.
The doctor wrote the order because her condition demanded continuous care.
That was the most dreaded of all events imaginable to my mother.
I visualized her world crumbling and I hurt for her.
The irony was moist in my mouth.
Now, when she had finally found her reason to live,
(a live-in lover who was my age)
she was entering a nursing home.
Before hanging up, I said, "I love you."
There was no reciprocal response; she just hung up.

I prayed for the Lord to lead my path
and hold me tight, for the journey would not be easy.

I'm Through Dancing

It was hard to pray for people I felt had harmed me—
it was hard to get past the anger.
However, I was determined to hold up my end of the bargain,
so I searched for help.

A book on spiritual warfare stated that
my spirit already dwelt with Christ in heavenly places.
This seemed true to me because on some level,
I experienced my spirit's communication as an intercessor;
it translated the divine when words were limiting,
or when concepts could only be understood spiritually.
It was a communication from heaven to earth
that is independent of the limits of language.

I wondered if my spirit was obliged to translate in reverse…from earth to heaven?
Did it translate my every thought as I struggled to understand?
Did it translate my blame, anger and feelings of wretchedness
I have against another?
Perhaps a person had harmed me.
Perhaps I feared they would harm me:
Would they drag me off to the lion's den
leaving me to be destroyed because they had the worldly power to do so?
Or because I would not acquiesce to the ways and means of the powerful,
would I inevitably face humiliation in their world?

Evil's intent had inhabited my thoughts as a consequence
of living spiritually blind in the world.
I had fear that I wanted displaced by love.
I didn't want to participate with evil any longer.

 Thoughts inside of my head railed continuously.
     "Stop!" I shouted. "Stop tormenting my mind.
     I am sick of it… sick of feeling bad…sick of the lies."
I demanded each negative assertion be examined for truth.
     "I want my life back—I am finished with lies."
I confronted each allegation that entered my mind
evaluating it against logic and the evidence I had already seen of my deliverance.
I refuted each lie.
It was an exhausting process, but I persisted until my mind stopped,
until I heard nothing when I paused.
I noticed it was strange to have my mind free and resting.
I wondered what would fill the void.

Normally distracted by workday demands that awaited me,
that morning I remained at peace

and in return was granted escape from the confines of my life.
In the quiet, I experienced the throne of God
and for a fleeting nanosecond,
I was captured by eternity.
I paused, as if on the threshold of a completely different reality.
Aware it was my choice to step over the threshold, I nonetheless resisted.
As if drawn by a logic warp in the physics of my mind,
I wanted to enter this heavenly place, but I did not.
There was nothing restricting my entry,
yet I was aware of my separate nature.
I simply couldn't fathom such boundless peace, joy, beauty and love.
It was inconceivable and therefore frightening.
The beauty and love overpowered my ability to control my understanding.
I feared what I could not control
and willingly slipped back into my known "reality."

The Bible says Satan does not dwell in heaven,
yet Satan accuses believers before the throne of God.
How can that be?
Now that I had experienced the throne,
I understood my spirit dwelt there
and my soul had communion with my spirit.
My soul often raged against others and myself.
It cried to the Lord about injustice and anger and fear.
    "Is it my words that accuse at the throne?
    Have I unwittingly bought into the lies
    and like a spy who has had a bug planted on her body,
    have I helped the enemy's cause?
    Do I bring the accusations before God?"

I felt so cheap and dirty,
so disgusted with myself,
as if I had slept around and woke up realizing the consequence of my actions.

I understood why I must pray for my adversaries;
to do otherwise is to further the kingdom of darkness.
Dancing with the ruler of this world was revealed in all its horror.
A desire arose within me to pray fervently for the healing and wholeness
of those who had harmed me.
I wanted them brought into the light.
There, I hoped, we would both live in God's peace.
I think perhaps it is the only way to bring God's peace to earth;
we must refuse to dance with evil's intent.

IN THE PRESENCE

I dedicated myself to the daily discipline of releasing myself to God.
Just as surely as my body found its existence on a planet
spinning within the enormity of our universe,
I was certain of a quiet place in eternity where my spirit dwelt.

It is amazing to me that the majesty of our cosmic reality
can be so easily ignored.
Still, we lose ourselves in the minutiae of living, producing and planning,
as if all of life depends on our concern for such details.
When we die, the living, producing and planning continues without us.
But we are kept busy for a time,
for the time of our life.

It is silly, preposterous, tiring and eventually boring to be so consumed.

I have on rare occasions of spiritual meditation,
ceased my earthly fixation and escaped to a place
where I watch myself
and others,
as if standing outside of myself.

Although I was certain others could not perceive it,
from my perspective,
all things seemed to move in slow motion:
    wind as it touched my face,
    cars passing on the dirt road,
    people speaking,
everything moved in a different dimension of time.

All of life became cloaked in a vibrancy previously hidden from my sight.

I was aware of the stable, continuous energy that holds all things
within this exquisite dance called life.
My own body settled into its rhythm.
    I moved,
    and felt it was not I who moved.
    I spoke,
    and felt it was not I who spoke.

This was life within the presence of God.
It was enchanting, endearing, peaceful.
One would willingly die to remain there
knowing that death would hold no harm.

When I returned from meditation,
I remained in the altered state of tranquility for several days.
But it eventually ended,
and I came back to my "right" mind and noticed I was once again impatient.

We say it is good to live in the present.
But it is exceedingly better to live in the presence
of God.

LEGACY

It is said that the sweet smell of God's presence fills the temple
and beckons people home
into the Holy of Holies,
the innermost place where the Spirit dwells.
It entices us to draw near.
It is where we find our home in perfect condition.

I believed that no matter the condition of the clay jar in which my body dwelt,
or how my soul had been scorched,
Christ lived on in my innermost being.
The Holy Spirit's heavenly aroma filled me with hope.

I claimed my adopted status.
No longer the child of my parents' lust,
I became spiritually christened as the creation of God's perfect love.
I could be free from the legacy I unwittingly absorbed.

Living is a lot about legacy.
What you don't get early on
impacts you in untold ways.

It's about life's experiences.
Messages you are given and expected to receive.
Some people are more sensitive to receiving signals,
some block them out efficiently.
How you respond affects not just you,
but your children as well.

Although my legacy seemed impossible to beat,
I knew I could not give up.
No matter how the thoughts inside my head wished me harm,
I would continue to refute their findings.
I had been delivered!
The land of promise was mine.
I would live in a new place and resist the bondage of old scripts.
I had been set free!
I would live free!

I was grateful for the Light that caused me to see.
I can't imagine how children who are abused physically or sexually
ever leave the darkened corners of their minds.
How do people of color fight to preserve their sense of self?
What if you are poor,
or disabled?
Our world is not a soft and gentle place.

Even if I never totally defeat my own demon,
I could work to slay the demon passed to my children.

I had already made significant steps with Corissa.
She does not doubt that I think she is precious, beautiful, intelligent, gifted,
trustworthy, important, lovable, loving, strong and capable.
She is what life is meant to be.

I have prayed fervently for my sons.
I am certain they carry demons from times earlier.
Yet the Lord has proven faithful.
God has touched their hearts and marked them for eternity.
They are beautiful, loving men.

No doubt, we are all in process.
But I will never relinquish myself to the darkness.
I will continue the fight
because my children's children depend on it,
as do the children of others.

ASSURANCE

January in northern Minnesota
is usually cold.
It is cold like a loveless mother,
callous and cruel.
At four degrees below zero,
your forehead aches,
a rational reaction to bodily fear.

Still, I had to return.

It had been a snow-less winter.
As I checked in, the receptionist at Naniboujou Lodge commented:
"It's finally snowing. How wonderful. We have waited so long for the snow."
She was right.
It did appear a welcome and unusual guest,
given the very low temperature.

Wasting no time,
I quickly put on my long johns, wool socks and hiking boots
and headed across the highway for the trail head to the Devil's Kettle.

It was four o'clock on a sunless afternoon.
The sky, as gray and lusterless as a pewter tray,
cast an insipid shadow on the day.

Much of the trail was iced over
making it difficult to hike.
As I often do when hiking alone,
I wondered if I had made a sane choice.
If I slipped and knocked myself out,
or broke something,
I would freeze to death before I was found.

I paused and looked up to see snow falling tenderly,
as if to kiss my cheek softly,
and whisper that the forest had slumbered while it awaited my return.
Like visiting a wise and kind grandfather,
it felt good to be back.

But just as a child outgrows her grandfather's knee,
my heart told me I had moved past the period of struggle and uncertainty
that had called me back so often looking for solace and direction.
Forever, I would hold reverence for what happened at the Devil's Kettle.

Yet, growth implies new experiences,
and it was time to move forward into freedom.

I had never seen the falls in the dead of winter
and was curious to witness the once raging molecules of water
frozen into a still plummet over the cliff.

Standing on the edge,
I laughed aloud
and heard my voice return to me,
volleyed from the river's frozen crust.

The half of the river that had
taken the visible and predictable route over the falls
and down the stream,
was predictably frozen into a solid sheet.
It emitted no sound from beneath its glacial course.

The Kettle half of the river,
however,
was a contorted sculpture
of gnarled, twisted and cochleated
attempts to form a contiguous whole
across the Kettle's cavernous pit.
Similar to the opening of a snail shell,
a deep groove transversed the Kettle's rim.
From the abysmal depths
the sound of water plunging into the precipice
could still be heard.
I imagined a conch shell;
if I held it to my ear,
the entire volume would roar forth declaring:

"Remember.
    Nothing can stop my love,
      not even steel doors.
Remember."

I remained in stillness
while the forest,
given breath by the north wind,
lifted its voice in chorus with the Eternal.
Tears of joy and thankfulness fell warm against my icy cheeks.

I was grateful for my time and place in eternity.

Chapter 16

LIVING IN HOPE

Freedom's Purpose

Blessed beyond comprehension,
I was healed and had found rest in the lush valley of Christ's love.
It was a euphoric place,
free from strife.
I didn't want to leave,
but staying there seemed a withdrawal from the challenges of living out
my faith.
That didn't feel right;
what is faith if it is not tested?

I was compelled to remember the compromise I had asked God to make.
I would be given rest and space to regain strength,
after which time, I would respond to the women's voices crying.

I had to admit God had done a spectacular job of
    upholding,
    supporting,
    strengthening,
    and establishing me.
Everything had fallen into place without much effort.
I was making more money than I would have ever imagined.
Not one person had sought to diminish my value.
Even John, the president who distrusted me, now complimented my work.
And, after more than 40 years of wrestling with my body ailment,
it seemed to have found homeostasis on its own.

I could never have conceived of this place,
a state of being so removed from past evils as to make it unimaginable.
Yet I was living in the promised land.

I was beginning to feel certain that I had been created
for a specific time and purpose.
I didn't know what, though.

Who were these women crying?
Why were they crying?
What was I supposed to do about it?
I had no idea.

Then 9/11 happened.
An article in the newspaper reported
Chilean women despairing because they could not feed their children.
It was just one of many consequences of 9/11.
A marketing firm in the towers had contracted with this group of women
to hand knit scarves that would be sold in the U.S.
The women, anticipating payment on the contract,
had already spent most of the contract fee in credit at the local food store.
Now they owed for the food,
and couldn't pay because the marketing firm no longer existed.
To make matters worse,
they questioned how they would continue to feed their children
in the absence of such a contract.
The women cried.

I thought to myself,
"That is stupid; for the lack of a market, their children will be hungry!"
It wasn't that the women refused to work,
or lacked skills.
What they lacked was the ability to define marketable products
and distribute those products to customers willing to pay.
How calamitous!

How remarkable that I, a marketer,
was in the process of proposing the creation of a service bureau
to distribute Heinz's products to their customers.
Amazing!
The exact two things missing:
marketing support,
and a means to distribute products.

Fate?
Destiny?
Plan?

It was of no significance what I believed about the theoretical discussion
supporting or refuting the notion of destiny.
The relevant issue was that I possessed a certain set of skills,
with a certain base from which to contribute.
I could make the choice to say in disbelief,
"No, that couldn't be what God meant."
Or, I could make the choice to believe and act on my belief.

In my mind's eye I could see the suffering women cry.
I understood their pain and struggle.
In many respects we shared the same story:
When no one else believes,
they must believe.
When no one has hope,
they must have hope.
When they are too tired to move,
they must get up and try again.

THE WOMEN WHO CRY

It didn't take long to find these women.
They seemed to be everywhere and were known by everyone.
Several others joined me in the search.
The mere mention of our intention
sparked enthusiastic offers to connect us to groups in such diverse lands as:
    India,
    Russia,
    Mexico,
    Africa,
    Bosnia,
    Serbia,
    Peru,
    Honduras,
    Tibet,
    Thailand,
    and Haiti.
The list of possibilities quickly became overwhelming.

Everyone we met had a story to tell.
Missionaries beamed with joy at the prospect of helping those they served.

A husband and wife team, returning to work in Haiti,
tumbled and tripped over each other
as they passionately recounted the travesty they sought to remedy.
Desperation lingered after their words
as they described women who,
without options,
and seeking to bring security to their husband-less families,
compromised themselves further by involvement with any man
they thought would stay;
their situations grew far worse with each failed encounter.
Adolescents, leaving villages to find work in Port-Au-Prince,
find only prostitution.
They live on the streets,
while back in their village
their mothers cry.

We asked the couple if it was realistic
to believe women in such circumstances
could consistently produce quality products within a deadline.

This saddened them further
because they knew Haiti when it was largely a female dominated
agricultural economy.
Later, urbanization hit Haiti,
rocking their world
and leaving behind disintegrated families.
The women who remained in the villages
painted colorful depictions of idyllic life
on tin cans that are sold to cruise ship tourists.
These women don't argue the fraction of a cent they earn.
What are they to do?
Move to the city?
Then what?

I, along with two friends, spent the evening with the couple;
a banker and nurse, both Haitian born.
They were returning home with a sense of possibility, despite the despair.

In parting, they remarked,
"There is no hopelessness in people who believe."

We were shown examples of work from women in Haiti.
They were beautiful!

Immediately our minds raced toward the vision
of incorporating their skill and design work into unique products.
Pricing the products appropriately
would allow us to pass a large share of the margin on to our women partners.

Freedom!
It was beginning to smell very sweet.

ENTHUSIASM FUELS VISION

We couldn't wait to take the next step.
Could our women partners' talents be translated into unique
products that would sell?
To answer that question,
we held a session with volunteers
and charged them to identify product concepts.
The objective was explained to the group:
> "We must apply our partners' skills to unique product formats
> that will be ever-changing and evolving.
>
> Remember, we are looking for concepts that will be profitable and can be
> positioned at a high price point.
> This is important for a number of reasons.
> In our culture, price and value are closely correlated;
> if we are to communicate her value,
> her products cannot be a bargain-priced commodity.
>
> If she is to achieve economic freedom,
> we must pay her accordingly.
>
> Our desire is to reach as many women as possible;
> this will take reinvestment from profits.
>
> Our pricing must take all of this, and more, into consideration."

Our eager participants were off and running.
Hand painted tin cans became painted shutters, stools, mailboxes, margarita glasses…
Hand stitching on cotton squares became spa sets, coordinated linens for B&Bs,
wedding invitations…
Ideas kept coming.
More than 50 categories of product concepts were identified in one meeting.

We told our enthusiastic participants more about our vision.
> "The products will be released in sequence,
> as if to tell a story, the story of her life.
> We believe the product must involve you in her life.
> All products will be identified by our logo,
> signed or thumb-printed by the woman partner,
> and numbered in the same manner as limited edition prints.
> One of each of her product categories will be archived for display.

Someday we envision building a center,
a cross between an art gallery,
history museum,
and cultural exhibition.
The progression of her work will be displayed in the center.
You will experience her within the context of her environment.
Large murals will place you in her world;
a sunrise on her village,
the people she loves,
her dwelling,
her passions.

A series of coffee-table books,
one for each group,
will explain how the product concepts were derived and evolved.
You will see her making the product; perhaps the one you purchased.
Photos will detail the chronology of her creations,
all against the backdrop of her life story.

We hope she will become real to you.
As you hold the results of her efforts in your hands,
you will feel her life's energy.
The product will reflect her story."

Our volunteers were hooked.

Wherever we told the story
people wanted to be a part of the adventure and volunteered their help.
They observed that the U.S. market is flooded with products produced in
sweat shops, or trinkets of little value purchased and later discarded.

"Sweat shops and trinkets do not foster economic independence for workers.
Your idea," they said, "is refreshing."

We agreed that freedom cannot be bought that cheaply.

However, beating the rules that govern the free market
would be nearly impossible;
it would require divine intervention.

NEW RULES

Several successful businessmen asked me about the vision.

They told me market realities wouldn't support such a concept.

I explained,
    "A new model is required.
    Instead of usury, indentured servitude, and fear-driven dependence,[22]
    we intend to form partnerships that foster respect
    and personal growth.
    More than products,
    we will sell investment in the story,
    and involvement in the epic journey to freedom."

"Sounds like charity," came the retort of several business leaders.
"Will this business, what do you call it, Set Free International?
Will it be a nonprofit?
It should be," they asserted.

"No," I responded.
"It will be a for profit business.
Our women partners are not charity cases.
We will not communicate such a message;
not to them,
or to the world.
It is time for a new business model.
Before micro-loans,[23]
the world of finance assumed people living in poverty were a different class,
not reliable or trustworthy like those of us who live in wealth.
That has been proven wrong.
It is time to prove that people living in poverty
can be driven and capable of securing their own freedom."

One gentleman shared an experience.
    "I invested heavily in my wife's clothing store.
    It was never profitable.
    She didn't take it seriously—it was just fun for her."

    "I can understand your perspective,
    "but I am not motivated by fun," I countered.

Another was curious.
"Where will you get the money to start?"

"More than four years ago when I turned my company over to the Lord,
I had no idea where the money would come from,
but it came.
We'll start with earnings from my company,
keep salaries low and invest in our growth.
Instead of buying boats or taking vacations,
my husband and I have agreed to invest in freedom for these women."

A skeptical one said,
"People won't believe you.
They'll think it is a scam."

"We will have full disclosure of our financial reports on our website," I retorted.

The practical thinker cautioned,
"But once you get the products into the U.S.
how will you warehouse and distribute them?
Who will accept orders from customers and send invoices?
I think that is going to be a big problem."

"I am glad you asked.
For the past two years my son and I have been working on that piece."
I began to share the story.

UNLIKELY BEGINNINGS

As I told the story,
I reflected back to two years earlier.
In retrospect,
I did not see the hand of the Lord at work
and I had to admit the plan took shape without consciousness,
or for that matter,
much cooperation on my part.

I had been blessed to work for Heinz under a consulting contract,
but when 9/11 happened and the economy slumped,
Heinz turned a critical eye on consulting agreements.
I knew that anchoring myself to something
more tangible would secure my income,
yet I had no desire to establish an answering service requested by Heinz.
The service would accept orders for dispensers from food service customers
and then email the orders to a warehouse
where the equipment was being stored.
The warehouse would ship the equipment and invoice the customer.
Our only responsibility would be to receive the calls and relay the orders.

For my part,
I was extremely reluctant to tie myself to a desk and a phone.

Andy, on the other hand, jumped at the chance.
He had just returned from a year of mission work in inner-city Chicago.
Feeling disconnected from his former college career plan,
and needing to see an opportunity on the horizon,
this appeared to be the perfect solution.
From his perspective, Andy believed that with a laptop and cell phone
he could manage the expected call load as he went between classes.
He was excited and confident about the opportunity.

Suffering from a lack of interest,
I put together a proposal for Heinz that was quickly rejected.

I was relieved.

Andy felt dejected.
Several weeks later, while sitting side by side on the sofa,
he and I had a heart-to-heart talk.
We ended in prayer and asked for God's guidance.
As we finished praying, the phone rang.
It was Heinz—they had changed their minds and accepted my proposal.
Andy was elated and ran out the door to register for classes at the university.

We expected the number of calls would be minimal, and therefore manageable.

Soon the orders outpaced Andy's ability to keep up, so we hired help.

A year later, Heinz asked if we would expand our service
to now include warehousing, shipping, and invoicing their customers.
This would require a space larger than the bedroom
Andy was using as an office.
That room had ceased to function as a bedroom when equipment infiltration
forced him to stand his bed against the wall and sleep on the floor.
He said this was not a bother since sleeping conditions in Chicago
were often worse.

Regardless, warehouse space would be required.

Andy was encouraged by the possibility of expanding the business.
I love my son and his eagerness was hard for me to ignore—
he had that effect on me.

I told Heinz I would agree to the expansion under two conditions:
Number one, I would own the business.
Number two, we would use the same space
to develop a concept for a new business
that was just beginning to form in my mind.
(I explained Set Free International using the story of the Chilean women whose
children went hungry.)

Heinz accepted.

ASSOCIATED RISK

I had asked to own the business,
so it was up to me to create it.
I leased warehouse space devoid of offices
and contracted the build-out.

Eric, a brilliant software programmer, agreed to help us out.
He created a remarkable database structure
that expanded as we grew until it eventually rivaled the big boys
like Amazon.com.
Graciously, he did this at a fraction of the cost because
he saw the bigger vision.

Bill agreed we could use our home equity to cash-flow the process,
including the monthly operation of the Heinz service bureau.
It wasn't long until I understood the full impact of an important business axiom;
money comes with a price—interest.
By the end of the year I had gone $83,000 in the wrong financial direction.
Much of the investment was on our home equity loan,
the remainder on a business bank loan.

To make matters worse,
I realized I owned something that had no equity and little marketable value.
The only one benefiting was Heinz, and they were benefiting in a big way.

I justified the situation by telling myself we were developing some core capabilities
I would one day need for Set Free International.

Most nights I found myself wide awake at 2:30 a.m. praying and thinking.
What was I doing?
All of my time was absorbed in getting the Heinz operation off the ground.
I had no time remaining to dig myself out,
or for that matter,
to spend on developing the business I really felt compelled to start.

Then, the night before I was to meet Janelle, a friend, for lunch,
when I was once again wide awake praying,
the Lord suggested I ask Janelle to join me—
I should offer her a job.
(Janelle was one of the women who came forward to
support my claims at Goliath.)
I told God I thought the idea was crazy.
In fact, I knew God was wrong on this one.
Although Janelle hated her job at the Goliath company,

I thought she would never be free to leave the salary and benefits behind.

At lunch I waited,
listening to Janelle talk,
not wanting to bring up the subject
and thinking that maybe hearing God was actually brought on by psychosis.

Astonishingly, she blurted out:
"Yesterday when I was driving down the freeway,
God told me to leave my job.
You know, it was really loud and clear.
It was as if he were really trying to get my attention this time.
What do you think about that?"

A lump formed in my throat.

"I don't want you to think more of this than you should,
but at 2:30 this morning…"
I went on to tell her my story.

We looked at each other with a mixture of bewilderment, excitement and
stunned comprehension.

Not wanting to bear the guilt of the financial risk she would take by leaving Goliath,
I told her to wait until I could support her salary.
Once we got things moving,
whenever that would be, she could quit and join us.

Janelle didn't take my advice.
She quit immediately after returning from a business trip to Europe,
the first such international tour she had ever been asked to take by Goliath.
People wondered how she could leave after 24 years with the company.

At her farewell gathering in one of Goliath's cafeterias,
she boldly told the story of God calling her out.
She told them of our plans for Set Free International.
Some people cried.
Everyone shook her hand and wished her luck.

I was beginning to learn that faith without works was dead,
and works without risk doesn't exist.
I also saw my supreme arrogance in assuming I knew more than God.
It was a constant struggle to let go of control.

GOOD FAITH

I had taken the risk and did all Heinz asked me to do without a contract,
without a guarantee of income or reimbursement of expenses.
I had nothing other than a verbal agreement.

I was working with a new marketer at Heinz,
who had the very best intentions.

I explained to her that I wanted Heinz to be responsible
for the portion of the financial burden
that was supporting their benefit.
She felt that was fair and appropriate.

Her management said my financial burden was the investment I made,
and just like any investment,
it should be paid back over time within the cost of the service
I was providing them.
Ouch!
That was easy for them to say.

It was obvious;
I was in over my head and needed help.

I found Mark, a lawyer, listed in my church's business directory.
He was every bit the image I held of a Minnesota Scandinavian.
They don't beat their chests,
or make a big show,
they just quietly help others and expect nothing in return.
In fact, the only hard part about working with Mark
was getting him to accept payment for his service.
Some might say he is generous to a fault.
If that were true, his fault was my blessing.

Before long his wife, Angela, also a lawyer,
was volunteering her legal opinion.
Angela told Mark about an accounting firm
that could help package the financial portion of the contract.
She had met the owner of the firm at a conference for Christian business owners.

During the first meeting with the owner of the accounting firm,
I wasted no time describing the mess I had gotten myself into.

The situation intrigued him.
Knowing I could not pay their hourly rate,
the owner offered a contingency arrangement
wherein they would get paid their full rate,
if Heinz signed off on the contract.
If we failed at contract negotiations, he would wave their fee entirely.
I bristled at the notion of not paying at all,
so we compromised on a discounted rate.

Then the owner assigned Roman, a CPA, to develop the model.
Roman worked a miracle!
What Rembrandt did with oils,
Roman could do with numbers.
When he got through analyzing the business,
Heinz was even better off!

Together, Mark, Roman and I developed a proposal for
Heinz that was hard to refuse.

Heinz signed a three-year contract reimbursing my costs
and establishing us as a one stop, full service, customer centered agency.

When Andy called from the warehouse
to say they had just received the signed contract by fax,
I hung up the phone and cried for two hours.

We have been surrounded by capable professionals
all of whom share the vision.
They have become dear friends, almost family to us.

With a foundation of core competencies in place,
and committed passionate people working with us,
Set Free International will be given birth.

Cautious, skeptical, and practical business minds
may still think our vision unachievable,
and they could be right.

I know faith will set the standard for our achievement,
and only time will reveal the truth.

Safe Passage

It seemed I had traveled a lifetime in those two years
and an eternity during my life.
In that same two-year period,
everything also changed in my family.

Odd, as a mother I had never looked toward the day
all my children would leave home to find their own lives.
Since I had fought like a she-bear to keep my family intact,
there seemed no reason to do so.
When the time finally came, I was caught unprepared emotionally.
The first was the hardest.

On the day of Ben's wedding to Norma,
I had a hard time understanding the mix of emotions I felt.

Their ceremony was a touching and heartfelt testimony .
of their faith in Christ and their love for each other.
Family and friends laughed as they experienced renewal of hope in their love.

During the reception
willing attendees were asked to stand up,
microphone in hand,
and say a few words about the bride or groom.

Norma's family presented written, well prepared speeches
that described the joys of life within her family.

Andy gave a hilarious and loving account
of Ben's dependability and strength.

Corissa testified to the goodness of the man she knew as her older brother.

As I sat and listened, knowing my turn would soon come,
images of Ben flooded my mind.
A red-faced three-year-old,
hair wet from sweat,
riding on Grandpa's back,
laughing and hollering
as he tugged on the blanket that hid the "ooze-monster" beneath.

An adorable six-year-old best man at our wedding,
looking very grown-up as he pulled our rings from his vest pocket.

Dependable and brave,
he never made a big deal of any misfortune—he just adapted.

When I dropped him off to start his freshman year of college,
he waved good-bye with a casualness that typified him.
My heart ached as he turned and jogged off to his dorm.

He would always be mine.
I didn't connect that each step in his independence
would someday lead to his wedding day.
It didn't occur to me.
I had placed him,
and our trauma endured together,
into the most remote part of my heart—
untouchable by myself or anyone.
It was sacred ground.

When they asked me to stand and say a few words about Ben,
my heart wrenched and twisted and convulsed.
Was it possible to tell them how inseparable the memories were from my soul?
How could I tell them without ripping it from my heart?
They would never understand…
never know how precious…
how unbelievable it was to arrive at this day
alive and well.

As I held Bill's hand,
and looked into the crowd,
I saw Ben and Andy's father—
my ex-husband.
I choked on words that lodged in my throat.

I felt dizzy at the recognition of my family's deliverance;
our healing,
and wholeness,
our ability to love
and be loved.

What words could I say to express the miracle of this day?
I could not find them.
I gave the microphone to Bill and held back tears.

He did a wonderful job delighting in our son.

As the microphone was passed to my ex,
Bill put his arm around me and held me tight.
I cringed.

We all feared the worst.

We were shocked.

He praised Bill and me for the job we did raising the boys,
and confessed he had nothing to do with the way they turned out.
And, even though he had no time for faith,
he had to wonder if there was more to it than he would willingly admit
since both Ben and Andy were decent men.

The glory and beauty of forgiveness was visible in that moment.

Ben and Norma moved to Canada to live in the town where she grew up.

Andy married Kearstin and together they bought a house,
while Corissa, awarded a scholarship, left for college in Boston.

Breathless with wonder,
those two years marked enormous change in my life.

Although my children have all moved on to claim their futures,
I don't feel lonely—I appreciate the blessings they have given me.
It is their lives that have caused me to reflect on my own with joy and thankfulness.
They manifest the enormity of deliverance and hope.
They are the beauty of life.

I have become certain that God hears the cries of women,
and mothers for their children,
because I see clearly and profoundly
that mine were heard.

AUTHOR OF STRENGTH

With gratefulness and awe,
I reflect back on the seven years that have passed
since the Lord caused me to hear the cries of women.

At the time,
I resented the idea of being strong.
Broken, weak and tired,
I believed it was my destiny to be forever challenged,
never conquering;
to live the remainder of my life
absent of victory over the fears within,
and pulled by the destructiveness of the world outside.

I could not see the way out of the downward spiral.
Now I realize that on that fateful evening seven years ago,
while completely lost in my brokenness,
grace spoke softly and gently
calling me to find my place and purpose in something larger than myself.
Still incomprehensible to me,
I marvel that my weakness was turned to strength
as I acted in faith to respond to the cries of others.
I did not foresee that being emptied
meant finding everything.

When I stumbled to get back on my feet and try again,
faith alone motivated my movement.
I was given no clear vision to direct my path—
I was to trust that all things would be revealed in time.
I walked blindly.

I still walk blindly by faith—the future is unknown.
I have no guarantee that I have listened and responded correctly.

I know I have been set free in the process,
and some things have become clearer.
I no longer resent being called to be strong.
There is beauty in such strength that can only come from God.

A strong woman can admit she is broken.

She challenges what the world tells her about herself and others
and finds definition in eternal truth.

A strong woman loves her children
because they are the torch of truth declaring life cannot be denied—
that light and creation coincide eternally.

Destruction stands in opposition to creation.
The power that created the infinite variety of the universe lives within us.
A strong women dares to find and express
the unique creative gift that resides solely in her,
a contribution no other person can bring to the world.

A strong woman does not close her eyes
nor turn her back on reality;
she looks straight at it
and moves away from harm.

A strong woman can risk being vulnerable to love again,
despite previous hurt.

A strong woman wages war against the powers of darkness
that threaten to steal and destroy.
She stands against the mercenaries
who for a buck or a little power
seek to destroy her or others.
She fights to claim the abundance of life promised to all.

A strong woman leaves a better legacy than the one she was given.

A strong woman will never give up.
She cannot,
no matter how long it takes.
Because the Spirit of God dwells in her,
she will claim the victory in Christ.

SET FREE

I have been set free
by the Spirit of truth that lives within me.

I seek daily to live in a place of freedom,
a place of beauty and peace,
of love and hope.
A place where time is eternal,
and truth is not obscured by the lie.

It is a place of choice;
each day I can choose to enter.
When I enter,
I see differently.
I see a reality free from the distortions caused by darkness.
I know what I see can be, and will be, because it already exists.
But one must have eyes to see it.

We choose daily how we will see the world,
with eyes born of freedom, or eyes veiled by lies.
When we fear,
we are trapped in bondage to a suffocating delusion.

There was a price paid to set us free.

Freedom.

Free from the insatiable and oppressive demands
of corporations who slay the soul
to feed voracious appetites—
cravings that will not be satisfied by truth.
Masked as an ever-increasing demand for profit,
the corporation becomes a slave master who,
with mouth salivating for more,
shelters his millions while the lives of others are forfeited to the cause.

There is only one good cause.

Freedom.

Freedom from the intrusion of others who
would write darkness as an epitaph on your soul.
With their hearts and minds unprotected by hope,

they become hard and bitter by evil's intent.
Driven by fear,
they refuse to be vulnerable to truth.
They spread their view of reality like a virus.
They cannot see differently.

There is only one truth.

Freedom.

We are told it is naïve to believe in what is good and right and true.
It cannot and will not happen.
"Just look around," they say,
"evidence suggests otherwise."
We are encrusted by our lack of belief
and succumb because we cannot see in darkness.

There is light to see a different reality.

Freedom.

It is fear that binds us to a life half lived.
It is a lie.
We have been given life to live it fully, intensely,
without compromise.

For freedom we have been set free.

Freedom.

Some may fear tomorrow will bring a return
of the harm and hurt of the past.
If we pull back and guard our insecurities,
the battle will be lost.
To participate in the promise,
we must believe it is true—real—although we cannot see it tangibly.
This is a blessing born of love and placed in the heart.
Inside belief,
hope is never lost and patience is rewarded.

Freedom.

FULLNESS OF LIFE

My work is no longer separate from my life;
it is the living out of my purpose.

I believe we become partners with the divine
when we live passionately,
taking the risk to find our life outside of the programming of the world.
In that place,
all other choices seem a dull compromise.

I have discovered that a life focused on the Spirit
is a life of adventure,
beauty,
grace,
love eternal,
power,
purpose.
It offers a view of another reality that extends past the edge of the universe.
It is breathtaking!
Majestic!

A life lived fully, truthfully, and with faith, grants its own bountiful reward.
Nothing is forfeited.
Everything is gained.

I pray we meet someday on the journey into freedom,
for this is not the end,
it is only the beginning.

EPILOG

CRANINESS

I told Bill I would kill him if he bought me a Harley for my 50th birthday.

So what if I also told him in moments of extreme agitation
that I wanted to ride off into the sunset on one.
And I know that I said the rumbling sound of the engine
transported me to open roads far from the aggravation of the day.

But so what? People say a lot of things under pressure.
I had seen past the material things of the world and changed my mind.
I could do without a Harley.
I fully expected he heard the desires of my heart,
which were to invest in Set Free.

He agreed and decided on a dinner and night of polka dancing at the Gasthaus.
It would be just family and a couple of friends.

Janelle got to the restaurant before us and said the others
were waiting downstairs.
Stepping aside, she graciously allowed Bill and me to go first.

I opened the door to a room full of people I didn't recognize.
They were all dressed in black leather, tattooed and looking rowdy.
In the midst of the group,
a red Dyna Wide Glide sat shining like a rare jewel.
She floated in a cloud of vapor while spot lights beamed off her exhaust pipes.

No one in the room said a word.
They didn't laugh,
or yell, "Surprise!"
They just looked tough,
actually—scary.

Thinking I had opened the door to hell,
I went from face to face in desperation and shock
looking for someone familiar.

When I recognized Ned
(my former boss who went out on a political limb for me),
I shrieked, laughed, and slammed the door on Bill.

Bill, caught between the door and the wall,
persuaded me to open the door.
It was all a perfectly orchestrated surprise.

Deb, the neighbor down the road,
and Bill were the masterminds,
but they had a lot of help.
The kids knew while we spent the afternoon visiting my mother,
yet they never said a word.

Deb and Janelle whisked me off to the ladies' room to change into biker garb.
I chastised them both severely for going along with Bill,
and didn't cooperate with the apparel change
because I was too busy arguing finances.
They gave up and sent Bill into the ladies' room leaving the two of us alone.
He promised the purchase wouldn't compromise our dream for Set Free.
He assured me he had it all figured out.
Deb and Janelle stood outside the ladies' room,
ears plastered against the door,
waiting until it was safe to enter.

Andy rolled Ms. Dyna Wide Glide outside
and allowed me the honor of starting her.
The circle of family and friends surrounding the bike
backed up a couple of feet.

Oh, she RUMBLED and ROARED.
Her GROWL was beastly.
I heard laughter from the circle as I bounced up and down, giddy with delight.

Although it was a rainy, cold October night,
I begged Andy to take me for a ride.
He said she drove like a Cadillac.

I named her Irene
after my neighbor and adopted godmother.

Everyone had a good time.

Bill and I hugged and kissed.

Several days later,
I told Bill I was going to sell Irene in the spring because we couldn't afford her.
His eyes shone a brilliant blue in response.

NOTES
The Book in Context
Data based on U.S. Statistics and Observations

Chapter Two: Engagement and Marriage (page 50)

1. More children are now being abused and neglected than in 1986, and their injuries are more serious. In 1993, an estimated 1,553,800 children in the United States were abused or neglected under the Harm Standard. Well over half a million of these children were seriously injured or harmed due to this abuse, nearly quadrupling similar occurrence estimates from 1986. The majority of these children (78 percent) were maltreated by their birth parents. Of all factors, family income is the strongest correlate of incidence in nearly all categories of abuse and neglect, with the lowest income families evidencing the highest rates of maltreatment. -U.S. Department of Health and Human Services, National Center on Child Abuse and Neglect. Third National Incidence Study of Child Abuse and Neglect Final Report (NIS-3). Washington, DC: Government Printing Office, September 1996, 8.3-8.9.

Chapter Three: The Long Dark Tunnel (page 81)

2   In 1999, an estimated 203,900 children were the victims of family abductions; roughly one in every 344 children. Just over half (53 percent) of these children were abducted by the biological father. Twenty-five percent were abducted by the biological mother. Family abductions were much more likely to occur in families where children were not living with both parents - the circumstance that gives rise to motives for family abduction. The most common serious elements (intents of abduction) were attempts to prevent contact (76 percent) and intent to affect custodial privileges permanently (82 percent). It is also noted that, although children of any age can be victims of family abduction, younger children appear to be particularly vulnerable. In 1999, 44 percent of family abducted children were younger than age six. - U.S. Department of Justice, Office of Juvenile Justice and Delinquency Prevention. National Incidence Studies of Missing, Abducted, Runaway, and Thrownaway Children (NISMART-2): Children Abducted by Family Members: National Estimates and Characteristics (NCJ-196466). Washington, DC: October 2002, 4-6. http://www.ncjrs.org/pdffiles1.ojjdp/196466.pdf.

"Research has begun to demonstrate what therapists and left-behind parents have known for some time, that children are deeply and permanently affected by family abduction... The emotional scarring caused by these events requires that officers recognize family abduction not as a harmless offense where two parents are arguing over who 'loves the child more,' but instead as an insidious form of child abuse. The history of the issue has also demonstrated that law enforcement has a much broader responsibility than the simple act of 'retrieval.' By responding promptly, professionally, and efficiently to reports of family abduction, officers and the agencies they represent become, in effect, a means of protection for the child."
- Missing and Abducted Children: A Law Enforcement Guide to Case Investigation and Program Management. Steidel, Stephen E., ed. Alexandria, Virginia: NCMEC, 2000, 63.

Chapter Four: Rights are not Guaranteed (pages 99, 104, 114, 115)

3   In the 1960s through the late 70s, domestic abuse was identified as a recurring criminal justice problem, especially for police: "Spouse abuse was viewed by police and the courts as an intractable interpersonal conflict unsuited for police attention

415

and inappropriate for prosecution and substantive punishment. In fact, many police departments had "hands-off" policies prior to the 1970s, and police training manuals actually specified that arrest was to be avoided whenever possible in responding to domestic disputes." - Fagan, Jeffrey, "The Criminalization of Domestic Violence: Premises and Limits" (Presentation at the 1995 conference on criminal justice research and evaluation) (NCJ-157641). Washington, DC: July 10, 1995, 8. http://www.ncjrs.org/pdffiles/crimdom.pdf.

4   The American Medical Association estimates that over 4 million women are victims of severe assaults by boyfriends and husbands each year. About one in four women is likely to be abused by a partner in her lifetime. -Sara Glazer, "Violence Against Women" CQ Researcher, Vol. 3, No. 8, Congressional Quarterly Inc.: February 1993, 171.

Intimate partner violence is primarily a crime against women: During 1999, females experienced 671,110 (85 percent) such violent victimizations; whereas males experienced 120,100 (15 percent). Females were also more likely to be murdered by an intimate partner than their male counterparts. In 1999, 1642 persons were slain at the hands of an intimate partner; 74 percent of these were female (1,218 incidents). "Women separated from their husbands were victimized by an intimate at rates higher than married, divorced, widowed, or never married women... In general, separated females experienced intimate partner violence at rates significantly higher than women in any other marital category."
- U.S. Department of Justice, and the Bureau of Justice Statistics Special Report: Intimate Partner Violence and Age of Victim, 1993-99 (NCJ-187635). Washington, DC: October 2001, 1,3,5. http://www.ojp.usdoj.gov/bjs /pub/pdf/ipva99.pdf.

"Several sources of information indicate that a woman's risk of victimization from a boyfriend or husband does not necessarily end or even decline when the relationship is ended... That separation or divorce is associated with continued or greater risk for intimate partner violence from ex-husbands or ex-boyfriends has been documented [by several sources dating from 1984 to 1995]... One estimate of risk associated with separation or divorce is that as many as 50 percent of women who leave their abusive partners are stalked and/or assaulted by them after they end the relationship." - National Violence Against Women Prevention Research Center, Wellesley Centers for Women. Prevalence and Incidence Estimates for Intimate Partner Violence, by Vera E. Mouradian, Ph.D. Wellesley College: 2000. http://www.musc.edu/vawprevention/research/ipvestimates.shtml.

5   "Until the legal reforms of the late 1970s, a woman could not obtain a restraining order against a violent husband unless she was willing to file for divorce at the same time. When protective or restraining orders were available, their enforcement was weak, penalties for violations were minor, and use in emergencies was not possible."
- Fagan, Jeffrey, "The Criminalization of Domestic Violence: Premises and Limits" (Presentation at the 1995 conference on criminal justice research and evaluation) (NCJ-157641). Washington, DC: July 10, 1995, 8. http://www.ncjrs.org/pdffiles/crimdom.pdf.

The National Violence Against Women Survey, conducted between 1995 and 1996, provides compelling evidence of the link between stalking and other forms of violence in intimate relationships. The survey found that husbands or partners who stalk are four times more likely than husbands or partners in the general population to physically assault their partners, and are six times more likely to sexually assault their partners. The survey also found that ex-husbands who stalked (either before or after the relationship ended) were significantly more likely than ex-husbands who did not stalk to engage in emotionally abusive and controlling behavior toward their wife. - The National Institute of Justice, Centers for Disease Control and Prevention. Stalking in America: Findings From the National Violence Against Women Survey (NCJ-169592), by Patricia Tjaden and Nancy Thoennes. Washington, DC: April 1998, 8. http://www.ncjrs.org/pdffiles/169592.pdf.

6   In America, a woman is raped every 37.5 seconds. A man is raped every five minutes. (Although rape is legally defined as a gender neutral crime, females are the primary victims of rape occurring in childhood and adolescence, and males are the primary perpetrators.) - Calculations based on findings from the National Violence Against Women Survey conducted in coordination between the National Institute of Justice and the Center for Disease Control - November 2000.

It has been previously reported that rape in America is a "tragedy of youth" because the majority of rape victims are victimized before age 18. More than half (54 percent) of female rape victims and nearly three-fourths (71 percent) of male victims were younger than age 18 when they experienced their first attempted or completed rape. A tragic relation has also been noted between victimization as a minor and subsequent victimization. Women who reported they were raped before age 18 were twice as likely to report being raped as an adult.
Regardless of source, when the victim was under 12 years old, the likelihood of a family relationship was relatively high (46 percent of victims and 70 percent of imprisoned rapists.) Additional detail has revealed that 20 percent of victims under age 12, 11 percent age 12-17, and one percent 18 or older were raped by their fathers; the older the victim, the less likely the victim and offender were family members and the more likely they were strangers to one another.
- National Institute of Justice, and Center for Disease Control. Full Report of the Prevalence, Incidence, and Consequences of Violence Against Women (NCJ-183781), by Patricia Tjaden and Nancy Thoennes. November 2000. http://www.ncjrs.org/pdffiles1/nij/183781.pdf.

Chapter Six: The Beginning of Independence (page 137)
7   Divorce rates reached a peak between 1978-1980 at 40 divorces per 1000 marriages annually. The initial rise toward this high begins to show in the 1963-1968 time period. A total of 32 states implemented no-fault divorce legislation during this boom between 1965 and 1974. -U.S. Department of Commerce, and the Bureau of the Census. Marriage, Divorce, and Remarriage in the 1990s (P23-180). October 1992. http://www.census.gov/population/socdemo/marr_div/p.23-180.pdf.
-Americans for Divorce Reform, Why Divorce Rates Increased. http://www.divorcereform.org /why.html.

"No-fault divorce laws allow one person to dissolve a marriage without the consent of the spouse. In most states before no-fault, divorce required consent of both or proof of fault by the non-consenting spouse. 'Under no-fault wives can always threaten to walk out without the husband's permission, changing the power balance in the relationship,' says Professor Justin Wolfers. The husband, understanding the lowered threat point, behaves himself, thereby reducing the incidence of domestic violence and spousal homicide - and increasing women's well-being." - Chang, Helen "No-Fault Divorce Laws May Have Increased Women's Physical Well-Being." Stanford Graduate School of Business: January 2004. http://www.gsb.stanford.edu/news/research/econ_divorce.shtml.

Chapter Seven: Risking it All Again (page 173)

8   There were 66 million working women in 2001, a significant increase from 5.3 million in 1900, and 1.4 million in 1950. Today, about 60 percent of all women are in the labor force, including three-fourths of all mothers. Even among mothers with young children, 70 percent work for pay. - Business Professional Women of America. Women in the U.S. Labor Force. 2003. http://www.bpwusa.org/content/PressRoom/101Facts/101_LaborForce.htm.

Chapter Eight: Moving On (page 197)

9   Women earn a greater number and proportion of bachelor's degrees than they did 30 years ago. Between 1970-71 and 2001-02, the number of bachelor's degrees that women earned more than doubled, from 364,100 to 742,100. Women earned 43 percent of all bachelor's degrees in 1970-71, but in every year since 1981-82, they have earned at least half of all bachelor's degrees awarded. In 2001-02, women were awarded 57 percent of all bachelor's degrees. Women have also made gains at the graduate level. In 2001-02, women earned 59 percent of master's degrees, compared with 50 percent in 1984-85 and 40 percent in 1970-71. At the doctoral level, women earned 46 percent of all degrees in 2001-02, up from 34 percent in 1984-85 and 14 percent in 1970-71. -U.S. Department of Education, and the National Center for Education Statistics. The Condition of Education 2004 (NCES 2004-077). Washington, DC: US Government Printing Office, 2004. http://nces.ed.gov/pubs2004/2004077.pdf.

"Women and men with college degrees earned about 76 percent more than those with only a high school diploma, in 2002. Nonetheless, female college graduates who were full-time wage and salary workers had median earnings of $809 a week, compared with $1089 for men." - U.S. Department of Labor, and the Bureau of Labor Statistics. Women in the Labor Force: A Databook (Report 973). February 2004. http://www.bls.gov/cps/wlf-databook.pdf.

Chapter Nine: Introduction to Corporate America (pages 225, 238, 239, 240, 241)

10   Despite a decade of battling for increased awareness and an end to sexual harassment in the workplace, 2003 statistics show that annual sexual discrimination charges filed with the Equal Employment Opportunities Commission have had no significant drop, declining only 1/10 of one percent (in its ratio to overall charges filed) since 1992. In 2003, 30.0 percent of all charges filed were due to sexual harassment complaints. In 1992, this fraction was 30.1 percent. - U.S. Equal Employment Opportunity Commission. Charge Statistics FY 1992 Through FY 2003. (2004). http://www.eeoc.gov/stats/charges.html.
In 1993, Governor Mario M. Cuomo of New York ordered a task force to conduct a comprehensive examination on institutional responses to sexual harassment. The task force responded with the following: "Our survey tells us that the problem in not epidemic; it is pandemic - an everyday, everywhere occurrence... Nearly half of our survey respondents say that they (or a woman they know) have quit a job or have been fired because of the problem."

"In the 1990s, polls and studies of many different designs and magnitudes continue to report consistently that sexual harassment is a common and widespread problem in almost every type of workplace... More than 60 percent of the respondents had been harassed ... Perhaps most troubling of all was the finding that only one out of five women believed that most complaints of harassment are given justice."
- New York State Division for Women, the Governor's Task Force on Sexual Harassment. Sexual Harassment: Building a Consensus for Change (1993): Chapter 4. http://www.mith2.umd.edu/WomensStudies/GenderIssues/SexualHarassment/NYTas kForceReport/Chapter04.

11   A recent Catalyst study of women in corporate leadership shows that women have: "Made more trade-offs and adopted more strategies to achieve balance than their male counterparts... To facilitate their advancement, the majority of women (81 percent) also developed a style with which male managers are comfortable."
- Catalyst. Women and Men in the U.S. Corporate Leadership: Same Workplace, Different Realities? PricewaterhouseCoopers: 2004.
http://www.catalystwomen.org/publications/executive_summaries/wicl4executivesummary.pdf.

Joyce Fletcher, a Professor at the Center for Gender in Organizations at Simmons College, likewise concludes that women must often adapt to male dominated paradigms in order to achieve upper management positions: "'The masculine image of the heroic leader is amazingly resilient, in spite of the needs in today's economy,' says Fletcher. She notes that some women who have made it to the top have indeed 'mimicked a male role' - that is, they may be single, or have no children or have a stay-at-home spouse who ends up taking a secondary career role or none at all. In fact, among the top five women on last year's Fortune list of the '50 Most Powerful Women in Business,' four have husbands who don't work."
-Wells, Susan J. "A Female Executive Is Hard to Find." HR Magazine, June 2001.
http://www.findarticles.com/p/articles/mi_m3495/is_6_46/ai_76940928/pg_1.

12   "While minorities and women have made strides in the last 30 years, and employers increasingly recognize the value of workforce diversity, the executive suite is still overwhelmingly a white man's world. Over half of all master's degrees are now awarded to women, yet 95 percent of senior-level managers of the top Fortune 1000 industrial and 500 service companies are men. Of them, 97 percent are white. African Americans, Hispanics, Asian and Pacific Islander Americans and American Indians also remain woefully under-represented in the upper echelons of American business." -The Federal Glass Ceiling Commission. A Solid Investment: Making Full Use of the Nation's Human Capital. Washington, DC: November 1995, 6.
http://www.witi.com/center/researchstatist /glassceilingrep/recommendations.pdf

13   "The typical Fortune 500 company loses $6.7 million annually, or $282 per employee, to sexual harassment in the form of absenteeism, increased staff turnover and reduced productivity, as quoted in a *Working Woman* magazine survey in 1988. Morale declines and divisiveness increases among co-workers. Worker's compensation and unemployment claims increase, along with increased potential litigation."
- Millersville University. The Costs of Sexual Harassment: Time and Productivity. New Media Learning, LLC: 1998. http://uweb.milersville.edu/~humres/shnon-sup/1028d.htm.

Due to the Civil Rights Act of 1991, a federal commission was enacted whose mandate was to investigate the notorious glass ceiling of American businesses which

prevents women and minorities from advancing to upper-level positions. The commission returned with the following conclusions: "It is not only a matter of fair play, but an economic imperative that the glass ceiling be shattered. It matters to the bottom line for businesses and to the future economic stability of America's families. Independent research has shown that companies that go the extra mile in hiring and promoting minorities and women are more profitable. A study of the Standard and Poors 500 by Covenant Investment Management found that businesses committed to promoting minority and women workers had an average annualized return on investment of 18.3 percent over a five-year period, compared with only 7.9 percent for those with the most shatter-proof glass ceilings."
-The Federal Glass Ceiling Commission. A Solid Investment: Making Full Use of the Nation's Human Capital. Washington, DC: November 1995, 5.
http://www.witi.com/center/researchstatist /glassceilingrep/recommendations.pdf

14 Sixteen Points for Change by Debra Krueger
1. Act with a sense of urgency.
2. Make a policy concerning confidentiality during an investigation and communicate it across the company.
3. All supervisors should be aware of their responsibility when an employee reports allegations of harassment/discrimination.
4. Clearly communicate to divisional management the liability to the corporation if such matters are not handled properly-do this before the problem, not after. The corporation cannot afford the political power plays of divisional managers.
5. Give your lead person in Employee Relations more power and authority.
6. All cases of reported harassment/discrimination should be reported to a corporate panel for an immediate, confidential review, with frequent progress reports required.
7. Provide intensive training for HR managers here from other countries-cultural differences leave them lacking understanding.
8. Provide education and sensitivity training for all HR managers on the human consequences of harassment and discrimination.
9. Protect the victim's rights.
10. Support the victim-they are isolated.
11. Don't blame or fault the victim-put ownership of the inappropriate behavior where it belongs.
12. Don't put the burden of changing the harasser's behavior on the victim.
13. Don't put the victim in an insanity trap.
14. Don't reward/award the perpetrators.
15. Pain is a great motivator for change-the consequences to the perpetrator should be a strong signal of intolerance of such behavior.
16. Don't patronize-this is a serious issue for women and minorities.

Chapter Twelve: Return to the Work World (pages 298, 315)
15 According to a Catalyst survey of eleven different corporate sectors, the health care industry is reported to maintain the highest percentage of senior executive women. It has also been acknowledged however, that despite this advance, there still remain only a small number of women at the highest ranks of health care's corporate involvement—in levels such director or trustee. - Roberts, Jennifer. "More Women Lead Health Care Industry." PR Newswire, February 3, 2004. http://www.findarticles.com/p/articles/mi_m4PRN/is_2004_Feb_3/ai_112858215.
- Women Business Leaders of the U.S. Health Care Industry Foundation. An Examination of Women Business Leaders of the U.S. Health Care Industry:

Pre-Retreat Questionnaire Results, by Lynn Shapiro Snyder and Jennifer Roberts. Epstein Becker & Green, P.C. and the U.S. Health Care Industry Foundation: January 2002. http://www.womenleadinghelathcare.org/nonflash/wbl_question-naire_results.pdf.

In 2000, the American College of Health care Executives conducted a study in collaboration with Catalyst, Inc., and documented the following: "At the end of 1995 study, we reported that some parts of the gender gap were narrowing. With regard to salary, however, we see that the gap has not really changed in the past decade. Moreover, we see that while most women (90 percent) believe that efforts should be made to increase the proportion of women in senior management positions, only 53 percent of men agree. Without some consensus on this issue, it will be difficult to pursue policies to redress the documented inequities."
The study also noted that the personal lives of employees, in an attempt to balance work and family responsibilities, were more often taxed among women workers than their male counterparts: "Overall, fewer women than men health care executives are married which may suggest that women more often have to choose between having a career and having a family... Indeed, our survey uncovered clear evidence that women bend more to facilitate their husbands' careers than vice versa." -The American College of Health care Executives. A Comparison of the Career Attainments of Men and Women Health care Executives. 2001. http://www.ache.org/pubs/Research/genderstudy_execsummary.cfm.

16   In 1999, a study was conducted examining the career gender inequality among priests in the Episcopal Church. Paul Simmons, the studies coordinator, noted the following: "Contrary to my initial expectations, this study found resistance to the ministry of women to be undiminished over the past 20 years both in the aggregate and in its effect on individual careers. Also contrary to expectations, this unchanging resistance was found to be located entirely in congregations, and not at all in decisions o the church hierarchy or other clergy. On both counts it appears that male/female inequality among the clergy is not due to formal institutional discrimination but is a result of embedded cultural values, values that are particularly resident in congregations and that show no indication of changing. That the disparities regarding women clergy are 'cultural' in a direct sense is evidenced by the obvious fact that such disparities are by no means confined to religious organizations."
- Sullins, Paul. "The Stained Class Ceiling: Career Attainment for Women Clergy." Sociology of Religion, Fall, 2000. http://www.findarticles.com/cf_0/m0SOR/3_61/66498055/print.jhtml.

"As community, the whole Church is to teach one another, support one another, forgive one another, engage in theological self-reflection on its own ministry to each other... Only when men and women are peers in the Church can we create human relationships that express authentic communication and exorcize the evil spirits of injustice and dehumanization that turn women and all oppressed people into fantasized symbols of the negative self... Our anthropology must cease to be modeled after sexist doctrines of male hierarchicalism and polar complementarity and become centered in the full human personhood of every individual. For each of us unites all those dualities of thinking and feeling, activity and receptivity, falsely polarized as 'masculine' and 'feminine.' We can begin to relate to each other out of all sides of our being in truly reciprocal ways." - Ruether, Rosemary Radford. "Male Clericalism and the Dread of Women." (Excerpted from Women and Orders) Robert J. Heyer, ed. Paulist Press: 1974. http://www.womenpriests.org /classic/ruether2.htm.

Chapter Thirteen: Boundaries Require Defense (pages 321, 322, 323, 329)

17   Elie Wiesel, From the Kingdom of Memory:Reminiscences (New York: Schocken Books, 1990), 69

18   "All of the numeric gain in enrollment in the MDiv program across the past 25 years has been due to the increasing enrollment of women. While women are not enrolled in theological schools to the extent that they are present in American law schools (just over 50 percent in 2000) or medical schools (just under 50 percent), they are dramatically more present now than they were 25 years ago."
Also of importance in recent theological enrollment is the observation that: "Women students appear to differ from men in the forms of ministry they intend to pursue. A slightly higher percentage of men than women intend to pursue parish ministry after graduation. Women [on the contrary] are more likely than men to pursue hospital or other institutional chaplaincies. Women are less likely than men to anticipate ministry in church planting or evangelism, or youth ministry."
-The Association of Theological Schools in the United States and Canada. Fact Book on Theological Education, 2002-2003 (ISSN 0363-7735). Edited by Chris A. Meinzer and Nancy Merrill. Association of Theological Schools: 2003. http://www.ats.edu/archive/fbarch/2002-03.pdf.

In 1995, approximately 11 percent of all ordained U.S. clergy were women. "A widely-known multi-denominational study on women clergy, Women of the Cloth (Harper 1983), found that female and male clergy held similar entry-level placements, but that sharp gender differences appeared when they moved to midlevel positions, with men tending to move upward while women moved laterally. They attributed the differences to a variety of influences from passive socialization to tendencies by congregational search committees not to generalize positive experience with women clergy into receptivity toward subsequent female candidates. A comparative update of this research by Zikmund et al. (1997), as well as other recent studies, shows that these earlier trends have remained consistent across denominations, resulting in a 'glass ceiling' effect for women clergy interested in the senior leadership of a large congregation or denominational leadership." "Traditionally, opportunities for women clergy have been primarily in small, poorer congregations that have been unsuccessful in attracting men, often in rural locations. In response, women clergy have developed a legacy for building up congregational membership and financial resources - the two criteria traditionally considered by male clergy as measures of occupational 'success' - but often have found themselves replaced by men, either by congregations newly able to afford a man or through denominational reappointment." - Hartford Institute for Religion Research, and Hartford Seminary. Encyclopedia of Religion and Society: Clergy. William H. Swatos, Jr., ed., Clergy, by Paula D. Nesbitt. AltaMira Press: February 1998. http://hirr.hartsem.edu /ency/clergy.htm.

19.   "...the editorial board came together in the Fall of 1990 to undertake a rendition of the whole New Testament and the Psalms that was inclusive with regard to gender, race, religion, or physical condition, but yet that did not violate the meaning of the gospel...The result is another step in the continuing process of rendering the Scripture in language that reflects our best understanding of the nature of God, of the humanity and divinity of Jesus Christ, and of the wholeness of human beings." -Victor Roland Gold et al., The New Testament and Psalms: An Inclusive Version (New York, Oxford: Oxford University Press) ix.

20. "Surveys measuring the incidence of extramarital relationships are difficult to compare because sample characteristics create wide variations in self-reports. Comparable findings in a number of studies suggest that a reasonable estimate for lifetime incidence of extramarital intercourse in 25 percent of women and 50 percent of men. However, the incidence of actual extramarital involvement is increased by 14 to 20 percent if sexual intimacies and emotional involvements are included." -Glass, Shirley P., Ph.D., and Jean Coppock Staeheli. Not "Just Friends": Protect Your Relationship from Infidelity and Heal the Trauma of Betrayal. The Free Press: 2004. http://www.shirleyglass.com/introduction.htm.

Chapter Fourteen: Breaking Free (page 355)

21. In 2002, estimates showed that there were approximately 10.1 million privately-held businesses that were majority or 50 percent women-owned. These firms represent nearly half (46 percent) of all privately-held firms in the U.S. and are shown to be growing and expanding faster than the economy in general. -Center for Women's Business Research. Completing the Picture: Equally Owned Firms in 2002. Underwritten by Pitney Bowes Inc., Wells Fargo, and NAWBO (Philadelphia Chapter). April 2003. http://www.nwfbo.org/CompletingthePicture.htm.

Data supplied by the Center for Women's Business Research has documented that: "Women-owned businesses are just as financially strong and creditworthy as the average U.S. firm, with similar performance on bill payment and similar levels of credit risk."
It should also be noted that: "The workforce of women-owned firms shows more gender equity. Women business owners overall employ a roughly gender-balanced workforce (52 percent women and 48 percent men), while male business owners employ, on average, 38 percent women and 62 percent men." -Business Professional Women of America. 101 Facts: Women Entrepreneurs. 2003. http://www.bpwusa.org/content/PressRoom/101Facts/101_Entrepreneurs.htm.

Chapter Sixteen: Living in Hope (page 395)

22. The maquilas of El Salvador are popular among many large brand name companies sold in American markets, as a means of cheap garment manufacturing and production. These maquilas employ approximately 60,000 workers, nearly 80 percent of which are women between the ages of 16 and 30 years old. Approximately half of these women are single mothers who must support their families through their meager incomes.
In 1999, a National Labor Committee study documented the plight of these workers. The following are their findings: "While most maquila workers in El Salvador do earn the legal monthly minimum wage of 1,260 colones, [approximately $144 in June of 2004] this amount is barely sufficient to meet basic food requirements as defined by the Salvadoran government itself. In fact, the cost of the government basic food basket - a bundle of 11 food items (plus cooking fuel) that fills a minimum caloric intake requirement and is used by the government to set the extreme poverty line - for a family of 4.3 in December 1998 was exactly 1,260 per month. In other words, a family must spend 100 percent of one wage earner's income just to eat. As one NGO activist told us, 'Paying a worker the minimum wage effectively condemns her to extreme poverty.'

Indeed, a 1997 government household survey estimated that 12 percent of urban households are in extreme poverty, while 26.7 percent are in relative poverty. Barely scraping by, workers are unable to satisfy their most basic needs. No worker we spoke with was able to save any amount of their income for long-term planning or emergencies." -The National Labor Committee for Worker and Human Rights. The Case for Corporate Responsibility: Paying a Living Wage to Maquila Workers in El Salvador. New York: 1995.
http://www.nlcnet.org/campaigns/archive/elsalvador/sipareport .shtml.

23. "Muhammad Yunus was born in Bangladesh and earned his Ph.D. in economics at Vanderbilt University. After returning to Bangladesh to teach, he was inspired by the country's crushing famine of 1974 to leave academia to help the poor. His revolutionary microcredit concept began by giving out loans totally twenty-seven dollars to forty-two villagers with no collateral. Microcredit has now spread to more than fifty countries worldwide. With a repayment rate of 98 percent and two million borrowers, Yunus's $2.5 billion Grameen Bank has expanded into dozens of other projects for empowering the poor, including telecommunications and venture capital. Grameen Foundation USA, www.grameenfoundation.org, (888) 764-3872 Michael Collopy and Jason Gardner, Architects of Peace: Visions of Hope in Words and Images (California, New World Library, 2000), 188